THE RIVER CAFÉ

WINE PRIMER

THE RIVER CAFÉ WINE PRIMER

Joseph DeLissio

FOREWORD BY ROBERT MONDAVI

LITTLE, BROWN AND COMPANY
BOSTON NEW YORK LONDON

First Edition

Library of Congress Cataloging-in-Publication Data

DeLissio, Joseph.
The River Café wine primer / Joseph DeLissio. — 1st ed.
p. cm.
Includes index.
ISBN 0-316-18592-2
1. Wine tasting. I. Title.
TP548.5.A5D45 2000
641.2'2—dc21

10 9 8 7 6 5 4 3 2 1

Q-FG

Designed by Jam Design
Maps by Michael St. George
Printed in the United States of America

In loving memory
of my father,
Joseph John DeLissio

Dedicated to
Krista, Joseph, and Julia,
who are the bright and most beautiful stars in my universe,
and to my wife, Janice, for all the love and support she has given me

CONTENTS

FOREWORD

When Joseph DeLissio was thinking about entering the wine profession in the mid-1960s, I was starting the Robert Mondavi Winery in Napa Valley. We've been in touch over the years — I remember well when he came to the winery when he conceived the successful California Classics wine program for The River Café.

Two factors have been important for both of us during this period: we recognize the importance of education and we are both committed to excel in the paths we've chosen.

The River Café Wine Primer provides an excellent wine education for the novice and has a lot of good information for the wine knowledgeable. In addition, Joe's personal insights and comments are valuable for all of us interested in wine. By investing more than twenty years tasting, buying, studying, recommending — and enjoying — wine, Joe has become a true wine professional.

Education is also a key concept at the Robert Mondavi Winery. We have always felt that our staff, whether in production, sales, or public relations, is basically a teaching cadre to encourage the moderate enjoyment of wine.

I always knew that in Napa Valley we had the soils, the climate, and the grape varieties to make wine that ranked among the best wines in the world. We invested in research and education, and happily the vision of the 1960s became the reality of the 1990s. We can make better wines more consistently in Napa Valley than in any other region, and we made a commitment here to make the best wines we can, with the belief that there would be a market for those wines.

Joseph DeLissio was one of the first to recognize that commitment, and matched it with one of his own — to bring the best wines he could find to his patrons. He has certainly earned the recognition he's received and the success he's had.

The wine industry enters the new millennium at a very high point in the seven-thousand-year evolution of wine. And the wines we will be making will be even better — we haven't tasted anything yet!

ROBERT G. MONDAVI
Napa Valley, July 1999

ACKNOWLEDGMENTS

Below are the names of some very special and dedicated people who, through their generous gifts of time, guidance, knowledge, opinions, and friendship, greatly helped me with this book. To each and every one I offer my deep appreciation.

Michael (Buzzy) O'Keeffe, owner of The River Café, for taking a chance on "a young kid from Brooklyn" over twenty-two years ago. And for giving me all the support, resources, and flexibility needed to create and develop the wine program at The River Café.

My mother, Jean, for introducing me to the wine business

Patricia Woodruff, for ending all my run-on sentences and smoothing out all those rough edges

Robert Mondavi, for all his support

Mario Daniele, for over twenty years of solid friendship and sound advice

John Sheldon, for gently placing me under his wine wing in the early years of my career

Joseph Heitz, for all his kindness

Frank J. Prial

Kevin Zraly

Neal Rosenthal

Mitchell Nathanson, Wine Market International

Joshua Greene, *Wines & Spirits* magazine

Robert Chadderdon

Mark Lartigau, Château & Estate Wine Company

Chuck and Julie Feinberg

Clicquot, Inc.

Sotheby's

Washington State Wine Commission

California Wine Institute

Sonoma County Wineries Association

Wines of Spain

Al Bassano and Bloomberg Multimedia

Jack Poust & Company
German Wine Information Bureau
Food and Wines from France
Champagne Information Bureau
The Wine Enthusiast
Rupert Symington
Beaulieu Vineyard
Alan Fechter
Larry Pattinger and Lou Macolino
Markham Vineyards
Robert Mondavi Winery
Bo Barret and Château Montelena
Sonoma-Cutrer Winery
Shafer Vineyards
Terry Robards
Eunice Fried
Wine Spectator
Tim Biancalana
Craig Graves
Rory Callahan
Vigliano Associates
Jennifer Josephy and Little, Brown and Company
Harvey-Jane Kowal
Noah, wherever you are
Rudi Weist and Cellars International Inc.
Matthew La Sorsa, Heights Château Wine Shop
André G. Shearer and Cape Classics
Jorge Ordonez—Fine Estates from Spain
Miguel Valdespino
Michael Belardo
Morrell & Company
Sherry-Lehmann
Michael Yurch
Jan Petrow
Vineyard Brands
The Quality Cork Council
Tonnellerie Demptos
Maureen Hayden Andariese
James Caulfield
Lilian Budesa, for the world's best eggplant
Anthony DiDio of Lauber Imports

Rick Laakkonen, one of New York's finest chefs
The entire River Café staff, both past and present
Dr. John E. Sarno, Dr. Lionell Bissoon, and Dr. Paul Gazzara

And a special thanks to three good friends who have always been there:

James Basile
Rocky Graziano
Robert (Mitchell) Glaude

INTRODUCTION

Growing up in Brooklyn during the sixties, I shared a ritual with my brothers, Michael and Gerard, and friends who lived on the block — stickball. This was a game very similar to baseball, except that the ball was rubber and the bat was fashioned from the handle of a broken broom or mop. Stickball was played on Brooklyn's narrow streets and was no doubt the major contributor to broken windows and dented cars in the neighborhood. After our games, somehow or other we often ended up talking about what we would be when we grew up. Our choices were typical for American children and ran the gamut from police officer to major league ballplayer to astronaut. As for me, I was going to be in a band *bigger* than the Beatles.

Thirty-five years have come and gone, and my childhood dreams remain just that. And while I haven't performed with the Rolling Stones, Paul McCartney, George Benson, Frank Sinatra, or U2, I *have* selected wines for them. Wine tasting is my profession — in simple terms, I sample, select, and recommend wine. Back in 1966, if we had had a crystal ball, wine tasting would have seemed the oddest of possible professions. I can imagine what we would have said. A wine taster, what's that? Who drinks wine? Who *pays* someone to drink wine? In the sixties, beer and liquor were the adult beverages of choice. Few drank wine, and fewer still drank wine from wine bottles with corks. Not many restaurants offered a wine list, and wineshops — well, few existed.

Wine just didn't have a major role in America in the sixties. This was one of the few areas in which we lagged behind Europe, where wine has been an integral part of culture as well as of the economy for thousands of years. When we fast-forward from the sixties to the nineties, we find much that has changed. Wine has become the new drink of choice, enjoyed not only for its taste and pleasures but also as a healthy and natural beverage. Americans have also discovered what Europeans have known for centuries: wine is most wonderful when served with food. Today wine has a new image: bottles of wine are given to show appreciation; fine wines are cellared for many years as an investment; and knowing one's way around a wine list impresses clients, dates, and employers.

While the consumption and enjoyment of wine are at an all-time high, the subject of wine itself is still enveloped in an intimidating aura. This is particularly unfortunate because wine is actually a rather simple beverage. My goal in writing *The River Café Wine Primer* was to dissipate the aura surrounding wine and to give you all the information you need to feel comfortable in any wine environment. Ordering wine in a restaurant should be easy, not intimidating. Selecting wine in a local wineshop should be enjoyable, not anxiety provoking. Remember that tasting wine is a personal, subjective experience requiring personal judgments that can be formed only by you, the taster. Many inexperienced wine consumers lose sight of this fact and willingly yield their palates to the guidance of wine professionals. Sometimes the neophyte is lucky and is introduced to the pleasures of wine by a caring and knowledgeable wine clerk, critic, or restaurant wine server. More often than not, however, the beginner encounters people who are all too comfortable presenting their opinions as the law.

When you've finished *The River Café Wine Primer*, you'll be your own taster, confident in your own judgments. What you'll find in the following pages are all the tips, strategies, tricks, lessons, and insights I've accumulated during my twenty-two years in the wine business. It is my fondest hope that you will find *The River Café Wine Primer* what I intended it to be: straightforward, honest, unintimidating, informative, liberating, and—above all — enjoyable.

PART ONE

Understanding Wine

Wine can be an overwhelming and intimidating subject for the novice. It is my experience that the subject of wine is best approached in two distinct yet equally important parts or phases. *The River Café Wine Primer* has been designed in such a fashion. Part One, "Understanding Wine," concentrates on teaching the basics necessary in making anyone feel comfortable in all environments involving wine. Here the subjects of tasting, purchasing, cellaring wines, as well as a basic understanding of vineyards, and wine-making practices are discussed. Part Two, "The Wine Regions," concentrates on the world's finest and most famous wine-producing countries and their wines.

COURTESY RIEDEL GLASSWARE

1

HOW TO TASTE AND EVALUATE WINE

Tasting wine is an extremely personal experience. Although you may need some information and guidance to refine your judgments at first, tasting and evaluating wine involves your own perceptions, just as with watching a play, reading a book, or looking at a painting. There are no "right" or "wrong" perceptions. No one can tell you what — or what not — to like.

Many people picture the ritual of wine tasting as a group of experts huddled around an old barrel in a dusty European cellar. This is, however, a romanticized image and most certainly not the norm. Most wine tasting, in fact, is done while sitting or standing at a table with only a few accessories at hand. It is my hope that *The River Café Wine Primer* will demystify the wine-tasting experience. After you read this chapter, you'll be ready to taste wine right away. After you finish the book, you'll be well on your way to becoming a pro.

Let's get started. There are six basic steps to tasting and evaluating wine:

1. *Observing.* Look at the wine.
2. *Sniffing.* Take a quick sniff for "off" odors.

3. *Aerating.* Rotate and swirl the wineglass in a circular motion in order to release the wine's aroma.
4. *Smelling.* A variation on the sniff, done after aeration, in which you concentrate on the wine's bouquet, smells, and aroma.
5. *Tasting.* Aerate the wine in your mouth and swallow.
6. *Savoring.* Concentrate on the wine's finish (the sensation and flavors left in your mouth after swallowing).

Looking at Wine

Sight is a sense we access so automatically that we often take it for granted. We see something, formulate an opinion, and move on. Have you ever observed the exact same thing — a painting, say, or a movie — more than once? Did you notice anything new the second time around? With each look at a glass of wine, we can gather more information. First, though, we must learn *how* to look and *what* to look for.

Why do you look at a wine? Looking at a wine can tell us many things. A clean, clear, brilliant appearance can be a strong indication of good winemaking practices, while a very cloudy aspect may indicate that something has gone wrong along the way. More specifically, observing a wine can give us some clues about its age.

The color of a very young white wine (two years old), for example, will be a very pale yellow with light green highlights around the edges. By the time this wine is four years old, though, it most likely will have begun to shed its green highlights and become more yellow or golden. If you notice that a wine is beginning to brown or develop an orange tinge around the edges, it is probable that this is an overly aged white wine and one that would best be avoided. There are always exceptions to the rules, of course, and Sauternes — a lusciously sweet French white — displays many different shades of orange as it ages to perfection.

In addition to noting a wine's color, you should also pay attention to any deposits that may have accumulated at the bottom of the glass. In a red wine, sediment may indicate that a wine has not been overly filtered (a common process that helps stabilize wine by removing its many small particles). The filtering process also removes some of the wine's natural flavors and will often soften a wine's body (more about the terms *soften* and *body* later on).

Sediment in a white wine may manifest itself in the form of small, glasslike crystals that adhere to the inside of the bottle or to the cork. These particles are called *crystal tartrates.* The presence of crystal tartrates is both good and bad: good because their presence indicates that the wine has not been overly processed — or "stripped" — and bad because they can be a sign that at some point in its lifetime the wine may have become too cold. Crystal tartrates themselves are quite harmless and do not usually affect wine significantly.

How do you look at wine? When you look at a wine it is important to take your time. Too often I have seen people rush through this first stage of wine tasting without properly observing the wine's color and taking note of the information it can provide. Still . . . how do you look at wine?

Let's consider the environment first, starting with light. Proper lighting is essential because we can't inspect a wine correctly if we can't see it clearly. The best kind of light is natural sunlight, shining through plain glass if you're indoors. Fluorescent light is not an honest light, nor is any light that has a hue or color that might distort the real color of a wine. And while dim lights and candlelight are indisputably romantic, these are the very worst lighting conditions under which to look at wine. The light cast by standard light bulbs is acceptable.

The amount of light present is also important. There should be enough light to read a book without straining.

Now, let's pour the wine. Remember, we are *tasting* wine, not just drinking it, so there are certain procedures we should follow to make certain we get the most out of every sip. First, fill the wineglass to about one-third full. You will notice that sometimes the more wine you pour, the deeper its color appears in the glass. So if you are going to taste and compare more than one wine at a single session, make sure you pour an equal amount of wine into each glass. This will help you properly evaluate a wine's color. The reason you don't fill the wineglass all the way to the top is that soon you are going to *swirl* the wine, and you don't want wine spilling all over the table.

Speaking of the table, any table will do. The tablecloth, however, must be white. On television you may have seen a wine taster pointing his glass skyward and observing the wine from underneath. This is an incorrect procedure. Wine should be viewed from above, at a slight downward angle, against a white background. A plain white tablecloth is strongly recommended, because any other color will influence your impression of a wine's color. If a white tablecloth is not available, a white napkin will do just fine.

Sniffing the Wine

The purpose of sniffing is to detect strong off odors, or obvious flaws in a wine's aroma. For example, occasionally a wine will smell like vinegar or nail polish remover. This is an indication that the wine has turned. Oxidized wines (wines that have suffered from overexposure to air) smell stale and are similarly unacceptable. Any foul smell, in fact, is a good enough reason to pass on to the next wine. But again, you must first learn what smells are considered foul in wine and how much of these off odors is too much.

Sniffing wine is pretty simple. The proper way to sniff is to bring the glass to approximately one inch below your nose. You do not need to — and should not — stick your entire nose into the glass. Two or three gentle sniffs should be sufficient to tell if the wine is bad or "off." Be aware, though, that an unexpected odor should not be confused with an off odor. Sometimes a perfectly good wine will smell different from what you expect. As you sniff and sample a variety of wines, you will become able to distinguish the wonderfully unusual from the frankly bad. The sniff is a preliminary step in tasting wine. We will get a much fuller picture of a wine's aroma after we complete step three of wine tasting: swirling.

Swirling the Wine

Swirling wine is not as easy for most of us as sniffing and will require some patience and practice to get right. In the beginning it is quite normal to feel ridiculous, uncoordinated, or both. But soon you'll be swirling with the best of them.

There are two main reasons for swirling. First, we swirl to aerate the wine. Good or bad, smell doesn't expose itself until it is mixed with air. Aerating, then, helps a wine release its aroma or, in the case of an older wine, its bouquet.

The second reason we swirl is so we can observe the way the wine adheres (or doesn't adhere) to the side of the glass. This coating is called the wine's *legs* and can supply us with some more clues about the wine. If the coating is thin and falls quickly from the side of the glass, the wine in question is most likely light-bodied. If the coating is thick and slow moving, it tells us that the wine has a fuller body and, possibly, a higher alcohol content. Sugar is another element that adds to a wine's viscosity. Sweet wines tend to have thicker and slower-moving legs than their drier counterparts.

The first step in swirling the wine is to take hold of the glass by the stem (usually with the thumb, index finger, and middle finger) and, without lifting the glass from the table, slowly and gently make small, circular motions in one direction. You should notice the wine moving up and down the side of the glass in a continuous wave. If your motion is too vigorous, the wine may spill over the top of the glass. If your motion is too timid, on the other hand, you will not create a continuous wave around the glass. Five seconds of swirling is usually about enough. If you are tasting a very young wine, though, swirling for a few more seconds may be helpful, as younger wines tend to be more "closed up" and require more contact with the air. Sometimes, if the wine is fully mature, you may want to do slightly less swirling, so you do not risk too much aeration. Do you need to do this before every sip of wine? I find it helpful, but, of course, it's a personal choice.

No matter how awkward you feel at first, pretty soon this procedure will become second nature, and then it will be time for you to master the next step: the fine art of swirling wine off the table. This will require a little getting used to. But fear not — it will come.

Smelling the Wine

Our sense of smell Often unappreciated, the sense of smell is one of the most evocative — and useful — of our five senses. Millions of hairlike receptors found inside the nose detect odor particles in the air. These receptors then transmit signals to the brain, where they are interpreted. Thus the nose — conveniently located right above the mouth — is designed, in part, to act as our body's first alert system, warning us if something we're about to eat is spoiled or in some other way inadvisable. Smell also provides us with many of life's pleasures, from the smell of the sea air or of a freshly mowed lawn to that of a wood-burning stove in winter or the precious scent of a newborn baby. We spend millions of dollars each year on perfumes and colognes because they smell pleasant and make us feel good, not to mention their aphrodisiac quality. In addition, our sense of smell is one of our strongest memory triggers. A whiff of a familiar odor can transport us back in time as quickly as a photograph or a song.

Memory is key when tasting wines, and since our sense of smell so strongly influences our sense of taste, we need to have an ability to detect and remember different scents. (Recall is important because you must be able to recall your perception of a wine in order to compare it with other wines, or even to the same wine in a later stage of development.) Be warned, though: our sense of smell can be quite lazy and sometimes lets our eyes do most of the work.

If I see lemon, for instance, I smell lemon. Once I was part of an experiment in which I was blindfolded and offered different things to smell. Although I did fairly well, I was also confused by more than a few scents, not because I wasn't familiar with them, but because I was unable to connect the scent with its source. Banana was one of my mistakes. I suggest you try it using different fruits, flavorings, flowers, and herbs. The point is simple but important: Pay attention to your sense of smell by practicing its use, not only with wine, but with anything that you come in contact with daily. More than 50 percent of my judgment of a wine is based on its aroma and bouquet, so this is a skill you'll want to master.

How to smell wine Smelling the wine is done immediately after swirling. When you finish swirling, bring the rim of the glass to one or two inches below your nose, and smell. You do not need to take a deep, long inhalation. Your inhalation should be easy, consistent, and comfortable. Voilà! You are now *smelling the wine*. What do you smell? How would you describe it? At first, use any words that you feel accurately describe the wine.

Start out by asking yourself if you like what you smell. Does the wine smell fresh or old, fruity or floral? Can you smell any wood, like cedar pencils or oak? Is the aroma smoky or toasty? If the wine smells fruity, what fruit does it remind you of? It may be apples, cherries, bananas, tomatoes, strawberries, raspberries, or black currant. Does the wine have an earthy smell like soil, wet earth, mushrooms, nuts, or hay? You may smell fuel oil, sea salt, sauerkraut, tar, or stewed vegetables. The wine's aroma may even remind you of a barnyard. These would all be correct perceptions as long as they are *your* perceptions.

Although there are no right or wrong descriptors, after a while you may begin to notice some similarities with certain wine types, and that is when you will start to become a wine taster. You may discover that many Chardonnays have a strong scent of apples or that many Sauvignon Blancs seem weedy or grassy. You may find that many California Cabernet Sauvignons have similar scents of cherries or that many German Rieslings smell like peaches.

These observations can come only after much tasting experience, but there is no rush. You have your entire life to enjoy and analyze wine. In a later chapter I will provide some common descriptions used to define the major wine varieties. A listing of both good and bad smells follows. (Some of them are obvious — who would want to drink something that smells like nail polish?)

Good Smells

apple	wood
cherry	smoke
strawberry	bacon
raspberry	soil
vanilla	mushrooms

chocolate
cassis
apricot
pepper
melon
nuts
coffee
cinnamon
lemon
flowers

Bad Smells

glue
nail polish
vinegar
excessive oxidation
volatile acidity
excess wood
stewed fruits
garbage
sauerkraut
gas
chemicals
cork
sulfur
garlic
bitter almond
high alcohol
banana
leaf (or leaves)
skunk
other foul smells

Tasting the Wine

Here's where all the fun begins. Well, *almost*, because first we must learn how to taste. Our taste buds are tiny taste receptors that are grouped on the tongue. Each receptor in a taste bud responds best to one of the four basic tastes: sweet, sour, bitter, and salty. You can remove salty from these choices, because while some wines — Manzanilla Sherry, for example — may smell salty, there are no commercial wines that taste salty. That leaves us with only three taste sensations: sweet, sour, and bitter. There are, however, hundreds of possible combinations of these three sensations. It is the proper combination of sweet, sour, and bitter that we are looking for when tasting wine. When these tastes are in harmony, we have a *balanced* wine.

To be balanced, a wine must fall within certain guidelines or prototypes of the particular wine we are tasting. For example, if we are tasting young red Bordeaux from France or California Cabernet Sauvignons, we should expect — and even desire — a certain amount of bitterness or tannin. That same bitterness, though, would be considered undesirable in a German white Riesling or an Italian Pinot Grigio. Chardonnay can be produced many different ways stylistically, but all Chardonnays should be bound together by certain varietal characteristics, such as the flavor and aroma of apples or a sensation of creaminess with a crisp finish.

Tasting wine also provides much information about the body of a wine. The body is the weight of the wine on the tongue and is more of a sensation than an actual taste. To describe body, I offer an experiment I saw Joshua Wesson (a well-known wine consultant) perform. Get three empty glasses and pour skim milk into the first, whole milk into the second, and heavy cream into the third. Now take a sip of the skim milk and allow it to rest on your tongue. Just concentrate on the sensation of weight on your tongue for a moment and then spit out the milk. Now rinse out your mouth with water and follow the same procedure with the whole milk and then with the heavy cream. What you should have experienced is the difference between light body (skim milk), medium body (whole milk), and a very full body (heavy cream). Interestingly, the water you had between the different milks is as close as you can come to the sensation of no body. Remember these sensations because they will serve as a useful guide in describing the weight, or *body*, of a wine. Following is a partial list of some of the different elements that can affect a wine's body:

1. alcohol content
2. sugar content
3. grape type
4. grape yield (amount of grapes produced)
5. age of wine
6. level of filtration
7. amount of time in contact with oak barrels

There are two schools of thought concerning the importance of swallowing wine in order to analyze it properly. The first is that swallowing the wine is not necessary for a true assessment. These tasters choose to spit out the wine without consuming any. The second school of thought is that swallowing at least a small amount of wine is essential in all wine evaluation. Personally I fall into the second group. There is, however, merit in the opinion of the first. When you are tasting wine (red, white, and sparkling), swallowing does present its problems. The consumption of too much alcohol can certainly dull your senses as well as alter your judgment. A sensitive stomach can quickly become upset from the high acidity that is often found in wines (especially young ones). Tasting a number of young red wines in succession can quickly bring on palate fatigue (the inability to distinguish among different wines; literally, the exhaustion of that ability) as a result of the high levels of tannins usually associated with these wines. When you are tasting wines out of the barrel, the wine can be unsettled (meaning certain chemical reactions remain unresolved). In this case, spitting out the wine after tasting makes sense. Once a wine has been bottled and made available for consumption and review, however, I feel strongly that at least a very small amount of wine must be consumed in order to evaluate it properly. The final stage — as well as one of the most important and enjoyable — in wine evaluation is called the *finish*. It would be impossible to describe accurately the finish of any wine without consuming at least a small amount of that wine. Please remember, though, that wine is an alcoholic beverage, and moderation is strongly advised.

Tasting wine properly is physically the most challenging of all the steps and requires some patience and practice. It is quite easy at first to choke on the wine or even for the wine to dribble out of your mouth. So dress appropriately and practice before trying to impress the boss.

The steps: Pick up the wineglass immediately after smelling the wine and bring the rim of the glass to your mouth. Now raise the glass so that the wine slowly enters your mouth. (Approximately half an ounce is fine.) Then permit the wine to lie on your tongue for a few seconds so that you can assess the body of the wine. Now bring your lips into a small circle and, keeping the wine still, slowly draw in some air through your lips. You should begin to hear a gurgling sound and feel a slight motion of the wine in the front of your mouth. This procedure is similar to gargling, but it takes place at the front of your mouth instead of the back of your throat. After a few seconds of this, stop, and while keeping your head tilted slightly downward, breathe in the air and then let it out. Now you may finally swallow the wine. This may seem like a lot of work, but there are reasons for this ritual. When you bring in the air and mix it with the wine (the gargling sound), you are actually aerating the wine and helping it release its flavors. You will be quite surprised when you discover how much flavor can be picked up just by breathing in the air before actually tasting the wine.

The Finish

The finish of a wine is the last step in wine evaluation. It comes after swallowing the wine. The sensations and flavors left to savor after tasting and swallowing the wine (as well as the length of time these flavors and sensations linger with us) are all part of the wine's finish. Depending on how long the flavors linger, a wine may be described as having a short, a medium, or a long finish. A wine with a short finish leaves very little flavor or sensation in the mouth after it's been swallowed. The finish of a short wine dissipates in about three to eight seconds. This does not mean that the wine is bad — only that it lacks length. Simple and inexpensive wines often have short finishes. A wine with a medium finish is more flavorful and leaves a longer impression of itself (a finish of approximately eight to fourteen seconds). Wines with a medium finish are more desirable than wines with a short finish.

Finally, we have the Holy Grail of wine finish: the long finish. Wines with a long finish can linger in your mouth anywhere from fifteen seconds to a minute or longer. I once had a sweet dessert wine called Pedro Ximénez from the cellars of Valdespino, in the Sherry region of Spain, that was over 120 years old. To this day I cannot recall any other wine I have ever tasted that possessed the length of finish or thickness of flavor of that Pedro Ximénez. Obviously that tasting experience left a lasting impression (pun intended) on me and, I hope, helps illustrate the importance of a wine's finish. I know you're saying to yourself, "Good for him, but will I ever taste a rare wine like that?" The answer, sadly enough, is probably not. Nor will I ever again. I am sure, however, that you will taste many wines in your lifetime that will provide you with similar experiences.

How is the finish achieved? Although many factors come into play, here are the main ones.

Balance We have already discussed the importance of a wine's balance. From the time the wine is made until it is consumed, balance remains the key. If a wine lacks acidity, it will lack finish. If it lacks fruit, it will lack finish. "Balance, balance, balance" is the wine taster's credo.

Sweetness Sugar adds viscosity — or thickness — to a wine. The sugar content is manifested in a thick coating that sticks to our tongues and mouths, resulting in a lengthening of the wine's flavor. To illustrate this point, get a glass of water and a spoonful of honey. When you drink the water, the finish and taste sensations will dissipate almost immediately. Now put the spoonful of honey in your mouth and instantly you will feel its viscosity. You will also experience the sweet and lasting coating and flavor impressions left by the honey.

Alcohol Alcohol is produced as a by-product of the fermentation of sugar and yeast. It is at this stage that raw grape juice is transformed into wine. The amount of alcohol produced during fermentation depends on the sugar level of the grapes. The more sugar the grape juice has, the more alcohol it can produce. However, the highest level of natural alcohol that can be achieved from the fermentation of grape juice is approximately 16 percent (considered much too high for table wine), and at this level the fermentation process — if left alone — ceases naturally. The amount of alcohol in a wine increases its viscosity and the length of its finish. Too much alcohol can leave a hot finish (a burning sensation), which, for obvious reasons, is considered a fault in a wine. Remember, a long finish is desirable only if it is pleasant. While alcohol can add to the wine's length, enhancing its finish, too much of it takes away from the wine's overall balance and decreases your enjoyment in drinking the wine.

What's Needed for Wine Tasting

Wine opener There are many types of wine openers. I recommend the compact waiter's type.

Table With white tablecloth or white napkins for proper viewing.

Proper wineglasses See examples of wineglasses, page 16.

Empty bucket For spitting and pouring out remainder of wine.

Plain crackers or bread To neutralize the palate between tastes of different wines.

The wine Any type.

Pencil and paper For note taking.

Anyone you care to invite

GLASSWARE

Proper glassware is essential in both the evaluation and the enjoyment of wine. Quite often the importance of serving wine in the proper glassware is overlooked. There are different glasses for different wines in the same way that there are different utensils for different foods. You wouldn't use a butter knife to cut a steak, would you? Nor should you serve a white wine in a fluted Champagne glass. Before we discuss the different types of wineglasses, let us first understand some basic information that applies to all glassware.

Cleanliness Regardless of which glass we use, it must be clean and neutral. The glass should be free of any soap spots or food stains. Soap often leaves a residue that cannot be seen, and when a wine comes in contact with this residue it will negatively affect the taste and smell of the wine. The best way to clean wineglasses is by hand with plain hot water, preferably immediately after use. While plain hot water may seem easy to come by, it is important to know that water itself can leave undesirable off odors such as sulfur or chlorine on a wineglass. This can be avoided by using bottled water.

Just writing down this information reminds me of one occasion when I was reviewing some rare California wines in northern California. When the wines were presented, I noticed that all of them smelled odd and "off," and although wines sometimes do go bad, it would be very unlikely for all of these wines to be bad. I contacted the host, informed him of my concern, and politely asked him if the wines had been properly stored. His response was to lead me immediately to an impeccable, temperature-controlled wine room. I sat back down and started to retaste the wines. I took a sip of water from the water glass, and I immediately noticed that the glass of water had the same off odor as the wines. When we checked the source of the water, it became clear that the water used in washing the wineglasses had extremely high levels of chlorine, thereby contaminating and altering the wine. After rerinsing the wineglasses with a more neutral warm water, the tasting resumed without a hitch.

The lesson here is important and should be remembered: Always smell the glasses before you pour the wine, because if the glass has an odor, so will the wine. Smell the glasses at home, at wine tastings, and especially in restaurants. Restaurants usually wash their wineglasses together, using the same hot water that is used to clean dishes, pots, and pans. This creates a horrible environment for glassware. Smelling the glasses beforehand will quickly become second nature and save you from many an embarrassing situation. This simple procedure also sends a strong signal to the dining room staff that you are a serious taster.

Storage Have you ever experienced the strong smell of moth balls while pulling clothes out of a closet? How about the smell of tobacco on your clothes after being in a public place that permits smoking? You may not have smoked, but you still smell of it. Scents do seem to stick to things, and glasses are no different. If you store your wineglasses in a new oak breakfront, you can be sure that they will smell of wood when you take them out. Glasses stored in the basement can pick up the musty smell that many basements have. Brand-new glasses right out of a cardboard box will continue to smell like cardboard until they are rinsed properly. So try to store your glasses in as neutral an environment as possible, and remember: When in doubt, rinse.

Thickness Thin glasses, in general, are preferable to thick, heavy ones. Thin glasses allow the taster a truer and more natural evaluation of the wine, and they have less influence on the wine's temperature.

Etchings Glasses that are etched, painted, or tinted may be quite attractive as well as expensive, but they will affect the true appearance of a wine and are therefore inappropriate for wine tasting.

Shape There are many shapes and sizes of wineglasses, and one must be careful not to confuse a good, proper glass with a fashion statement. For Champagne and sparkling wines, the best glass is the tall, tapered flute glass, which is designed to keep the bubbles active. The worst glasses for Champagne and sparkling wines are the small, flat, wide saucer-styled glasses that are often used in catering halls. This type of glass exposes too much of the wine to the air, causing a premature release of the gases needed to sustain the active bubbles that one associates with these wines.

The best all-purpose white-wine glass should be approximately eight to fourteen ounces (remember, we fill the glass only one-third full, so in effect an eight-ounce glass will hold only about three ounces of wine). The bowl should be of medium size and should taper inward at the top. Tapered glasses are designed to help direct and focus the wine's aromas inward toward the nose.

A good red-wine glass should be approximately ten to sixteen ounces, with a slightly larger and rounder bowl than the white-wine glass. It should be slightly tapered in at the top. I have sometimes witnessed older and more mature red wines being poured into extremely large-mouthed glasses. While these glasses may look impressive, they can actually hinder the wine's aroma. Unlike young wines that can actually benefit from being exposed to a lot of air, older and more mature wines possess complex aromas and nuances that can dissipate prematurely as a result of such excessive exposure. How sad it would be to miss out on the pleasures that long-term aging and proper cellaring can produce because of using too large a glass.

Pour amount To properly swirl a wine in the glass, it is important to fill no more than one-third of the glass with wine. Champagne can be poured higher (two-thirds).

How to hold All wineglasses should be held by the stem. This is true whether you are drinking wine with dinner or are involved in a serious wine tasting. Wineglasses should be held in this way because if the bowl of the glass is held, the heat from your hand can cause the wine in the glass to heat up. (The exception here is the drinking of Cognac and brandy, where this warming is considered desirable.) Another reason to hold a wineglass by the stem is to keep the bowl of the glass clean and void of any odors from colognes, lotions, or nail polish.

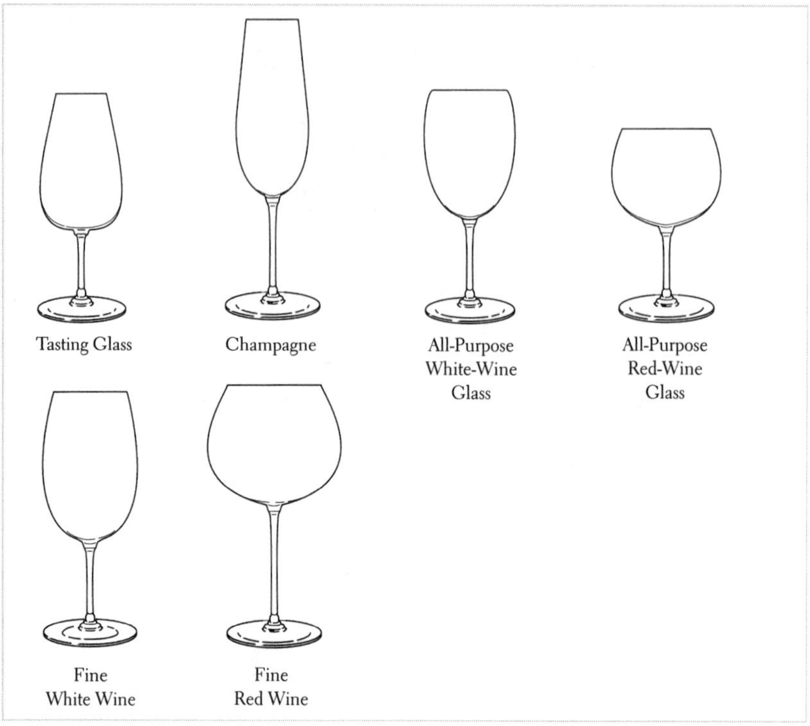

Wineglasses

Wine-Tasting Guidelines

When setting up a wine tasting, you will find it helpful to follow several basic and important guidelines. I have listed the most important ones here, each with a brief explanation. As you gain more experience as a wine taster, the reasons for these guidelines will become more apparent to you. I do recommend that you start out with only two or three wines at first. It is better to taste fewer wines completely than many wines incompletely.

1. *Taste white wines before red wines.* Red wines possess much more tannin than white wines, which often results in more bitter, full-bodied wines. Once these elements have been introduced to the palate, they can influence your impression of the wines that follow.
2. *Always taste unoaked or lightly oaked wines before more heavily oaked wines.* Again, heavily oaked wines can influence your subsequent impressions of unoaked or lightly oaked wines.
3. *Always taste dry wines before sweet ones.* Sweet wines are very thick and coat the mouth and palate. This coating can stay on the palate, falsely influencing the impression of the wines tasted afterward.

4. *Always taste similar wines at the same temperature.* White wine: 50 to 60 degrees. Red wine: 55 to 65 degrees.
5. *Always taste the same wine types together.* Chardonnay with Chardonnay, Pinot Noir with Pinot Noir.
6. *Always taste softer wines before stronger wines.* The impression of a strong or big-style wine will alter your impression of a softer, less structured wine.
7. *Always taste low-alcohol wines before high-alcohol wines.* High alcohol also coats the mouth and palate, making it difficult to judge wines that follow with substantially less alcohol.
8. *Go back and retaste all wines.* Before making final evaluations, quickly retaste all the wines. You will notice that many of the wines have evolved and are displaying different characteristics from those they revealed when you tasted them initially. This change, called "opening up," occurs as the wine sits in the glass over a period of time.
9. *Neutralize your palate.* Before and after tasting each wine, neutralize your palate by taking a sip of water or eating a plain cracker.
10. *Keep a written record of your impressions and remember, wine is an alcoholic beverage, so use discretion in consumption.*

Wine Terminology

A list of the most commonly used wine-tasting terms and their meanings follows:

LOOKING AT A WINE

White wine color range Pale green, light yellow, yellow golden, golden, golden orange, orange brown, brown

Red wine color range Dark purple, purple ruby red, red, brick red, red brown, mahogany, amber

Rosé wine color range Onionskin, light pink, pink, light red, orange

Brilliant A wine that is extremely clear and sparkling

Clear A wine that appears clear and transparent with no cloudiness or sediment

Cloudy Unclear and hazy

Crystal tartrates Glasslike crystals that sometimes form when a wine has not been overly processed

Dense Difficult to see through

Dull Cloudy, lackluster

Hue Particular shade or hint of color

Legs A coating that forms around the bowl of the wineglass

Maderized A negative chemical reaction that causes a wine's color to turn brown

Sediment Sandlike deposits found mostly in red wines

Viscosity Thickness of a liquid (can be an indication of high alcohol or sugar content)

Youthful When a wine displays a color that makes it appear younger than its actual age

SMELLING A WINE

Acetic Vinegar odor (considered a fault)

Aroma The smells of a young wine

Barrel-fermented An aroma that is produced as a result of fermenting the wine in wood

Bouquet The smells of an older wine

Candy apple The smell of candied sugar (often a sign of a process known as *chaptalization*)

Charred The smell of charred wood

Cigar box Another wood aroma (cedar)

Clean Void of any off odors

Complex Many different flavors or aromas combined

Corked The smell of a defective cork

Floral (all types) Geranium, honeysuckle, hyacinth, lilac, rose, stock, violet

Foxy Grape jelly aroma, found in some American grape types

Fruity The fresh scent of different types of fruits: apple, apricot, banana, blueberry, black cherry, black currant/cassis, cherry, coconut, grapes, lemon, lime, melon, peach, pomegranate, raspberry, strawberry

Green Unripe smell

Heady A wine that possesses an excess of alcohol

Herbaceous A green, unripe, vegetal odor

Hot Term used when a wine is considered too high in alcohol

Hydrogen sulfide The aroma of rotten eggs (considered a fault)

Mature The smell of a properly aged wine

Mineral The smell of different minerals

Musty Damp basement smell (often confused with corked)

Nose The combined aromas of a wine

Nuance A slight complexity

Off When a wine smells of a defect

Open The aromas of the wine have become obvious

Oxidized The smell of a wine that has been overexposed to oxygen (when excessive, considered a fault)

Pine The smell of pine sap

Salty/brine The smell of saltwater

Smoky The aroma of smoke

Spices/herbs Basil, caramel, coffee, chocolate, cinnamon, clove, coriander, lavender, mint, mustard, nutmeg, pepper, sage, spearmint, sugar, burnt sugar, vanilla

Steely Flinty, slightly metallic

Stewed The smell of overripe or overcooked fruits

Sulfur dioxide The smell of sulfur (burnt matches) (considered a fault)

Tar The aroma of warm tar (found in some red wines from Italy)

Toasty The aroma of slightly burnt wood

Varietal When a wine smells true to its grape type

Vegetal The aroma of vegetables (considered a fault)

Vinegary The smell of vinegar (considered a fault)

Volatile acidity The unpleasant smell of glue or nail polish remover (when excessive, considered a fault)

Weedy The smell of wet weeds (can be a fault)

Woody The presence of wood aromas

Yeasty The smell of yeast as found in baking bread

TASTING A WINE

Acid Sharp, tart, crisp taste of a wine

Approachable Can be currently enjoyed and consumed

Astringent The hard, biting sensation in the mouth caused by tannin

Balanced When all of the elements of a wine are in harmony

Big Refers to the size and body of a wine

Bitter Taste of bitterness (considered a fault if excessive)

Body The weight of a wine on the tongue (light, medium, heavy)

Closed The aromas of a wine are not apparent or obvious

Cloying Describes a wine that is sweet and lacking acidity

Coarse Rough textured

Complex When a wine contains many different flavors and nuances

Crisp Refreshing, lively

Elegant Refined, well balanced

Fat Heavy, thick

Faulty A flawed wine

Finish The flavor of a wine after it has been swallowed (short, medium, long)

Firm Good structure and acidity

Fleshy A wine with high extract

Fresh Youthful

Fruity A taste of fresh fruit

Hollow Empty, little substance

Hot Refers to high alcohol

Lean Thin, high in acidity

Length The amount of time a wine's flavor remains after swallowing

Meaty Thick, chewy

Oaky Flavors of oak barrels

Rough Hard

Spritz Sensation of fizz, carbonation

Tannic Bitter and dry sensation of red wines

Toasty Toasted or roasted flavor

The Progression of Tasting Wine

Today's quick-fix society demands that we achieve the highest possible level of expertise in the shortest amount of time. And although it's great that we tend to approach new endeavors with both energy and enthusiasm, we should be aware of the pitfalls we will face if we try to do much too soon. To properly absorb both the simplicities and the intricacies of wine, one must begin with the knowledge that acquiring such an understanding requires time, patience, and practice. Wine is best understood when learned about in separate stages, or levels, over time.

It would be unwise to assume that any stage of learning can be bypassed or leapfrogged simply by purchasing expensive, highly rated wines in order to go immediately to the head of the class. Such thinking can actually hinder your enjoyment and development as a taster. The following examples should make my meaning clear.

Let's say that someone recommends you buy a bottle of a top-rated French Bordeaux, a current vintage of Château Lafite-Rothschild, for example. Excited, you return home, invite over some friends or associates, and uncork your prized wine, only to discover the wine is harsh, bitter, and mouth-puckeringly hard and dry. Disappointed, you lose faith in the clerk and wineshop that recommended the wine, vow never to buy such a wine again, are embarrassed in front of your guests, and — as if all that weren't bad enough — you get to pay dearly for the experience. In reality there was nothing wrong with the wine. You just had no right to open it. More often than not, young, top-rated Bordeaux needs years of cellaring before it becomes approachable, but you hadn't learned that yet.

At the other end of the spectrum, let's say you're in a fine restaurant, celebrating a profitable business transaction. You order the oldest, most expensive wine on the list, regardless of the fact that you're accustomed to drinking more current wines. For some reason many of us believe that older wine is better wine, when in fact that statement is a gross exaggeration. The wine is opened and poured. You notice the wine is not perfectly clear and there are tiny particles in it, and when you taste the wine, you find it is not nearly as fresh and fruity as you expected. It even smells slightly oxidized with old flavors. Is this wine bad? Do you send it back? No on both counts. The wine is actually displaying many of the signs associated with an older wine. But because you haven't experienced older, mature wines on a regular basis, you think the wine is bad. If you had more tasting experience under your belt, you might find this very same wine and its characteristics to be delicious and proper. If you had stayed within your tasting range and ordered a wine you were more comfortable with, you would have enjoyed both the wine and the evening much more and saved a considerable amount of money. Training your palate cannot be rushed. Be patient, take your time, nurture your palate, and I can assure you many pleasures along the way.

With so many different labels, regions, vintages, and wine types, where does one start? How does one begin? To ease you on your way, I have outlined three progressive levels of wines that will expose you to different styles and tastes in an organized manner. Each level contains a minimum of ten red and ten white wine types for you to taste. This is a general guide, and a good wine salesman or wine waiter should be able to suggest additional choices. Save money by trying half bottles instead of full ones, and when dining out, try different wines by the glass.

I strongly recommend that you spend a minimum of three to six months experimenting with the wines of each level before proceeding to the next. While each level will introduce you to more complex tastes and aromas (and at higher costs, I might add), it is important to realize that each level does contain unmatched applications and pleasures that will last a lifetime. In other words, no one level is more important than any other. Good tasting, and please, take your time.

Exposure Level One (recent vintages)

White Wines

German Riesling QbA and QmP Kabinett
American Chenin Blanc and Riesling
Lightly oaked California Chardonnay
French Mâcon, Bourgogne Blanc

French Alsatian Pinot Blanc, Riesling
Lightly oaked Australian Chardonnay
Spanish Albariño
Slightly sweet Champagne and sparkling wines
Most Italian white wines
Oregon Pinot Gris

Red Wines

Basic French Beaujolais, Bourgogne
French Bordeaux Supérieurs, Cru Bourgeois
Sweet-style rosé wines
Washington State Merlot, Cabernet Sauvignon
California Pinot Noir
Italian Dolcetto, Chianti, Barbera
Spanish Rioja Crianza
South African Pinotage
Côte du Rhône
Basic California Cabernet Sauvignon

Exposure Level Two

White Wines

French Pouilly-Fumé and Sancerre
French white Bordeaux (dry and sweet)
French white Burgundy (AOC level)
French Alsatian Grands Crus wines
Drier Champagne and sparkling wines
Most California Chardonnay and Sauvignon Blanc
German Riesling (Spätlese and Auslese levels)
Full-style Australian Chardonnay and Sémillon
Italian Tunina and Vin Santo
New Zealand Sauvignon Blanc

Red Wines

Most California red wines
French red Burgundy (AOC)
Most Australian Shiraz/blends
Oregon Pinot Noir
French Côte du Rhône (Côte Rôtie, Hermitage, and Châteauneuf-du-Pape)
Classified French Bordeaux

Italian DOC and DOCG wines
Italian Super Tuscan wines
All other rosé wines
Most Spanish wines

Exposure Level Three

White Wines

Spanish Fino and Manzanilla Sherry
Premier Cru French white Burgundy
Grand Cru French white Burgundy
Older French white wines
French Sauternes
French Savennières
French late-harvest Alsatian wines
Very dry French Champagnes
Hungarian Tokaji
German Riesling (Beerenauslese, Eiswein, Trockenbeerenauslese)

Red Wines

Top classified French Bordeaux
French Premier Cru Burgundy
French Grand Cru Burgundy
Aged red wines (ten years plus)
Top Spanish Ribera del Duero, Rioja
Top Italian Amarone, Barolo, Barbaresco, Brunello, Chianti
Top Australian Shiraz/blends
Top California Cabernet Sauvignon
Top French Rhône wines

Wine cellar
COURTESY OF ROBERT WEIL, GERMANY

2

THE WINE CELLAR/BUYING WINE

The words *wine cellar* evoke two images. One is an elaborate maze of wine racks that gently cradle an assortment of rare and expensive bottles of wine in a temperature-controlled room. The owner of this cellar is in the corner making notes, compiling a current inventory of his liquid assets. The second image has more of an Old World flavor, a dungeonlike cavern whose walls and ceiling are covered with mold. The bottles in this cellar are old and coated with a thick layer of dust. While these two types of wine cellars *may* exist, each is quite an exaggeration of the norm.

Both of my grandparents were born in Italy in the late nineteenth century, when wine on the dinner table was as commonplace as bread on a sandwich. One of their first goals when they arrived in the New World was to create a wine cellar. Their wine cellar may seem quite primitive to us today, but it was actually quite functional. Let me re-create it for you.

My grandparents built their wine cellar in the loneliest corner of the basement, away from the furnace and clear of any windows, in a room six feet by six feet with no light source. A two-inch layer of moistened gravel covered the floor, and there were large pails of water on both sides of the door. The wines were stored simply, in wooden milk crates, and the used corks were kept in a container by the door, ready to be reused. As humble as this cellar was, it was actually quite practical, as we will see.

First of all, my grandparents selected the basement because it was underground and thus offered the coolest and most consistent temperature in the house. This environment was further enhanced by the fact that there were no windows. The wine cellar was kept dark, because light can have a deleterious effect on wine. It was also far removed from any work areas, where the odors of paint or cleaning fluids could permeate the corks and get into the wine. Finally, the cellar was far from the furnace, so that the temperature could be kept as constant and as cool as possible. The buckets of water provided a proper level of humidity, and the gravel was moistened because it absorbed the water and then slowly released the humidity that would help age the wine as well as keep the corks moist. Upon examination, this simple and extremely inexpensive cellar actually provided quite an acceptable environment for wine storage.

Anyone can have a wine cellar, in the bottom of a closet or in a subcellar, from ten bottles to ten thousand. It can be created at little or no expense, as my grandparents' was, or many thousands of dollars can be lavished on it by the serious (and wealthy) collector. The following "Wine Cellar Guidelines" outline the perfect environment for storing and aging wine. Perfection is not always possible, of course, so you may have to make some compromises.

Wine Cellar Guidelines

Maintain constant temperature Not only should a wine cellar have a cool temperature (55 to 65 degrees is optimum), but the temperature should be as constant as possible. Erratic peaks and drops in the temperature will have a negative aging effect on the wine. While heat is the worst enemy of wine, excessive cold can also damage and even freeze wine. When a wine has been kept too cold too long, glasslike crystals called *crystal tartrates* can form, and, although they are harmless, they can affect the appearance of the wine and your enjoyment of it.

Maintain constant humidity High humidity is preferred (70 to 80 percent), because humidity will help the aging of wine as well as keep the corks moist. One downside of high humidity is the effect on wine labels, which tend to peel off the bottles. Because of this tendency, many châteaus in Europe will put labels on bottles only immediately before they are released. If the location you have chosen for your wine cellar is low in humidity, pails of water and humidifiers can be used.

Keep free of vibrations Constant vibration can cause wine to age prematurely and keep it from settling properly. Constant vibration has also been known to prevent the cork from attaining a proper seal, thus resulting in spoilage.

Keep away from strong light sources Where there is strong light there is heat, and heat is the number one enemy of wine.

Keep away from strong smells Strong odors can also get into wine, so position your cellar away from strong chemical smells — paint products, gasoline, and cleaning products, for example. Even pet odors can have a negative effect on wine.

Wine bottles must be stored on their sides The reason for storing wine bottles on their sides is to keep the wine in constant contact with the cork. If the cork becomes too dry it will become brittle and lose its ability to keep the wine airtight. Madeira is the only exception to this rule, because exposure to air is part of the process used in the making of Madeira. It should also be noted that the average life of a quality cork is ten to twenty years, at which point the corks should be inspected. If a cork is failing, a process known as *recorking* can be done.

Why Start a Wine Cellar?

The following questions and points are worth considering if you are interested in starting a wine cellar.

Are you purchasing wines for early consumption?
If what you want is a simple and ready supply of wine, you do not need an extravagant layout. Empty wine boxes turned sideways in the back of a closet provide an easy, efficient, and inexpensive way to store wine.

Are you looking to purchase and hold wine as an investment?
If this is what you want to do, see "Wine As an Investment" (page 40), and follow the wine cellar guidelines I've just outlined.

Wine collecting is a fun and interesting hobby.
It's the kind of hobby that can easily last a lifetime. Should you eventually decide it's not for you, you can simply drink up your collection.

Wine is a great-looking decoration.
If aesthetics is your main objective, I suggest you purchase the least expensive wines possible.

Will you buy wine by the bottle or by the case?
You can receive considerable savings when you buy by the case, but if you buy this way, you will obviously need to dedicate a larger space to your cellar.

How long do you intend to own the wine before actually drinking it?
The longer you intend to keep and age wine, the more carefully you must adhere to the wine cellar guidelines outlined in this chapter, as proper aging requires proper care.

Fun Reasons for Collecting Wine

One of the most enjoyable reasons to collect wine is to mark special dates and occasions. In France it's a common practice to purchase a case of wine at the birth of a child. Throughout the life of that child a bottle is opened at each of his or her special occasions — birthdays and graduations, for example. Imagine the child's delight in knowing that he or she has a personal cellar!

How about a gift of a special-vintage, dated wine to commemorate a special event such as a wedding? One case of wine would last twelve years if a single bottle is opened every year on the couple's anniversary. If this idea appeals to you, I recommend purchasing only age-worthy wines, vintage Ports, or vintage Madeira.

Finally, who doesn't like a good bottle of wine as a gift? Apart from the fact that people generally enjoy gifts of the vine, if you choose and cellar wine carefully, chances are good that by the time you give it as a gift, its value will have grown considerably higher than your initial investment. This will make you look good and save you money as well.

Wine Cellar Locations

Natural Basements or cellars provide the coolest and most constant natural temperatures in the house, which is especially important if you plan to age your wines. Don't forget, however, that it is also important to store your wines away from heat sources such as a furnace. If your basement is prone to flooding, you may wish to consider another location. Unfortunately, the higher floors of a house are considerably warmer than the cellar, especially during the summer.

Temperature-controlled units Temperature-controlled units solve many storage problems and come in all sizes, prices, and styles. They are usually equipped with cooling and humidifying systems, thus providing an excellent environment for short- and medium-term aging. Other options are also available — for example, indoor lighting and temperature alarms. Prices range anywhere from $500 to $5,000.

Temperature-controlled prefabricated wine rooms These are similar to temperature-controlled units except that they are entire rooms. They come in a large assortment of sizes and can be placed wherever they fit. They can accommodate large amounts of wine, making them ideal if you plan to purchase and store wines in their original cases. Understandably, the cost of these rooms is high, but it is not hard to justify this cost if you view wine as a long-term investment and hobby.

Leased space in a commercial wine storage facility For the serious collector who doesn't need to have his wine on the premises, commercial temperature-controlled warehouses are available. The prices vary, as space may be leased by the room or by the case. One downside to this method of cellaring is that your access is limited. Most users of this type of facility store only their full cases. I strongly recommend that you check out these facilities in person to insure their security as well as the quality of their storage conditions. I would further recommend that you discuss the insurance coverage, if any, that is included.

A wine rack in the living room Wine racks come in many styles and, as living room accessories, look great. They look great, but as living room temperature usually fluctuates, I would not recommend this location for any length of time. If you do choose to store wine in your living room, I would recommend that you find a quiet spot away from radiators and direct sunlight.

The back of a closet For the city dweller, the back of a closet may be the best choice. It is dark, has a constant temperature, and is probably cooler than any room. Try to select a closet away from heating units and outside walls. As wine is sensitive to strong odors, remember to take out the mothballs.

The kitchen While stored wine may be aesthetically pleasing in a kitchen, this is one of the worst locations possible. Stoves and ovens can cause temperatures to skyrocket, and of all the different environmental factors to which wine can be exposed, heat is the worst. I have been in too many homes where the wine rack is located directly above the refrigerator, where constant heat and vibration will quickly take their toll on a wine's quality.

A designed space You can hire a design firm to create a custom wine cellar for any area in your home. While the results can be stunning, so will your bill.

Filling Your Wine Cellar

Okay, you're finally going to start filling your wine cellar. But where do you begin? What do you buy? And how much should you buy? Now that you know the basics about cellar locations and are familiar with the guidelines for providing good storage, all you need to know is *what* to put in your wine cellar. Following are some safe, affordable, and simple cellar hints.

Start out small Don't buy a lot of wine right away. If you drink one bottle of wine a week, start your cellar with four to six bottles (a four- to six-week supply).

Buy half bottles Half bottles are always cheaper than whole ones, so when you're trying a wine you haven't yet tasted, always invest as little as possible. Once you've found something you like, you can then purchase the larger version. Having half bottles in your cellar will also accommodate those times when you need or desire only a glass or two.

Don't spend a lot It's smarter to purchase more bottles of different, inexpensive wines than just a few bottles of expensive wines. If you follow this practice, you can try many different wines.

Buy by the bottle, not the case As tempting as the discount on a full case may be, never — I repeat, *never* — buy a case of a wine that you have not tasted. Give your palate a chance to develop.

For a starter cellar, try buying a case of assorted wines When you're down to the last three bottles, it's time to purchase another mixed case. Obviously, the more you drink, the more you will need to replenish. By using this method, you will never run out of wine.

Sample Case

WHITE

1 bottle French Chardonnay (Mâcon)
1 bottle California Chardonnay

1 bottle New Zealand Sauvignon Blanc
1 bottle German Johannisberg Riesling (sweet)
1 bottle French Vouvray (Chenin Blanc)
1 bottle Sparkling Wine

RED

1 bottle Spanish Rioja (Crianza)
1 bottle California Zinfandel
1 bottle French Bourgogne Rouge
1 bottle Italian Barbera
1 bottle Chilean Cabernet Sauvignon
1 bottle Washington State Merlot

Once you have acquired a mixed case you can begin practicing the most important and easiest procedure described in this book, tasting and enjoying wine. Keeping simple tasting notes as you taste these wines will help you remember what wines and which styles of wine (dry, sweet, red) you enjoyed, as well as which ones you didn't. The more you taste, the quicker your palate will develop. By tasting, you will also begin to acquire your own impressions about different producers, wine-making styles, and vintages. You will be well on your way to becoming a skillful taster.

Good Value Wineries

Following is a partial list of wineries located around the world that in my opinion offer good value to the consumer. Remember that good value does not necessarily mean inexpensive.

United States

CALIFORNIA

Beaulieu Vineyard
Beringer Founder's Estate
Byron Vineyards
Carneros Creek Winery
Chateau Souverain
Domaine Carneros Sparkling Wines
Estancia Estates
Fetzer Vineyards
Franciscan Winery
Guenoc Winery
J. Lohr Estates

Joseph Phelps Winery
Markham Winery
Monterey Vineyard
Ravenswood
Robert Mondavi Winery
Roederer Estate Sparkling Wines

WASHINGTON STATE

Château Ste. Michelle Winery
Columbia Winery
Columbia Crest Winery
Hogue Cellars

OREGON

Argyle Winery
Erath Winery
Oak Knoll Winery

NEW YORK STATE

Hermann J. Wiemer
Dr. Konstantin Frank
Lenz Winery

Spain

Wines of Cune
Wines of Marqués de Caceres
Wines of Marqués de Murrieta
Wines of Muga
Wines of Torres
Wines of Tondonia
Wines of Conde de Valdemar
Wines of Vina Mayor
Ònix

Italy

Wines of Rainoldi
Wines of Vallana
Wines of Alois Lageder
Wines of Cosimo Taurino
Wines of Banfi
Wines of M. Chiarlo
Select wines of Antinori

Germany

Wines of Pfeffingen
Wines of J. J. Prüm
Wines of Robert Weil

Chile

Wines of Los Vascos
Wines of Santa Rita
Wines of Concha y Toro

Australia

Wines of Lindeman's
Wines of Hardy's
Wines of Richard Hamilton
Wines of Rosemount Estate

France

Burgundy wines of Bouchard
Burgundy wines of Joseph Drouhin
Burgundy wines of Louis Latour
Burgundy wines of Georges Duboeuf
Red Rhône wines of E. Guigal
Red Rhône wines of P. Jaboulet
Alsatian white wines of Domaine Trimbach
Alsatian white wines of Willm
Alsatian white wines of Hugel

Bordeaux Because most classified red Bordeaux have become overpriced in my opinion, it is difficult to list them as good value wines. However, some of the well-known châteaus often offer a second labeling or bottling at a considerably lower price. The grapes for these wines are usually from younger vines that may not have yet reached their optimum quality level. These wines are produced and bottled separately and can be of excellent value, especially if purchased near the time of their initial release. Following is a partial list of these wines, the châteaus that produce them, and the communes where the châteaus are located.

CHÂTEAU	SECOND BOTTLING	COMMUNE
Latour	Les Fortes de Latour	Pauillac
Lafite-Rothschild	Carruades	Pauillac
Lynch-Bages	Haut Bages Averous	Pauillac

Pichon-Baron	Tourelles de Pichon	Pauillac
Pichon-Comtesse Lalande	Reserve de la Comtesse	Pauillac
Gloria	Haut Beychevelle Gloria	St.-Julien
Lagrange	Les Fiefs de Lagrange	St.-Julien
Beychevelle	Amiral de Beychevelle	St.-Julien
Léoville-Las-Cases	Clos du Marquis	St.-Julien
Giscours	Margaux de Giscours	Margaux
Palmer	Reserve du General	Margaux
Margaux	Pavillon Rouge	Margaux
Phélan-Ségur	Frank Phelan	St.-Estèphe
Montrose	Dame de Montrose	St.-Estèphe
Calon-Ségur	Marquis de Ségur	St.-Estèphe
Haut-Brion	Bahans Haut-Brion	Graves
Fieuzal	L'Abeille de Fieuzal	Graves
Cos d'Estournel	Les Pagodes de Cos	St.-Estèphe
La Dominique	St. Paul de Dominque	St.-Émilion
Cheval Blanc	Petit Cheval	St.-Émilion
Lafon-Rochet	Numero 2 Lafon Rochet	Graves Rouge
Belgrave	Diane de Belgrave	Haut Médoc
Sociando-Mallet	Demoiselle de Sociando	Haut Médoc
Chasse-Spleen	L'Érmitage de Chasse-Spleen	Haut Médoc-Moulis

Other unclassified Bordeaux wines can be found and would be categorized as Cru Bourgeois (see discussion of Cru Bourgeois, page 211). Two good examples of Cru Bourgeois are Château d'Angludet from Margaux and Château Meyney from St.-Estèphe. Cru Bourgeois wines often represent some of the best values in Bordeaux.

Buying Wine at Retail

Not very long ago, if you wanted to purchase a bottle of wine, you had to go to the local wine and liquor store. Not so anymore. More liberal laws involving the sale of wine have been implemented, making the purchase of wine as simple as going to the supermarket. In some states even convenience stores can now sell wine. Think about it. You can pull up to a gas station, say, "Fill it up" to the attendant, and return with a bottle of Cabernet Sauvignon before your tank has been filled.

Convenience, however, does have its downside. Do you think these wines have been handled properly or stored correctly? The odds are that the clerk will not know the difference between a case of classified

Bordeaux and a case of Pennzoil. Will the stock person in the supermarket be able to tell you the difference between Chardonnay and Sauvignon Blanc? I think not.

It is important to remember that there are good wineshops and bad wineshops, and only you can decide if one particular store can satisfy your wine needs. To help you make an informed decision, I have outlined here what services are desirable.

A QUALIFIED AND COURTEOUS STAFF

A good salesperson should be able to guide you and answer your questions. He or she should be someone who has tasted the wine you are interested in and has the ability to accurately translate his or her impressions to you. A qualified wine salesman is almost as rare as a qualified sommelier. You do not want to work with a salesperson who relates only what score or awards a wine has received, since very few wines have *not* won some kind of award. You should also try to avoid wineshops where the staff gets paid a commission, because this seems to create a "sell the most expensive wine you can" mentality.

ACCESS TO MANAGER/OWNER

If you have a problem or the wine you want is hard to find, the regular sales staff may not be able to help you. Thus it's important that the store's manager or owner makes himself accessible to customers. Purchasing, return, and discount policies are usually set by the store's manager as well.

GOOD STORAGE FACILITIES

Good wine must be stored properly. What a shame that a wine can travel around the world in good condition, only to turn sour in a local warehouse. Ask the clerk if the wines are stored at an even, cool temperature (55 to 60 degrees is optimum) and away from sunlight, strong smells, and constant vibrations. I have been in too many wineshops where the "wine cellar" was next to the boiler. If you really want to make the clerk nervous, ask if you can inspect the store's storage facility. Even if this is not possible, you will come out ahead, because you have just sent a serious message that you are a knowledgeable buyer. One good way to check on a wineshop's dedication to proper storage is to show up just as the shop is opening during a summer hot spell. You can be sure that if the store is warm, the wine is, too.

FAIR PRICING

You could spend a great deal of time trying to find the least expensive price for a bottle of wine; the range of prices for the same wine is amazing. With a little research, however, you should be able to find a store with fair pricing. Stores that specialize in loss leaders lure you in with a known item at cost in the hope that you'll make additional purchases with higher markups. Beware of the store that attracts you with a loss leader, then tells you that a particular wine is not available or sold out and tries to sell you a different wine of lesser value and in all probability lesser quality as well. Many stores will give quantity bottle discounts, as well as case and multiple case discounts. While they may not always offer a discount, most stores will give you one if asked. Don't be shy about this. These savings can be quite dramatic, sometimes as high as 20 percent. It is important to keep in mind that the more you order, the more the store can order, and just as you receive discounts for large orders from the retailer, the distributors in many cases (no pun intended) offer quantity discounts to the retailers. Again, the smart retailer who is looking to keep you as a customer will pass on these savings to you. Exempt from these discounts are rare and hard-to-find wines. When purchasing such wines, expect to pay top dollar and understand that obtaining such a wine is part of your reward.

A RETURN POLICY

Sometimes a wine does go bad, be it because of a defective cork, improper storage, or bad wine making. It is the wise shopper who will discuss this possibility before it occurs. You may find that a store's return policy is not set in stone, and the better and more familiar customers get the most return bottle flexibility. This is another good reason for the store personnel to get to know you as a customer. In many cases the bad wine can be returned to the distributor for credit.

DELIVERY SERVICES OFFERED

Let's face it: wine is heavy, so why carry it if you don't have to? Some retailers will deliver for a minimal charge, while some will do it free of charge. I have even heard of some smart retailers who will deliver wine as gifts around the holidays to your friends and clientele. This can certainly make gift giving a lot simpler. But you won't know whether your retailer will do this if you don't ask.

PARTY PLANNING

Any good wine store should be able to help you with party planning. Party planning covers a wide range of services — from which wine to buy to how much wine you will need and recommendations on pairing wine with food. Don't forget that from discounts to better service, it is quite advantageous for you to do most of your business with the same store. You are best served, as the song from the hit TV show *Cheers* says, in a store "where everybody knows your name."

Top Retail Tips

- Inspect a bottle before you purchase it. The bottle should not feel too warm or too cold. Look at the top of the capsule: it should be dry and void of any wine stains, and the cork should not be above the lip of the bottle. All of these are signs of improper storage. With a slight firmness, press the cork downward with your thumb. The cork should feel firm but have a slight give. It is a sure red flag if the cork easily pushes down the neck of the bottle. A very hard cork may also be a bad sign, as the cork should be pliable.

  Next you should visually inspect the bottle. As a general rule I recommend that you not purchase any wine that appears to be cloudy or unclear or that possesses an excessive amount of particles, sediment, or crystal tartrates. Look at the wine's ullage (the air space between the wine and the bottom of the cork) and purchase the bottle with the least amount of air space, as air is also an enemy of wine. Wine should be stored on its side to keep the cork moist. If that is done, no air can penetrate and make contact with the wine.

- Start out with small purchases, and never buy a case of wine you have not tried. (As my grandfather used to say, "You should drive the car before you buy it.") Do not be overly anxious when buying wine. Try a bottle first; if you like it, buy a case.

- Ask about wine tastings. Quite often wineshops hold free wine tastings (check out state laws) for its customers. Let the shop personnel know that you are interested.

- Chill your own wine. Unless you plan to drink a bottle of wine right away, do not buy it out of a refrigerated unit. Constant cold temperature and vibration can affect a wine's quality, and there is no way of knowing just how long the bottle you are purchasing has been sitting there.
- If you're interested only in certain wine types or regions — red Bordeaux or Spanish wines, for example — call up different wineshops and ask them how strong their selections are in those areas before making the trip.
- Do not be talked into a sale. Tell the sales staff the type of wine you are looking for, as well as your price range. Then stick to it.
- Empty wooden wine cases can be made into attractive, inexpensive, and functional wine racks, and retailers will usually give them to their customers for the asking.
- Everyone enjoys a compliment, so when you have been given a good wine recommendation, thank the salesperson responsible.

Retail Pricing

Walking into a wineshop can certainly be an intimidating experience. Just passing wall after wall of so many different types of wine from so many different places has been known to send many potential customers running to the corner deli for a six-pack. And just when you start to feel comfortable in this environment, you take a look at those prices. A friend of mine who had set out to purchase a bottle of wine said to me: "I found myself trying to make a decision between buying a popular Merlot or paying my phone bill." He opted for the Merlot, but the message was clear: Good wine can certainly be expensive.

As noted earlier, you can find an assortment of different prices for the same wine at different wineshops. Standard retail markup in the city of New York is roughly 50 percent of the wine's cost, or a profit margin of 33 percent (this percentage will be less if the store implements any bottle or case discounts). What this means is that a bottle of wine that cost the retailer $10.00 will be sold to the consumer for roughly $14.99. Cost-cutting stores may sell the same wine for a lower markup of 25 percent, resulting in a price of $12.50 to the consumer for the same wine.

Now, I know what you're thinking. With such a clear savings, why would anyone pay the higher price for the same wine? While this savings may be real with the purchase of a single bottle, the cost-cutting store seldom, if ever, offers any quantity bottle or case discounts to the consumer as other retailers often do. And as mentioned earlier, this savings can be considerable — often between 10 and 15 percent. Another reason for not buying in such high-volume stores — and I cannot stress this enough — is *service, service, service*. Most of the sales staff in high-discount cost-cutting stores have neither the time nor the knowledge to be of any *service* to you, the customer.

One other retail pricing policy that varies from store to store is the passing on of the savings and discounts the store sometimes receives when it purchases wines in quantity. Often the distributor (the retailer's supplier) will offer the retailer quantity case discounts on multiple case purchases. These discounts can range from 3 percent on a two-case purchase to 20 percent on the purchase of ten cases. A 20 percent savings on a $10 bottle of wine is $2 per bottle, which is the equivalent of getting every fifth bottle of wine free. The smart retailer passes these savings on to you, while quite often the cost cutters do not. It is important to remember that such discount programs may apply only for a short time (say, for a month) and only on select wines, as some distributors do not offer such a discount.

Finally, rare wines that are hard to come by, or are in very limited supply, are rarely discounted. They are usually priced at the retailer's discretion and at perceived market value.

The Serious Wine Collector

There are two types of serious wine collectors. The first collects wines to guarantee his enjoyment of them in the future, because wines often become too scarce and expensive to purchase at later dates. The second is impressed just by the fact that he owns certain wines and you do not. He buys a wine, cellars it for years, and then sells it without ever tasting it. In other words, to this second collector wine is just an investment or a commodity, and collecting it is no different from collecting stocks or art.

Wine is a beverage that is created to be consumed; it's not meant to be merely a trophy. Those who collect it as a commodity are in my view a dangerous group, as the main purpose of owning a commodity is to make a profit. This mentality inflates the value of certain wines, leaving the loyal consumers who actually created the demand for a particular wine out of the loop or unable to afford it. Personally, I like the traditional way that wine is collected in England. There, many collectors/drinkers purchase wine knowing that they will drink only half of the stock and will sell the remaining half to bankroll future wine purchases. What I like most about this system is that these collectors are wine drinkers who collect wine as a way to insure drinking good wine in the long term. They are not hard-core collectors who have only monetary gains in mind.

What Makes a Wine Collectible

The laws of logic do not apply when it comes to what makes a wine collectible. Common sense dictates that quality alone should be the main determining factor; however, that is not always the case. Often, just being rare qualifies a wine as collectible, regardless of its quality. I've known salesmen who have made a good living selling wine by saying to their customers, "The winery made four hundred cases, and only ten have been allotted for New York City." Other times a wine is considered collectible because it has received a glowing review or a high score from an important critic. Sometimes just the fact that a popular public figure has been seen sipping a certain wine is all that's needed to create a flurry of demand for the wine. New wineries' first efforts are sometimes considered collectible, as are wines made by the current hot wine maker. Wines collected for these reasons seldom pass the test of time. For long-term, safe, and sure collecting, I always choose wines with a history and a good track record.

Wine As an Investment

If profit is your prime motive in collecting wine, you should be aware of the pitfalls. First you should know that only a small percentage of the wine that is made is of investment-grade quality. Another misapprehension in collecting wine for investment is that old wine means good wine. Old wine means good wine only when it has been made from an age-worthy grape type from an age-worthy region, when it has been produced from an above average vintage by a consistent and reliable château or producer, and, finally, when it has been stored properly. Collecting wine for investment and resale is not much different from investing in the stock market: the investor looks for a good solid company with a good track record. While the rewards can be great, the losses can be even greater. The wine cellar guidelines I gave at the beginning of this chapter must be followed closely, as proper storage is essential for investment wines.

Investment Tips

- Purchase and store wine in its original case. Loose bottles do not retain as much value as entire case lots.
- Purchase wines only from above average vintages.
- Purchase wines as futures or as close to the original release date as possible.
- Wines for long-term cellaring and investing must be stored under optimum conditions.

- A soiled and stained label is considered less desirable than a pristine one.
- The smaller the production, the rarer the wine. The rarer the wine, the higher the demand. The higher the demand, the greater the perceived value.
- A signed bottle by the wine maker or owner may decrease or increase a wine's value.
- Purchase only from a reputable source.
- The best wines to hold as investments are red classified Bordeaux, vintage Port, select red and more select white Burgundy, Sauternes, certain California Cabernet Sauvignons, and Italian and Spanish red wines. (See "Some Select Wines for Investment," page 42.)
- While I do not like to admit the importance wine ratings can have as a tool in investing in wine, extremely high ratings (96 to 100) do seem to create a higher premium and demand.
- Some wineries occasionally release a commemorative label or special bottling, which can sometimes add to a wine's value. An example is the red Bordeaux wine of Château Mouton-Rothschild. Every year its label is designed by a different prominent artist.
- Oversize bottlings generally carry a higher premium than the standard 750-ml bottle. One reason for this is that fewer oversize bottles are produced, and thus they are rarer. Another reason is that, with the exception of Champagne, most wines age better in larger bottles, since a smaller proportion of wine is in contact with the air. Half bottles are correspondingly less desirable when collecting for investment because the larger proportion of wine/air contact accelerates the aging process of most wines.

THE DIFFERENT BOTTLE SIZES

	BURGUNDY	BORDEAUX	CHAMPAGNE	PORT
hf.bt. - half bottle	0.375	0.375	0.375	0.375
imp.pt. - imperial pint	0.568	0.568	0.568	0.568
hf.ltr. - half liter	0.5	0.5	0.5	0.5
bt(s). - bottle(s)	0.75	0.75	0.75	0.75
ltr. - liter	1	1	1	1
mag. - magnum	1.5	1.5	1.5	1.5
m-j. - marie-jeanne	—	2.5	—	—
d.mag. - double magnum	—	3	—	3
jero. - jeroboam	3	5	3	—
reho. - rehoboam	—	—	4.5	—
imp. - imperial	—	6	—	—
meth. - methuselah	6	—	6	—
salm. - salmanazar	—	—	9	—
balth. - balthazar	—	—	12	—
nebu. - nebuchadnezzar	—	—	15	—

COURTESY OF SHERRY-LEHMAN WITH SOTHEBY'S

Some Select Wines for Investment

French Bordeaux

PAUILLAC

Château Lafite-Rothschild
Château Latour
Château Mouton-Rothschild
Château Lynch-Bages

POMEROL

Château Pétrus
Château Le Pin
Château Trotanoy
Château Certan-de-May

GRAVES

Château Haut-Brion
Château La Mission Haut-Brion

MARGAUX

Château Margaux
Château Palmer

ST.-JULIEN

Château Léoville-Las-Cases
Château Ducru-Beaucaillou

ST.-ÉMILION

Château Cheval Blanc
Château Ausone

ST.-ESTÈPHE

Château Cos d'Estournel
Château Montrose

French Red Burgundy

Domaine de la Romanée-Conti wines
Domaine Leroy wines
Henri Jayer wines
Domaine Dujac Grand Cru
Armand Rousseau Chambertin
Comte de Vouge Musigny
Hubert Lignier Grand Cru

French White Burgundy

Domaine Leflaive Grand Cru
Domaine Raveneau Chablis
Louis Latour Corton-Charlemagne
Domaine Ramonet Grand Cru
Marc Colin Grand Cru
Comte Lafon Meursault
J. F. Coche-Dury Corton-Charlemagne Meursault
Romanée-Conti Montrachet
Faiveley Corton-Charlemagne
Domaine Michel Niellon Grand Cru

French Sauternes (Sweet)

Château d'Yquem

French Alsace

Zind Humbrecht

French Red Rhône

Château Rayas Châteauneuf-du-Pape
Château de Beaucastel Châteauneuf-du-Pape
E. Guigal Estate's — Côte-Rôtie (La Landonne, La Mouline, La Turque)
Chapoutier — Hermitage
J. L. Chave — Hermitage
René Rostaing — Côte-Rôtie (La Landonne)

California Cabernet Sauvignon

California Cabernet Sauvignons have been the hot ticket at wine auctions of late. What is interesting about the astronomical prices some of these wines are fetching is that they seem a direct reflection of a winery's tiny production, not neccessarily the quality of its wines. While rarity and tiny production can increase a wine's perceived value, it is never — and I repeat *never* — a guarantee of a wine's quality.

Château Montelena
Heitz Wine Cellars Martha's Vineyard
Caymus Vineyards Special Selection
Dalla Valle Maya
Dominus (blend)
Opus One (blend)
Stag's Leap Wine Cellars Cask 23

Robert Mondavi Private Reserve
Bryant Family Vineyards
Silver Oak
Harlan Estate
Screaming Eagle
Araujo Estate — Eisele Vineyard
Colgin
Grace Vineyards
Spottswoode
Shafer Vineyards Hillside Select
Philip Togni Vineyards
Beaulieu Vineyard — Georges de Latour — Private Reserve
Ridge Vineyards Monte Bello
Dunn Vineyards
Mayacamus Vineyards
Phelps Insignia (blend)

California Merlot

Palmeyer Vineyards
Matanzas Creek
Duckhorn Vineyards
Duckhorn Vineyards — Three Palms

California Zinfandel

Ridge Vineyards — Lytton Springs
Ridge Vineyards — Geyserville
Turley Wine Cellars
Martinelli

California Chardonnay

Mount Eden Vineyards Estate
Kistler Estate bottlings
Stony Hill Vineyards
Talbott Vineyards
Peter Michael
Palmeyer Vineyards

California Other

Rhône-style wines of Sean Thackrey

Washington State

Leonetti Cabernet Sauvignon
Leonetti Merlot
Quilceda Creek Cabernet Sauvignon
L'École No. 41 Cabernet Sauvignon

Oregon

Evesham Wood Cuvée J. Pinot Noir
Domaine Drouhin
Beau Fréres

Spanish Red Wines

Vega Sicilia Unico — Ribera del Duero
Marqués de Murietta Castillo Ygay Rioja Gran Reserva
Cune Imperial Rioja Gran Reserva
Pesquera Janus
Muga Gran Reserva
Clos de l'Obac

Italian Red Wines

Solaia
Sassicaia
Gaja Barbarescos
Biondi-Santi Brunello
Topflight Barolo
Quintarelli

Australia

Penfolds' Grange Hermitage
Mount Langi Ghiran Shiraz

A Word About Insurance

I once knew a gentleman — I'll call him Harry — who upon purchasing a large house decided to build a wine cellar. Harry was rather well-off, so he spared little expense in the cellar's construction. He then filled it with a selection of rare and expensive wines. Many of his purchases were made by the case, and after a few years he had compiled quite a stellar collection. As time went by and much to his delight, the value of many of these wines increased dramatically. Harry had famous Bordeaux, rare red as well as white Burgundies, a strong selection of vintage Ports, and an excellent collection of California Cabernet Sauvignons. Then, while Harry was vacationing one Fourth of July weekend, a loose rocket hit his house and started a fire. Fortunately no one was hurt, but the water and fire damage to his cellar was quite extensive. While Harry had fire insurance for his home, his wines were not covered.

If you are a serious collector, you should learn from Harry's misfortune and inquire about insuring your collection by adding a rider to your policy. Remember to save all your bills, as the insurance company will need to see them before settling any claim.

Wine Auctions

Your initial reaction on hearing the words *wine auction* may be something like "rich man's sport" or "way out of my league." This impression of wine auctions is historically correct. Until a few years ago they were fairly stuffy affairs, held chiefly in London. Recently they have become quite common in many major cities across the United States, and the image of the well-off, aristocratic wine connoisseur, bidding in a gentlemanly fashion, has given way to that of the very average wine drinker who is simply seeking out mature wines to drink today as well as wines that are no longer available in the marketplace.

AUCTION TIPS

- Quite often the best buys at wine auctions are the less popular lots of wine. The rare wines from the top wine estates, especially those from the perceived great vintages, always command top dollar and attract the most attention. If investing is your game, you may have no choice other than to enter the bidding war. If, however, you're looking for good, solid wines that are ready to drink tonight, buying the less popular lots may provide you with the best value as well as the most pleasure.

- Do your homework before attending an auction by procuring a copy of the auction catalog ahead of time. Some of the auction houses sell subscriptions to their catalogs and will send them to you automatically. The auction catalog offers important information such as auction rules and regulations, fees, and an absentee bid sheet.

- If you're looking for a specific type of wine — California Merlots, for example — just concentrate on the Merlots being auctioned. Look for old and current reviews of these wines. If you have the time and inclination, you can even call the wineries for their perceptions of a particular bottling, as many wineries taste their current and older-vintage wines on a regular basis.

- I am always a little suspicious when eleven bottles of wine are offered (a full case is usually twelve bottles). It makes me wonder whether upon tasting a bottle, the seller decided the wine wasn't worth keeping.

- While auction houses assure us that the wines they auction have all been inspected to verify their condition and storage, they seldom — if ever — guarantee these things. Always ask to inspect the wine before the auction is held (this is a common request).

- Quite often preauction tastings are held. Be aware, however, that you may have to call ahead and make a reservation. There may also be a slight charge for such a tasting, but tasting a wine before purchasing it is always best. Preauction tastings will also give you an opportunity to taste different wines.

- There is a customer disappointment of 5 to 15 percent on the wines that are auctioned. This figure varies among the different auction houses and may reflect the quality and condition of the wines that each of these houses accepts for auction. Be prepared for the possibility.

- The estimated selling price, calculated on the most recent price a particular wine has sold for at an earlier auction, is set by the auctioning house along with the seller. It is actually a range of prices, and the lower end of the range is considered a good value. Many wines at an auction also hold what is called a *reserve price*, which in reality is the lowest price at which a wine can be sold. If the reserve price is not met, the lot will be withdrawn and either returned to the owner or put into the next auction. Sometimes there is no reserve price, and a lot of wine will sell for even less than the lower estimate. For this reason, I strongly recommend you put in any bid you are comfortable with. You never know what a lot may sell for.

- Going to the beach on the weekend of the big auction? No problem. Thanks to technology, you don't have to be present at an auction, as your bid can be phoned, faxed, or even mailed in ahead of time.

- Understanding auction terms and their abbreviations (see "Wine Auction Terminology," following) will afford you more time to concentrate on the wines you are interested in.

- The more experienced, savvy buyers at wine auctions position themselves at the back of the room. They do this so they can view the activity, demand, and bidding interest among the other bidders.
- If you *do* decide to go to a wine auction, you must remember two important things: Know your limit, and remember you're there to have some fun.

WINE AUCTION TERMINOLOGY

If buying wine through auctions appeals to you, there are some basic terms and abbreviations you should know before you become actively involved in the auction process. Below is a list of some of these terms, their abbreviations, and their meanings.

owc — the wine being auctioned is in its *o*riginal *w*ooden *c*ase
oc — the wine being auctioned is in its *o*riginal *c*arton
wc — the wine comes in a *w*ooden *c*ase
doz. — dozen bottles
hf.bt. — half bottle — .375 liter
bt(s). — bottle(s) — .750 liter
mag. — magnum — 1.5 liters
d.mag. — double magnum — 3 liters
jero. — jeroboam — 3 liters
reho. — rehoboam — 4.5 liters
imp. — imperial — 6 liters
meth. — Methuselah — 6 liters
salm. — Salmanazar — 9 liters
balth. — Balthazar — 12 liters
nebu. — Nebuchadnezzar — 15 liters

ULLAGE

The term *ullage* is bound to come up when older wines are being auctioned. Ullage refers to the level of wine in the bottle. The lower the ullage, the lower the level of wine in the bottle. A low ullage level is considered undesirable, as it is a strong indication of an aging wine or a failing cork.

Ullage Abbreviations

u. — ullage
n. — neck, within the neck of the bottle — normal for young wines

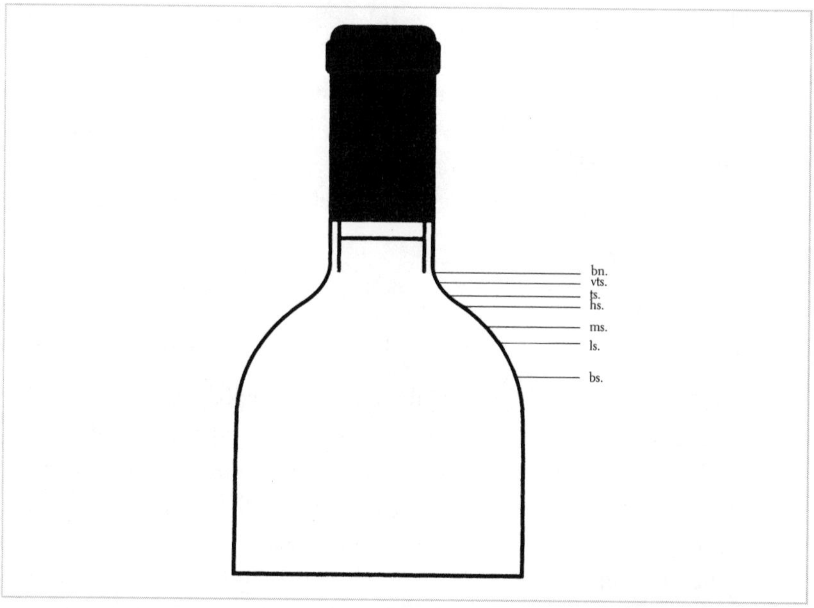

COURTESY OF SHERRY-LEHMAN WITH SOTHEBY'S

bn. — bottom neck — acceptable and proper ullage
vts. — very top shoulder — also acceptable ullage
ts. — top shoulder — acceptable level for wine aged over twelve to fifteen years
hs. — high shoulder — acceptable level for aged wine over fifteen years of age
ms. — middle shoulder — red flag — caution is advised
ls. — low shoulder — red flag — caution is strongly advised
bs. — below shoulder — avoid

Example of Auction Listing

LOT 522
6 bts. u.2bn. Heitz Martha's Vineyard Cabernet Sauvignon 1985
1 bt. mag. Ridge Monte Bello Cabernet Sauvignon 1987
1 doz. owc Dominus 1994
Estimate 1200.00–1600.00

Knowing auction language is not only necessary but timesaving as well. Using the abbreviations listed previously, you should have no problem deciphering this listing. The first item in Lot 522 consists of six .750-liter bottles of 1985 Heitz Martha's Vineyard Cabernet Sauvignon, of which two bottles have a wine ullage that goes to the bottom of the neck of the bottle, which is considered acceptable but not perfect. Also in the lot is one magnum (equivalent to two .750-liter bottles) of Ridge Vineyards Monte Bello Cabernet Sauvignon 1987. There is also one 12-bottle case of Dominus in its original wooden case. The estimate represents the perceived value of the entire lot, with the lower figure ($1,200) being considered a good value.

THE COSTS OF BUYING AND SELLING WINES AT AUCTION

When the hammer finally falls and the auctioneer calls out, "Lot forty-one sold to the gentleman in the third row for the sum of four hundred and ninety dollars," you might assume that you have just purchased Lot 41 for $490. You'll soon learn, however, that although the bidding may have stopped, the cost of Lot 41 will continue to escalate.

First the auction house adds its wine premium to the buyer's bill. This premium is usually a fixed percentage of the purchased lot price. It may vary from auction house to auction house, but it usually falls within a range of 10 to 15 percent. Added to that is the sales tax, or VAT tax if the wines are to be sent overseas. While auction houses will gladly arrange shipping for your purchase, they will also pass on the cost to you. You may also wish to purchase insurance when you ship the wine.

As you can see, the cost of your purchase has just increased dramatically. What you initially perceived as a good value may have turned into a bit more than you bargained for. Understanding the rules of buying wines at auction will always insure that you stay within your price range. I would recommend asking the auction house about these additional costs before the auction begins, because when that hammer falls it is too late.

If you plan to put your wines up for auction, there are additional costs that will be charged to you, the seller, as well. For starters, a seller's premium of 10 to 15 percent of the selling price goes to the auction house, plus sales tax, shipping, and insurance. If you have done your arithmetic, you can see just how profitable auctions are for auction houses, as collecting 15 percent premiums from both seller and buyer nets the house a hefty 30 percent of the proceeds from the entire auction. An auction that brings in $1 million may net an auction house $300,000. This is earned simply by providing a venue for the sale of wine, while offering little or no guarantee of its quality — not a bad way to make a living.

AUCTION HOUSES

An auction house cannot survive for any length of time without a spotless reputation for honesty and for possessing a great deal of knowledge about the commodity being auctioned. When seeking out an auction house with which to do business, it is of utmost importance that you make certain yours is a reputable house. Following is a list of a few established auction houses (marked with asterisks) as well as some of the newer wine auction houses.

Auction houses are sometimes affiliated with prominent retailers. An example of one such house in New York City is Sotheby's, which is associated with Sherry-Lehman. This affiliation may be different in different states, so always check. It is also not uncommon for a well-respected wine professional to serve as a consultant and sometimes as director for the auction house. Serena Sutcliffe of Sotheby's and Michael Broadbent of Christie's are two such professionals.

*Christie's — New York 212-774-5330
*Sotheby's — New York 212-606-7207
Davis & Company — Chicago 312-587-9500
Butterfield & Butterfield (purchased by eBay in 1999) — San Francisco 415-861-7500, ext 307
Morrell & Company — New York 212-307-4200
winebid.com

3

THE RESTAURANT WINE LIST

It wasn't long ago that the wine list in most American restaurants was little more than an accommodation. Most of the focus for both consumption and profits was on liquor-type beverages such as vodka, gin, rum, and Scotch. Today, however, the public has embraced wine not only as a much more appropriate beverage to consume with food but also as a much healthier choice. In America wine is now viewed as an elegant addition to the dining room table, as it has been in Europe for centuries. Wine also offers great profit potential as well as prestige to a restaurant, and many a restaurant has built its reputation on its wine list and commitment to wine. While almost every restaurant now offers some type of wine list, only a small percentage of these lists are drawn up in an appropriate manner.

What Makes a Good Wine List?

SIZE

Wine lists come in all sizes, from verbal selections given by your waiter to the intimidating, large, leather-bound book. While quantity can certainly be a factor in a good wine list, it is never a guarantee. A small list of well-chosen wines that work well with the menu is always better than a large, helter-skelter selection of wines thrown together with no direction or consideration for the food. It should not be assumed that the bigger the wine list, the better it is. Sometimes too large a list can actually hurt a restaurant's wine program, as a large list often results in a number of wines that simply do not sell. While some wines benefit by additional aging, the quality of most wines declines over time. As a result, more diners return their bottles of wine, causing a loss of revenue to the restaurant and, more important, lost confidence in the wine list by the consumer.

When a large list is organized, well selected, and in sync with the menu, it becomes a wonderful and impressive accommodation for the diner and a selling tool for the staff. A top-quality restaurant with a varied menu should have a sizable list so the menu's many different offerings can be matched and complemented. A large list might concentrate exclusively in just one wine-making country, such as France, Italy, or California; another might cover many wine-making regions. The type of restaurant and its clientele usually determine this. At The River Café, where there is a varied menu and a large international clientele, all of the great wine-making regions are covered in depth. What must be remembered when viewing a wine list is the quality of the selections offered, not the quantity.

APPROPRIATENESS TO THE MENU

It is important to remember that each wine list should be tailored to the restaurant and restaurant type. Regardless of its size, a wine list must work with the cuisine being offered. At a steak house, for example, hearty red wines, a natural accompaniment to steak, usually dominate wine sales. At this sort of restaurant, it makes sense to offer more red wines than white. White wines should not be neglected, though, as there are plenty of people who drink only white wine and order chicken or fish even in a steak restaurant. Another example would be a restaurant that specializes in seafood, where white wine sales dominate, and thus the wine list should favor white wine.

PRODUCER AND VINEYARD

Not listing the producer or giving any vineyard designation of a wine denies you valuable information. Clos de Vougeot (an expensive French red

---

Joseph DeLissio at The River Café
COURTESY OF BEVERAGE MEDIA

Burgundy), for example, is bottled by more than sixty different producers each year, and, understandably, some producers are better than others. Just knowing who the producer is can make the difference between choosing a great bottle of wine and choosing a mediocre one.

PRICES

A balanced wine list should offer good wines at different price points. Too often wine lists concentrate on only high-priced wines, which can intimidate the consumer. It also shows a lack of commitment by the restaurant, since there are many excellent wines available at affordable prices.

IMPORTANT WINE TERMINOLOGY

You will become familiar with these terms as you read through the book. They provide information that is essential when ordering a wine and should appear alongside each listed wine.

WINE'S REGION AND OTHER IMPORTANT INFORMATION

The region where the wine is made should be given in as much detail as possible. For example, "Pinot Noir Beaulieu Vineyard Carneros Napa Valley 1995" offers much more information than "Pinot Noir Beaulieu Vineyard."

VINTAGE

The difference in quality of a wine made by a producer from the same vineyards but from different vintages can be quite dramatic. Each wine's vintage should be included on the wine list. Be aware that prices often reflect the perceived quality and the availability of a particular vintage. You would not expect to pay the same price for a bottle of 1990 Lynch-Bages, a red Bordeaux from an excellent vintage, as for the 1991 Lynch-Bages, which is much less desirable.

QUALITY HALF BOTTLES

Half bottles have many applications in a restaurant. For example, they can be a good choice when a menu selection warrants a white wine with the appetizer and a red wine with the entrée. They also accommodate single diners who do not wish to order a whole bottle or to order wine by the glass. Half bottles are also tempting and affordable for the diner who would like to try something different without making a large investment.

SWEET WINE NOTATION

A special mark that indicates sweet wines on a wine list is helpful. It is an unpleasant surprise to order a wine you assume is dry, only to find it is sweet, or vice versa.

A BALANCED SELECTION

The type of restaurant and the menu it offers determine what a "balanced selection" is. "Balanced" does not mean that the list contains the same number of red wines as white wines or Champagnes. If the menu leans heavily toward white wines, it only makes sense for the wine list to reflect that. A wine list should not be redundant, however, by offering too many similar wines made in the same style or from the same vintage. There should also be a proper balance of prices so that everyone can feel comfortable purchasing a bottle of wine. A balanced selection should also provide a good representation of the wine region or regions listed.

DEPTH

A wine list's depth can be defined by the number of selections it offers representing one specific wine region or a number of different wine regions. It is an obvious commitment of direction by a restaurant. Another example of depth might be a restaurant that specializes in California Cabernet Sauvignon and offers many different styles and vintages by a number of different producers. Depth might also be defined as a restaurant's offering many different bottlings and vintages from the same château, domaine, or producer — six different vintages of Château Léoville-Las-Cases (a red Bordeaux from St.-Julien), for example. This is also called a *vertical selection.*

CLEAR PRINT AND EASY LAYOUT

I have seen some wonderful wine lists printed in such small type that I could barely read them. A friendly, clean, and easy layout is always preferable. It is also helpful when each wine is assigned a number. This eliminates a diner's fear of mispronouncing the wine when ordering.

Dissecting the Wine List

To be comfortable with a wine list, you should have a basic understanding of wine and wine terms. Once you have this knowledge, you must learn how to use it to dissect a wine list into minisections and cross sections. Regardless of its size, a wine list that has been broken down into sections will be much less intimidating and more manageable.

Let's say that you are seated in a restaurant that does not have a sommelier and are handed a wine list along with the menu. The first step is to avoid being rushed into a hasty decision, so ask the server to allow you a few minutes to review the menu and wine list. Let's say there are approximately a hundred wines on three pages. The first page is titled "Champagne and Sparkling Wines," the second "White Wines," and the third "Red Wines." Let me give you an example of how the process of dissection works on the page titled "Champagne and Sparkling Wines."

First you must know the difference between Champagne and sparkling wines. In order to be called Champagne, a wine must come from the Champagne region of France. Only certain grape types are permitted in the production of Champagne, and certain aging and wine-making requirements must be adhered to, making Champagne a highly regulated product. Sparkling wines, on the other hand, can come from anywhere in the world (including any region in France outside of the Champagne region) and may be made using many different grape types with little or no aging or wine-making requirements. While both products can technically be called sparkling wine, only wine made within the borders of the Champagne region can be called Champagne.

Next you must understand the different categories of Champagne. There are three levels of Champagne: nonvintage Champagne, a blend of many different vintages and usually the least expensive offering; vintage Champagne, made from the harvest of a single vintage and aged longer; and last, tête de cuvée, or prestige, Champagne, which is the finest offering of a particular Champagne house, usually a longer-aged, vintage Champagne and always expensive.

Champagne can also be categorized by level of sweetness. There are six levels, and knowing the sweetness level of the Champagnes on a menu can be very helpful when ordering. Ultra brut is the driest, followed by brut, which is the most common level and also dry. The remaining four, in ascending order of sweetness, are extra dry, sec, demi-sec, and doux, which is the sweetest Champagne offering. Rosé Champagne comes in many different shades, from a light onionskin to a pinkish orange to a light red. The color comes either from the addition of a small amount of red wine called *bouzy* or from contact with the red grape skins during fermentation. Like the Champagnes mentioned earlier, rosé Champagne can be vintage, nonvintage, or tête de cuvée.

Knowing some of the basic terms used to describe Champagne and sparkling wines is also helpful when making a selection. One such term is blanc de blancs, which translated into English means "white of whites." This is in reference to the fact that only white grapes (Chardonnay, if it is Champagne) are used in the production of that particular bottling. This is an important piece of information, because just knowing that the wine is made from the Chardonnay grape provides additional information about how it may taste. If you do not like the flavors of Chardonnay, you may wish to pass on this one.

Blanc de noirs is used to describe a Champagne or sparkling wine that has been produced from the white juice of only black grapes (in wine the color comes from the skins, as all grape pulp is clear and considered white). In Champagne the black grapes used are the Pinot Noir and the Pinot Meunier. Blanc de noirs wines are usually fuller in texture and bigger in style than the more elegant, refined blanc de blancs.

The term *méthode champenoise* or *méthode traditionnelle* refers to the traditional wine-making method used in Champagne. While this method may be applied in the production of sparkling wines made anywhere, it does not qualify a sparkling wine as Champagne.

Now that we know the basics about Champagne, let's turn our attention to sparkling wines. As mentioned earlier, sparkling wines can be made anywhere in the world, using any grape types and method of production. All of this variation can lead to a wine that is quite different from a true Champagne. This is not to say that there aren't many fine sparkling wines being made. You need only taste some of the sparkling wines being produced in California, Italy, Spain, and even New Mexico to appreciate their quality. When you order a sparkling wine, however, you should be aware of the differences. Champagne houses have joined forces with California properties — Roederer (Roederer Estate), Taittinger (Domaine Carneros), and Moët (Domaine Chandon) — to produce good-quality sparkling wines using the traditional grape types and production methods of Champagne. This type of collaboration can be an indication of a high-quality product, and the name of the associated Champagne house, which usually appears on the wine's listing, gives you a clue to its affiliation. Sparkling wines are usually much more affordable than French Champagne, and thus it is easier to enjoy this versatile product more often.

As you can see, once you are familiar with some basic facts and terms, the Champagne and sparkling wine page is no longer so intimidating. With this information and a little practice you will be fully equipped to dissect any Champagne list and, at the same time, indicate that you are knowledgeable to your guests or clients and the wine server. The terms used when dissecting red wine and white wine lists may be different, but the system of breaking down the list into sections and cross sections remains the same. (Again, you will become familiar with these terms as you read through the book.)

The Sommelier (se-mel-yay)/Wine Server

The sight of an approaching sommelier has been known to provide more than a passing moment of anxiety to many a diner. Is he friend or foe? Will she know that I don't know much about wine? Please, don't let me be embarrassed in front of my client! I hope he doesn't recommend too expensive a wine. Or, Here we go, one more tip!

How did the sommelier develop such an intimidating reputation? Any diner who has ever had a bad experience with an unqualified sommelier can tell you that, for the most part, the sommelier's poor reputation was earned when he acted in an intimidating and self-serving manner. This doesn't mean that qualified and caring sommeliers do not exist, because they do. Like good chefs, however, they are rare. Part of the problem is different perceptions of the position itself. There is a big difference, for example, between the traditional European and the American sommelier. Top restaurants in Europe consider the sommelier's to be a position of prestige, one that requires an extremely high level of training and experience. The sommelier can be one of the great assets of a fine restaurant. His competence and integrity can often make the difference in a customer's choice (especially a repeat customer's) of where to dine. In short, the sommelier's position is both noble and highly respected. With the acknowledgment by both management and ownership of his importance, it is not unusual for a talented sommelier to work at a single establishment for many years — even decades. And long-term employment is key in the development of a great wine program.

In the United States sommeliers are often viewed quite differently. Here too many restaurateurs view the sommelier as just another salary. Many do not seem to understand the importance of having a person on staff who is dedicated to the development of a wine program. I have always found that odd, as the wine and beverage program usually represents the most profitable area in any restaurant. Odder still is that the same ownership thinks nothing of employing a full-time coat check person, parking valet, or telephone receptionist. This type of nonsupport by ownership leads to job insecurity, which reduces this important position to little more than that of a transient worker. And while transient workers are not usually driven to be dedicated or caring to management or the consumer, they *are* driven by money. It does not take long to figure out that the more they sell, the more money they will make. With this dangerous mentality in place, the sommelier often recommends expensive wines and may overpour the wine so that a second — or even third — bottle will be needed.

Just one such sommelier can provoke disrespect, contempt, and total distrust from an entire group of diners. This type of employee will never be an asset to the restaurant, because he is seldom employed by one establishment long enough for a true wine program to be developed. It is sad to think that such a noble position, one that has endured for centuries, can be brought low so quickly by so few. The good news is that many of today's top restaurants are beginning to realize the importance of employing someone to be in charge of their wine program. The bad news is that change takes time, and until attitudes shift, wine and wine service in the American restaurant may never reach their true potential.

With that said, let's discuss the role of the sommelier. Above all, remember that the sommelier is there to help you. He should do this by gently and skillfully guiding you in choosing a wine to accommodate your tastes, menu selections, and budget. He should happily — and without intimidation — answer any questions you may have, regardless of how simple or silly those questions may seem. And as wine is meant to be consumed with food, the sommelier should have a good working knowledge of the menu as well as an understanding of food and wine pairings.

Qualities of a Good Sommelier/Wine Server

- Will not be intimidating
- Will answer all questions
- Should work within your pricing parameters, and if smart, will help you find the proper wine for less
- Will always ask the host before opening any additional wine bottles
- Should be able to offer more than one wine recommendation
- Should offer his expertise without insisting on it
- Should never embarrass or strongly correct the person ordering the wine
- Will know how to serve wine properly — will not overpour
- Will suggest decanting before doing it
- Will inform the table of any vintage, vineyard, or price change before opening wine
- Understands when a wine is bad and has the ability to explain why a wine is not
- Should offer the same professional service regardless of the wine's price
- Offers half bottles or wine by the glass when appropriate
- Has a good knowledge of the menu
- Should understand that sometimes the best recommendation is no wine at all (certain salads, artichokes, asparagus, very salty foods)

- Provides clean glassware
- Lets the table relax and enjoy themselves

ORDERING WINE WITH THE SOMMELIER/WINE SERVER

There are two basic scenarios that you can experience with a wine sommelier, and the first requires blind faith. While relinquishing control is difficult for most people (myself included), doing so in the gentle hands of a qualified and experienced sommelier can result in the most rewarding experience possible, for who better to match the food and wine than someone whose job is to do exactly that, someone with a working knowledge of the wine cellar as well as a very current awareness of what is going on in the kitchen? A qualified wine sommelier might just be the single most important connection between the restaurant itself and the diner. This type of sommelier is rare, but when you do find one, you will quickly understand his value. True to the laws of yin and yang, this same blind faith does have its dark side, as giving an inexperienced sommelier carte blanche can be disastrous as well as expensive.

The second, much safer scenario requires some input from you. Yes, you will actually talk with the sommelier, and after your first brave attempts, you will look forward to this exchange. It is important — as well as rewarding — that you set the parameters. Following is a list of information that will help the sommelier select a wine for you:

- Wine type. Are you looking for a red, a white, or a sparkling wine?
- Taste preference. Do you want a dry or a sweet wine? Do you want it to be fruity? woody? tannic? light? medium-bodied? (Of course you will understand these terms and many more once you've read this book.)
- Wine grape type. Chardonnay, Merlot, Syrah, Cabernet Sauvignon, Riesling?
- Region. California, Oregon, France, Germany, Spain, Italy, Chile?
- Vintage year. Do you have a preference?
- The table's menu selections.
- Price range.
- Bottle size. If this is not discussed, it will be assumed you are looking for a full .750-liter bottle.

Sequence of Ordering Wine in a Restaurant

1. Presentation of wine list and menu
2. Ordering of selection
3. Presentation of unopened bottle by the sommelier/wine server

4. Approval and opening of bottle
5. Presentation of the cork
6. The sampling
7. The approval
8. Pouring of the wine

TALKING TO THE SOMMELIER/WINE SERVER

Let's say that you're looking for a white wine to go with your grilled chicken and your guest's tuna. You tell the sommelier that you would like a wine that's very dry, medium-bodied with some oak, preferably something French made from the Chardonnay grape, and in the $25 to $35 price range. Armed with this much information, any wine sommelier or server should be able to recommend an appropriate wine for your table. You will most likely discover that the sommelier very much appreciates your input and direction. If he doesn't, be careful.

When the sommelier returns, he will present the unopened bottle to you for your inspection and approval. If there is any discrepancy with the vintage, producer, or price, it is the sommelier's job to inform you. Once you give a sign of approval (usually a simple nod of the head), the wine will be opened. It is tradition that when the wine server removes the cork, he places it by the person who has ordered the wine. At this point you may inspect the cork by sniffing for any off odors and by gently squeezing the cork for elasticity. It is important to know that any concerns you may have with the wine due to the condition of the cork must be reconfirmed by sniffing and tasting the wine, since a bad cork alone is not a valid reason for returning a bottle of wine. (I have had some wonderful wines with horrible corks.)

The server will now pour a small sampling (a half ounce) in your glass for you to taste and approve. I strongly recommend that before you taste the wine you take a small sip of water or a bite of bread to neutralize any strong flavors — salad dressing or salt, for example — that may be lingering on your palate. This is because strong flavors can interfere with your assessment of the wine. It is at this stage that any faults or displeasures with the wine should be brought to the server's attention. If you are not certain whether the wine is correct, you should mention it to the server and request a few additional minutes to see if the off odor or bad taste dissipates, as it often does.

Once you have decided that the wine is correct, tell or signal your approval to the server. The server will now pour everyone at the table a proper-size portion (a third to a half glass) of wine. Proper wine service dictates that ladies be poured first, followed by the gentlemen, and finally the person who ordered the wine. However, this rule is not etched in stone.

FREQUENTLY ASKED QUESTIONS ABOUT TIPPING, AND THE LIKE

Should all restaurants have a wine sommelier?
Although many top restaurants have sommeliers, most restaurants do not. At The River Café, for example, there is no wine sommelier; however, the maître d' and all the captains are trained to handle the wine service. While all restaurants do not need a wine sommelier, they do need a staff that is adequately trained in the handling of wine and wine service.

Should you tip the sommelier, and if so, how much?
It is important to remember that the sommelier is there to serve and properly guide you. A gratuity should not be considered automatic and should be earned by the sommelier. The amount given, of course, is up to you. Tips can be calculated on a percentage of the bottle cost or can be a set sum. Some customers prefer tipping a fixed amount per bottle. If you feel that no extra service or attention has been given, you may decide that a tip is not necessary.

Does the standard 15 percent tip for food apply to wines on the check as well?
There is much debate on this question, as most restaurant staff believe that wine costs are to be treated as part of the check. In France a standard 15 percent gratuity is added automatically to the entire check, including all wines. In America, however, a gratuity is not added automatically to the check, and many diners feel that wine — to some degree — has a different tipping standard. Does a wine server give a greater amount of attention when he opens a bottle of Dom Pérignon Champagne (at $160 a bottle) than he does when he opens a bottle of Veuve Clicquot Gold Label nonvintage Champagne (at $50 a bottle)? Again, the amount of the tip is up to you, and while the staff may feel that if you can afford the wine, you can afford the tip, it is your decision. Personally, unless I have had bad service, I tip on the wine as well.

How do you approach tipping in one of the many bring-your-own-wine restaurants?
In this type of restaurant the staff is not involved with wine choice but is very much involved with wine service. Usually a fixed tip per bottle is considered fair. The amount per bottle may be dictated by the cost of the wine or the amount of wine service required — decanting, for example. The staff in restaurants in larger cities seem to expect larger tips.

What do you do if the sommelier/wine server makes you feel uncomfortable?
Although it may seem a little impolite, either tell him how you feel or ask the maître d' or captain to handle your wine needs. If enough people do

this, you can be sure the sommelier will either adjust his attitude or risk being out of work.

What is the silver cup that sommeliers wear around their necks?
The silver cup usually worn around the neck of the wine sommelier is called a *taste-vin*. Traditionally, upon opening a bottle of wine, a sommelier would pour a little wine into this cup and taste it for soundness. The idea behind this custom was that the customer should not have to taste a bad wine. While this ritual is seldom performed today, the tradition of wearing a taste-vin has remained as a symbol of the sommelier.

DECANTING WINE

I've mentioned a couple of times a procedure called *decanting*. Decanting is the transferring of wine from its original bottle into an empty glass vessel. There are two purposes for this procedure. The first usually pertains to an older red wine that has developed sandlike particles called *sediment*. This is a natural residue that evolves over a period of time. Sediment can also result if a wine has not been filtered or fined. Although it is harmless, sediment can diminish enjoyment of a wine by making it appear cloudy and unclear. The second reason to decant is to aerate a wine. This helps soften the wine's texture and tannins and makes a hearty young red wine more approachable.

The procedure is performed by slowly transferring the wine from the bottle into the decanter. When the wine server is decanting to remove sediment, he will gently stop the flow of wine once sediment is spotted in the neck of the bottle. At this point the server will either give the sediment some time to settle at the bottom of the bottle or set the bottle back down for this same purpose and repeat the procedure when more wine is needed. Often a candle is placed between the bottle and the decanter to help the server spot the sediment. Today many restaurants are using specially made screened funnels that make the job of decanting easier.

Best-Valued Wines on the Wine List

Here is a hint list for the consumer who is looking for a good-value wine and is uncomfortable with making a decision when handed the wine list. Often the best-valued wines are the less popular types. Following is a list of some of the good ones.

WHITE WINES

Alsatian wines (France) Not only do Alsatian wines represent a good value, but they also complement many different styles of food. While these wines do not have the broad appeal and name recognition that Chardonnay has, they are much more versatile. Some examples are Riesling, Pinot Blanc, Gewürztraminer, and Pinot d'Alsace.

Mâcon (France) If you like Chardonnay yet are looking for value, try the white wines from the Mâconnais region of France. They are clean and very easy to drink, and it is often less expensive to order a full bottle of one of these wines than to order three or four glasses of house Chardonnay. They may be listed as Mâcon, Mâcon Superior, or Mâcon Village.

Chalonnaise (France) Another French region that produces good-quality Chardonnay is the Chalonnaise region. These wines often cost more than Mâcon but less than the Chardonnay produced from Chassagne, Puligny, and Meursault. While not as complex, they are often half the price. Some examples are Rully and Montagny.

Spain From the Galicia region of Spain, the Albariño grape produces a lovely floral and easy white wine that works as an aperitif with food. It is best enjoyed when young. These wines were a better value a few years back, as they have become more popular of late.

German wines German wines represent an excellent value, but remember that they are usually sweet. The noble grape of Germany is the Riesling. German wines have many levels of ripeness, with the most versatile and driest being the halbtrocken and Kabinett.

Italian wines Although not usually very complex, Italian white wines are in general reasonably priced and considered a safe choice. Pinot Grigio, Soave, Verdicchio, and Frascati are some good examples.

RED WINES

Chile Just beginning to be appreciated for its Cabernet Sauvignon, Chile produces an excellent wine made from France's most noble red grape. Chilean Cabernet Sauvignon gives you the most bang for the buck.

Italy There is value to be found when ordering Italian red wines if you are willing to go off the much traveled and popular path of expensive Barolos and Super Tuscan wines. Look for a simple Chianti, a fruity Barbera, or a Valpolicella. If you desire a bit more stuffing, seek out a Spanna, Inferno, or Ghemme — all representing good value.

Spain In my mind Spain offers the highest-quality wine for the least amount of money. Rioja Crianza is one such example. The well-known wines from the Torres winery in Penedés appear on many wine lists and are usually a tasty choice as well as a safe one.

Rhône region of France While fewer and fewer wines from France these days can be called a good value, the red wines from the Rhône Valley can be a great one. Wines labeled Côtes du Rhône are quite often a bargain, especially if made by the better producers like Guigal or Jaboulet.

Australia Australia is an interesting region that has recently stepped into the spotlight by producing world-class Shiraz for a fair price. My only hope is that they continue to hold their prices.

Napa Valley While the price for good-quality Cabernet Sauvignon and Pinot Noir has been steadily increasing, one winery has remained a leader in the production of good-valued wine — Beaulieu Vineyard. Although Beaulieu also makes high-end wines, it has continued to produce good-quality, affordable wines for decades. Bravo, B.V.

WINES BY THE GLASS

Wine by the glass has become a big part of the profit center of today's restaurant. Unfortunately too many establishments choose the cheapest available wines to realize optimum profit margins. Seldom does cheap wine turn out to be good wine, so be suspicious when ordering house wine. Some restaurants also use their wine-by-the-glass program as an opportunity to pour off declining inventory. Quite often it is less expensive and a lot smarter to purchase a half or full bottle from the wine list. Personally, I always choose this option, as there's a good chance of getting a higher-quality wine at a better price. Besides, I like a bottle of wine on the table. Another reason I prefer bottles is that I know I am not drinking wine from a bottle that was only partially consumed the night before. Some restaurants do offer a very good selection of wines by the glass, and in such cases further investigation with your server may reward you with quite a nice glass of wine.

Restaurant Pricing

It is amazing how wide the range of prices will be in different restaurants for exactly the same bottle of wine. I have been in restaurants that almost give wine away at cost; on the other hand, I have seen wine lists with prices that are outrageously inflated. What upsets me most is a wine that is easy to obtain and requires no cellaring that is marked up excessively. What *is* "excessive"? you may ask. Well, that depends on the type of restaurant you're dining in. A simple neighborhood restaurant or bistro should charge a markup between 2 and 2¼ times cost. For example, a bottle of Merlot that cost the restaurant $10 a bottle would sell for $20 on a 2 times markup. A 2¼ times markup would yield the restaurant $22.50, and anything above that would be too much. For a formal restaurant the costs of service, flowers, tablecloths, higher-quality glassware, and wine warehousing must be added to the mix. In this kind of restaurant, a 2 to 3 times markup is acceptable. A restaurant that marks up more than 3 times the cost of a bottle of wine is, in my opinion, charging excessively.

Many restaurants have a floating price policy whereby the more the wine costs, the smaller the markup implemented. For example, any wine that costs the restaurant over $25 will be marked up only 2 times, resulting in a selling price of $50 for a $25 wine. Restaurants that are able to purchase wine in large quantities can often save a fair amount of money. While some restaurants keep any additional profits, the smart restaurateur will pass on these savings to the consumer.

In defense of restaurants, the price of wine purchased after its initial release can be higher than it originally was. Many wineries will rerelease the same wine at a later date and at a substantially higher cost, and the restaurant must in turn pass on these higher costs to the consumer. The pricing of rare and hard-to-find wines — where the laws of supply and demand take hold — permits the restaurant to charge at will. What must be remembered with these rare and sometimes unbelievably high-priced wines is that "rare" seldom guarantees greatness. In closing, wine pricing can make the difference in whether or not a diner orders that second bottle of wine. The more a customer has to think about price, the more uncomfortable that customer will be, and when customers feel uncomfortable it is unlikely that they will return anytime soon.

Returning Wine in a Restaurant

The return policy at The River Café is quite simple: We take back any wine if it is bad. What is not so simple is *who* decides whether the wine is bad. When it comes to returning wine, the customer, in fact, may not always be right.

The wine list should not be viewed as a "free try until you find a wine you like" buffet. It should not provide an arena in which to show off your wine savvy in order to impress your boss, clients, or date. If the wine you ordered is sound, you should pay for it.

But now you need to know what a "sound" wine is. I describe a sound wine as one that properly represents the grape type and region it comes from, a wine that is free of any detectable flaws such as spoilage, being corked, improper storage, poor wine-making practices, or old age. Often a wine is sent back not because it is bad but because it is different from what the customer expected. The restaurant is not to blame for a diner's poor choice when he or she decides to try something different without seeking guidance from the staff.

A wine should never be refused because of the appearance or smell of the cork alone. You must smell and sometimes taste the wine before an assessment that it is bad can be made. I have tasted many great wines poured from bottles with horrible-looking corks. A corked wine has moldlike, chemical, stale, hard, unpleasant aromas. Unlike other off odors that may lessen with some exposure to air — for example, mustiness (basement smells), slight sulfur (burnt matches) — the smell of a corked wine does not dissipate and usually gets worse. Another major reason why wines are refused is dirty glassware. Dirty glassware is the sole responsibility of the restaurant and solid ground for refusal or compensation. I strongly recommend sniffing any empty glass before the wine is poured.

Return policies are different in each restaurant, and the price of a wine does seem to affect the policy. Many restaurants will not take back very old, rare, and expensive wines, even if they are bad, since replacement or compensation from the supplier for this type of wine may not be possible. Right or wrong, if this is the restaurant's policy, it should be brought to your attention before any such wine is opened or served.

The situation that causes the most confusion for both consumer and staff is a wine that is not obviously flawed yet does not seem to be correct. When a diner complains that a wine doesn't seem right, I recommend that it be given a little time (five minutes) to breathe in a wineglass. Sometimes an off odor that has built up in a closed bottle will dissipate, but this should happen within a few minutes. If after this brief intermission the wine has not improved, most restaurants will — and should — take it back. Personally, I feel that if the soundness of a wine falls into the gray area, the customer should be given the benefit of the doubt. The restaurant can either get credit from the distributor or simply pour the wine off by the glass at the bar.

Remember that you are responsible for neutralizing your palate before tasting the wine. Always eat a small piece of bread or take a sip of water before this procedure.

Inevitably, at some time or other you will find yourself in a stalemate with a wine server about who is responsible for the wine in question. When this happens, it is important to remain calm and ask to speak to the maître d' or the manager. You will find that people at higher levels of management often have more flexibility and are more inclined to see things your way. Another possibility, when such a deadlock occurs, is partial compensation (see following list). Both parties assume part of the responsibility and can negotiate a fair deduction. When all else fails, I recommend that you contact your credit card company or the State Liquor Authority for direction. However, such drastic measures are seldom necessary.

Correct Reasons for Refusing a Wine

- Excessive temperature, especially if the wine is served too warm.
- The server has not informed you of a vintage or producer change.
- The wine is corked. A faulty cork closure has caused moldlike, chemical, stale, hard, unpleasant aromas.
- The wine is excessively oxidized.
- The wine has turned (vinegar smell).
- The wine has excessive volatile acidity (strong glue or nail polish remover odor).
- The wine smells or tastes bad (subjective).
- The wine has excessive sulfur (burnt match smell).
- Excessive particles are to be found in the wine (somewhat subjective).
- An additional bottle has been opened without approval.
- The wine server has spilled or knocked over the wine.

Incorrect Reasons for Refusing a Wine

- The cork is dry.
- The cork smells corky.
- There is mold or dust matter on the cork.
- The wine is too fruity (when ordering a fruit-style wine such as Beaujolais).
- The wine smells like soil (when ordering a red Burgundy or Pinot Noir).
- The wine is sweet (when ordering a traditionally sweet wine like Sauternes).
- The bubbles in your sparkling wine or Champagne are too big.
- The wine is dry (when ordering a traditionally dry wine such as Chardonnay).
- The wine doesn't go with your food (subjective, especially if you ordered without assistance).
- You changed your mind. Once the bottle has been ordered and opened, you must assume responsibility.

Reasons for Partial Compensation

- Your server did not notify you of a change of vintage or producer until the wine was opened.
- The wine has been poured into glasses that have not been properly cleaned.
- The wine server has poured wine into the wrong glass.
- The wine server has spilled or knocked over the wine.

EXAMPLE OF A WRONG REASON TO SEND BACK A WINE

You order a bottle of Sauternes, a very sweet dessert wine from Bordeaux. Upon tasting it, you tell the waiter to take it back because it's too sweet and you want something dry. This is not an acceptable reason to return this wine, as Sauternes is supposed to be sweet and it is true to its wine type.

Label Removal

When you are dining out, you may come across a wine that you really enjoy and may want to purchase at your retail store. Once the bottle is finished, ask your server to soak off the label by placing the bottle in hot water. When you go to the store, simply present the label to the clerk. This will make locating the wine much easier, as almost all the information needed will be on the label.

Food and Wine

Having been in the restaurant business for more than two decades, I've had many opportunities to observe the pairing of food and wine. And while you might think that over time I've come up with definitive pairings of which wines to serve with which foods, what I've observed has had just the opposite effect. I've seen many seemingly illogical combinations that have, in fact, worked. I've also witnessed combinations that should have worked gloriously but were met with resounding disapproval.

Your perception of any particular combination of food and wine can be affected by many factors, including your mood and even your companions. Some people drink only white wine, others drink only red, and still others drink only sweet wines. Are they wrong? Of course not. The wine you enjoy with your food is, after all, a matter of taste (and don't let anyone tell you otherwise!). Although it is impossible to offer hard-and-fast rules on the subject, there *are* basic guidelines that can be helpful in putting food and wine together. Following is a list of hints that I hope will be helpful.

FOOD AND WINE GUIDELINES

- Before beginning to eat and drink, it is important to start out with a neutral palate. This can be achieved simply by eating a plain piece of bread or drinking a glass of water before you start your meal and between courses and wines.

- Certain foods and flavors do not work well with most wines: asparagus, artichokes, spinach, very salty foods, very spicy foods, chocolate, very oily fish like mackerel and bluefish, eggs, and most salad dressings. So it is important to remember that sometimes the best choice of wine may be no wine at all. One example of food that is difficult to drink wine with is spicy Chinese food. I enjoy it with a cold beer instead.

- When in doubt, drink white wine with white foods (chicken, fish, veal, and so forth) and red wine with dark foods (beef, lamb, game, and so on). While some consider this rule a bit too general, it serves as a quick and easy guide.

RED WINES WITH FISH

- For those who like both fish and red wine, there are options, and although this combination is a break from traditional thinking, there are many enjoyable pairings of the two. I do offer two pieces of advice, however. The first is to stay away from very oily fish, and the second is to stay away from big, rich, tannic red wines such as classified Bordeaux, full-style Rhône wines, Italian Barolo, and big-style California Cabernet Sauvignons and Merlots. Ignoring either of these suggestions will lead to a culinary mismatch more often than not. The following red wine types are safer and more versatile choices when ordering fish: French Beaujolais, Bourgogne Rouge, soft New World Pinot Noirs, Spanish Rioja, Italian Bardolino, and most semidry and dry rosé wines.

- Always try to match regional foods with regional wines (Italian food with Italian wine, French food with French wine), as they are likely to have evolved together.

- Sauces can drastically alter the taste of food and wine, so when dining out, always seek guidance and information from your server. In general, white wine should be drunk with white wine sauces and red with red sauces, but this is not an ironclad rule.

- The progression of wines is also quite important. Some helpful, but not absolute, rules include the following: young wines before old, white wines before red, lighter wines before heavy, and dry wines before sweet.

- While I do not know what you've planned for dinner, I can help you get started. The following wines are excellent aperitif or beginning wines. From France, Mâcon, Aligoté, Alsatian Pinot d'Alsace, Pinot Blanc, Riesling, dry Champagnes; from Italy, Pinot Grigio, Gavi, Pinot Blanc; from Germany, Riesling halbtrocken, Sylvaner; from California and Washington State, Chenin Blanc, Riesling, unoaked Sauvignon Blanc, sparkling wines; from Spain, Albariño, Cava (sparkling wines), Manzanilla, and Fino Sherry. Most of these wines can be successfully segued into first wine courses as well.

- Some wine types are more versatile and adaptable with more styles of food than others. Following is a list of five red wines and five white wines that are safe and affordable choices.

Five Most Versatile White Wine Types

Alsatian Riesling
German Riesling
Italian Pinot Grigio
Champagne and sparkling wines
White Burgundy (lightly oaked)

Five Most Versatile Red Wine Types

Spanish Rioja
Italian Chianti
French Burgundy (Côte de Beaune)
Pinot Noir
Australian Shiraz

I have included more information on wine and food pairings in my descriptions of wine regions (look for the heading "Enjoying Wines"). It is important that you approach this subject at your own pace, confident about your own judgments and perceptions. Your tastes are unique and need to be nurtured individually; no one can or should do it for you. Be confident in yourself and your experiences when matching wine and food. Your taste buds seldom lie, and the more different tastes and sensations they are exposed to, the more educated and experienced they will become.

4

THE VINEYARD AND THE VINTAGE

Soil and climate together create the fingerprints of a vineyard, and while these two elements will be discussed separately, they actually work in harmony. To see how climate and soil work together one need only consider the desert, where the lack of rain, combined with constant heat, results in infertile soil, where little life can be sustained. At the opposite end of the spectrum is the rain forest, where the balance of sun, high temperatures, constant humidity, and rain has created a soil so fertile that many believe life itself was nurtured here.

Man can do little to alter the climate and soil of a region, as Mother Nature and evolution are at the controls in the creation of these very individual conditions. Man can, however, work within the parameters of soil and climate by planting the grape varietals best suited to the specific conditions, climate, and soil composition of any particular plot of land.

Soil

Soil, known as *terroir* in wine circles, is the one constant in wine making. The soil of any particular plot is truly a reflection of its own evolution and regional history, and although soil can be fertilized and watered, little can be done to change its true properties.

It is from the soils and subsoils that the roots of a grapevine will extract the unique nutrients, nourishment, and minerals that will ideally transform a simple plot of land into a gifted vineyard. As mentioned earlier, the grape type planted must be suited to the soil, and finding just the right combination can take many years. In France wine makers in many of the established regions — Bordeaux and Burgundy, for example — are permitted by law to plant only certain grape types. These laws were implemented after centuries of experimentation with planting different grape types in various vineyards and wine regions. California, in contrast, has no such laws, and not too long ago Chardonnay, Cabernet Sauvignon, and Riesling could be found planted side by side within a single vineyard. Today California wine makers are still discovering which grape types are best suited to each region and soil type and have made considerable strides in their short history.

Another question that must be addressed is what differentiates the soil and subsoil of one region from that of another. One of the most extreme examples of unique soil composition is the solid, chalky, limestone-laden, white soils found in Champagne. Upon inspection, this impressively thick white chalk appears to be impenetrable by the soft roots of the grapevines. (Interestingly enough, this soil is so dense that many local buildings in the region have been forged from it.) Fortunately for us, resilient rootstock does penetrate this soil and extracts the special nutrients present in this rich and treasured limestone.

Let's take a look at the conditions that created Champagne's soil. Turning the clock back a few million years to the Cretaceous period, we find this entire region completely submerged in seawater and seething with an assortment of fish, shellfish, and mollusks. Champagne's limestone- and calcium-based soil was formed from the compressed shells and skeletons of these creatures. It's quite possible that this special soil is the chief reason the taste of true Champagne cannot be duplicated anywhere else in the world. From the gravelly, sandy soils of Bordeaux to the soft, spongelike textured soils that host the Palomino grape in the Sherry region of Spain, it is the soils and the subsoils of each vineyard that create the personality of the finished wine.

Rippon Vineyard, South Island, New Zealand
COURTESY OF RIPPON VINEYARDS

Drainage

The importance of soil and climate is well documented and often discussed. The drainage of the soil may be of equal importance, but it is seldom discussed. If the soil surrounding a grapevine retains water, there is little reason for the vine's roots to go deeper into the soil in their search for nourishment. Quite often these lower soil levels contain different minerals that unfortunately will not be extracted and reflected in the finished wine.

AN INTERESTING OBSERVATION

In a discussion of vineyard sites and soil composition, Robert Chadderdon (an importer of fine wines) made an interesting observation. "Isn't it curious," Chadderdon said, "that Europe's best plots of land were chosen and matched to the best possible grape types centuries ago? There was no help from wine-growing technology, as it didn't exist. Even more interesting, with all we know today about vineyards, soils, grape growing, and wine making, we still cannot duplicate or improve upon the quality of wine produced from these special and unique sites." This statement is amazingly accurate and yet puzzling at the same time. After much thought I can come to only one conclusion: God must like wine.

Vineyard Location

What makes the vineyards on the upper slopes produce better wine than those on the lower slopes? Why is a wine that is made up the hill so much more expensive than one made down the hill? Why is the yield so much greater in one particular part of a vineyard? Why do the vines near a lake have less of a frost problem than vines farther inland? Allow me some possible explanations.

A better grape may be produced on the upper slopes because these areas get longer sun exposure and the grapes ripen at a more even pace. Poor drainage may cause a greater yield of fruit in one part of a vineyard. The grapevines in this area enjoy a constant source of nourishment, resulting in a larger crop but one of diluted quality. As for the vines by a lake not being as affected by frost, that may be because they are protected from freezing by the slightly warmer temperature that surrounds a lake.

As you can see, many variables come into play within the borders of a vineyard. Knowing how to capitalize on special conditions requires that the grape grower and the wine maker have an intimate knowledge of the vineyard, soils, and region.

Climate

While the soil of a vineyard is fixed, its climate is not. Once an area is proven worthy of vineyards, only nature can produce the ideal balance of sun, rain, temperature, and humidity that insures a great vintage. Too much or not enough of any of these elements in a given vintage makes the difference between great, mediocre, good, or disastrous harvests. The gamble is real and must be lived year in and year out, as climate offers little guarantee of consistency. Following is a brief description of some of the major climatic elements and how they affect grapevines.

Sunshine The sun is essential to all forms of agriculture, including viticulture. Without the process of photosynthesis, by which light from the sun is absorbed through the leaves of a plant and transformed into the energy that allows growth and ripening, agriculture on any level could not exist. Too strong a sun can cause grapes to burn and spoil or become overripe, while a weak sun or none at all will result in grapes that aren't ripened sufficiently.

Temperature During the yearly seasons the grapevine goes through different stages of development. If the temperature becomes too cold or too hot during one of these stages, the crop for that particular harvest can be lost. In extreme conditions the grapevine can even shut down and die.

Rainfall Life does not exist without water. Even the hearty grapevine, which has been known to thrive and even flourish in harsh environments, must have water at certain stages of development. Too much water during the growing season can result in a crop of diluted quality or cause the fruit and vine to become susceptible to any number of undesirable, crop-destroying molds and rot.

It should be noted, however, that for certain types of wine certain types of mold *are* desirable. One such example is the *Botrytis cinerea* mold that is essential in producing certain sweet dessert wines. In the case of these wines, climate — with special attention to humidity — must be carefully matched with grape types that are susceptible to such molds. Not enough moisture can also cause an undersize and underripe crop that will result in a high-acid, green-tasting wine with little aging ability.

Frost and hail Not all types of moisture are friendly, and hail and frost are vineyard enemies number one and two. Hailstorms during the harvest season or at flowering (an important development period for the grapevine) can destroy an entire harvest in a matter of minutes. A sudden or prolonged period of freezing temperatures can destroy the grapevines as well as their crop.

Wind Even wind can be an important factor when selecting the site for a vineyard. If there is little or no wind in a vineyard that has a lot of humidity, rain, and high temperatures, grape rot can occur more easily than it can in a vineyard subject to a gentle breeze that dries the moist grape bunches. Too much wind can cause physical damage to both the grapes and the grapevines, resulting in an unacceptable crop, reduced yield, or windburn. Damaged and bruised grapes attract pests and birds that can further damage and — in extreme cases — even devour an entire crop.

Microclimate

You may hear the term *microclimate* in discussions of vineyards, so a brief description is in order. A microclimate is an area that falls within a larger area and possesses a unique balance of temperature, sun exposure, drainage, and soil that is capable of producing grapes of a quality different from that of adjacent vineyards on a consistent basis.

The Grapevine

The history of the wine grapevine can be traced back over seven thousand years. The Georgian region of Russia is thought to be home to the first wine-producing grapevines. History also shows that the grapevine was an important part of many early civilizations, such as those of Rome, Greece, and Egypt. This is apparent from wine carvings found on early structures, tombs, and engraved pottery.

The grapevine belongs to the plant genus known as *Vitis*, of which there are thousands of different species. Clearly the most important and most used species in the production of quality wine are those of the *Vitis vinifera* group, also known as the European vine. Included in this grouping are the most popular wine grape types — Chardonnay, Cabernet Sauvignon, Pinot Noir, Sauvignon Blanc, Riesling, Merlot, Nebbiolo, and Tempranillo, to name a few. In other words, all the good ones.

The grapevine is an amazingly hearty plant that seems to thrive under the most strenuous conditions. Its roots have been known to burrow to great depths — through even the most stubborn layers of soil, rocks, and subsoil — to satisfy their thirst. In doing so, they absorb and digest the many different types of minerals and nutrients found in these different layers. Maybe this is one of the reasons why such a premium is placed on old vines — as a vine ages, its roots go deeper into the soil — known in France as *vieilles vignes.*

How old is "old"? I would estimate that by European standards "old" starts at about thirty-five years of age and is capable of reaching sixty and even a hundred years of age. In America I have heard some grape growers describe twelve- and fifteen-year-old vines as old. The downside to an old vine is that once it is past about twenty to twenty-five years of age, its annual yield begins naturally to decline. While low yields are necessary in the production of great wines, they are unfortunately often viewed as lost revenue. Low-yielding vines are often pulled and replaced with younger and higher-yielding vines.

A lesser grape species is the *Vitis labrusca,* believed to be native to North America. In this group are to be found the less popular wine grape types such as Concord, Delaware, and Catawba. This group is identifiable by its strong aromas of grape juice and jelly — the Concord grape is used in the production of grape jelly — aromas often described as "foxy." While few professionals will disagree that the native American species produce wine of inferior quality, none would dispute the importance of its rootstock (the root system and structure of the grapevine that lies under the surface of the vineyard). These roots have become essential in the production of the high-quality wines made from the superior *Vitis vinifera.* To understand why, permit me a short history lesson on what has been branded the scourge of the vineyard — phylloxera.

PHYLLOXERA VASTATRIX

During the mid-1860s there was some interest in experimenting with native American grapevines in Europe, in the hope of learning more about non–*Vitis vinifera* grapevines. The experiment was to plant these vines and observe how they performed in French soils. Twenty years after these plantings, millions of acres of prime French grapevines had mysteriously sickened and slowly died, with millions more to follow throughout the rest of Europe. When the dust settled, the cause of this devastation was traced back to the roots of the experimental American grapevines that, upon inspection, were found to be infested with a small plant louse. The name of this small creature, which is no bigger than the head of a pin, is *Phylloxera vastatrix*, which when translated means "the devastator." These insects, when introduced into French soils, traveled throughout the vineyards, attaching themselves to the vulnerable roots of the French *Vitis vinifera* grapevines and feeding on them until they died.

Now, you ask, if phylloxera is so deadly to grapevines, why weren't American vineyards wiped out by this insect? Finding the answer to this question took some time, but eventually it was discovered that some native American rootstocks are much tougher and more resistant to phylloxera than their European counterparts. With this hard and expensive lesson also came the solution to Europe's devastating problem. Why not attach by graft (a connection by incision) the phylloxera-resistant rootstock of the native American grapevines to the fruit-yielding top of the desired *Vitis vinifera* grape type (Chardonnay, Merlot, and so forth)? This experiment proved a success, saving much of the grape-growing industry in Europe. As a result, today the rootstock of the inferior American grapevine can be found at the bottom of most European grapevines.

PHYLLOXERA TODAY

Most of us try to learn from our own mistakes, but the truly wise learn from the mistakes of others as well. While the French learned much from their bout with phylloxera, it seems the California grape growers did not. With the deadly history of phylloxera you'd think that using a proven phylloxera-resistant rootstock would be the first order of business when planting a vineyard. Why, then, during California's vineyard-planting boom of the 1960s and 1970s, was the recommended rootstock the AXR 1, a rootstock whose phylloxera resistance was known to be low? There certainly were better choices available at the time, so why weren't they used?

The decision to plant AXR 1 was clearly not based on its resistance to phylloxera. It was motivated chiefly by the growers' desire for a high-yielding grapevine. Yield — the amount of fruit a grapevine produces — translates into crop size, which further translates into profits. So when AXR 1 was found to produce a good-quality crop with a large yield, everyone shortsightedly forgot about phylloxera. In 1980 the growers were given a rude awakening when this resilient and persistent plant louse showed its ugly head in the middle of some prime Napa Valley vineyards. What had once destroyed the vineyards of Europe was now destroying many of the domestic vineyards planted in the high-yielding AXR 1 rootstock, which in hindsight seemed not to be so high yielding after all.

The solution this time was the same as it had been a century earlier — the use of phylloxera-resistant rootstock. All clouds have a silver lining, and so does this one. Granted, it will cost the wine industry millions of dollars, as well as lost crops for years to come, while the replanting process takes place. And this in turn will mean higher prices to us all. There is, however, a very positive upside. With all the knowledge that has been acquired and all the vineyard technology that has been developed over the past thirty years, grape growers can now select more appropriate wine varietals and rootstocks and better match them with the soils and growing regions, thus undoing mistakes that were made during the earlier plantings. Chardonnay, Riesling, and Pinot Noir, previously grown in Napa Valley (Rutherford and St. Helena), will most likely be replaced with Cabernet Sauvignon and Merlot. Cabernet Sauvignon, previously grown in the Carneros district, will most likely give way to the much more appropriate Chardonnay and Pinot Noir varietals. Growing up in Brooklyn, I learned to call this a do-over, and when it's done correctly, the do-over is often better than the original effort.

THE YIELD OF THE GRAPEVINE

One of the most important factors in the production of high-quality wine is the yield of a grapevine. Yield, as it pertains to wine, is the annual amount of the crop — in this case, the wine grapes produced by a grapevine. Left alone and given an unending water supply, a grapevine will produce as much fruit as possible. But in most cases, as yield increases, quality declines. We have already learned that the quickest way to produce a poor wine is to start with poor grapes. Too low a yield can also negatively affect the quality of the fruit, as the optimum balance between quality and quantity must be found individually for each vineyard site.

If money were no object and grape growers were given carte blanche to produce the highest-quality wine possible, the lowering of yields would likely be considered a top priority. A lower yield almost always produces a more concentrated wine. Sadly, the yield of most grapevines is determined by accountants and bankers, who view a lower yield as lost revenue instead of an opportunity to produce a higher-quality wine. Perhaps Joe Heitz, the legendary wine maker of Heitz Wine Cellars in California, said it best when he once told me, "We all know how to make the perfect wine, but the end result is usually reflected by the wineries' choice of compromise."

Yield per acre is a term used in the wine industry to describe how productive a vineyard is. It measures the production per acre in terms of tons; a yield would be described, for example, as four, five, or six tons per acre. In European vineyards production is described in hectoliters (100 liters) per hectare (approximately 2½ acres). For the purposes of this book, only yield per acre will be used. Following is a partial list of the controls a grape grower can impose on grapevines' yields.

Vine pruning A grape grower can drastically control a vine's yield through pruning. Pruning is performed after each harvest by selectively cutting a vine's canes. In doing so, a grower can dictate how many buds or clusters of grapes will be available for the next season's harvest.

Vine spacing One way to achieve lower yields per vine without losing volume of crop is through a vine-planting system called *close spacing*. The theory behind this concept is simply to plant more grapevines in a vineyard by placing them closer together. There is much debate within the wine community about the success of this system, as many feel that the root systems of the grapevines only wind up competing with one another for the soil's nutrients and the water supply.

Vineyard location The location of a vineyard has a great effect on the bounty of a grapevine. Mountain hillside vineyards always produce substantially smaller crops than vineyards planted with the same vine but located on a flat valley floor. Water retention and drainage of soil are two reasons for this. Water, always seeking the lowest level, runs downhill, offering the lower vines a much larger and more sustained source of moisture.

Vine age Once a vine is past twenty years of age, its production of fruit naturally begins to decline. The quality of these older vines' fruit, however, quite often improves. Unfortunately, many low-yield, higher-quality vines are pulled and replaced with more productive, younger vines.

Grape varietal Certain grape varietals are naturally more productive than others. Pinot Noir, for example, is low yielding, while Sauvignon Blanc is quite productive.

A Year in the Vineyard

Throughout the year grapevines and vineyards go through many different stages. Following is a description of the annual process, beginning with the harvest. The example I give is a French vineyard producing still (nonsparkling) wines. Other wine-making regions around the world may have different time frames, but the cycle remains basically the same.

Harvest (early September through mid-October) When the grapes contain proper sugar, acidity, and pH levels, the harvest begins. At this point the pace of the workers picks up dramatically as the vineyards and winery become very busy places. Picking crews are sent out to the sections of the vineyards that are to be picked first. Sometimes mechanical harvesters are used for harvesting, but for the most part the smaller wineries are hand harvested. This is the first-quality stage of the vintage, as the picking boss instructs the pickers to leave any unripe or damaged fruit on the vine. The unripe fruit may be picked at a later date. The fruit is then sent directly to the winery as quickly as possible to avoid any undesirable oxidation of the grape juice that can occur once it has been exposed to the air. Sulfur is often spread on the grapes to retard this unwanted oxidation.

Vineyard preparation (upon completion of harvest, late October through November) Once the grapes have been picked and delivered to the winery, the vineyard may be fertilized (often the remains of the skins, seeds, and stems are spread back onto the vineyard) and prepared for winter. Old and sick vines are replaced with new vines. The vines' long shoots, once the bearers of fruit, are cut off, and the leaves turn brown and fall off. The plant soon enters its dormant stage, as the sap of the plant retreats to the lower section of the vine for protection from the cold. In colder areas the base of each grapevine is covered with soil to give additional protection from the upcoming cold of winter, since grapevines can survive temperatures of only around minus five degrees Fahrenheit.

Vineyard care and pruning (late December through January) If topsoil has been washed away or down the slope, it must be retrieved or replaced. This task may be the hardest of all and is most common in the vineyards of Burgundy. Over the next few months, most wine-making regions now perform the important chore of pruning the grapevines. Pruning is itself a form of yield and quality control, as it dictates the number of buds that will be available to bloom in the upcoming spring. The number of buds eventually translates into the amount of fruit or grapes a vine is able to produce. If a grapevine is not pruned, it will produce as much fruit as possible, but unfortunately the fruit will be of a much diminished level of quality. In very cold areas the task of pruning may be put off until later in the early spring.

Vineyard preparation (February and March) It's cold outside, and most outdoor work is finished. The vineyard machinery is now prepared for the busy months ahead. Grafting vines onto rootstock can also be done indoors. As March approaches, it is time to get back into the vineyards to plow and aerate the soil. Toward the end of March, the grapevines begin to come out of their dormant stage, as the sap in the roots begins to flow. The protective covering of soil is also removed from the base of the vine in preparation for warmer weather. The threat of frost begins in early March and will last for the next two to three months.

Frost watch and vineyard care (April through May) The vineyards are cleared and cleaned up. The danger of frost begins. Year-old cuttings (new grapevines) can now be planted. Any wood cuttings, left over from pruning, are removed or burned in the vineyard. The buds left from the earlier pruning process start to break open as leaves begin to develop along with new cane growth. As May approaches, the soils are often worked again, with special attention to the killing and removal of weeds and other unwanted vegetation. This is an especially tense time because one prolonged period of cold weather, frost, or even a hailstorm can seriously undermine the upcoming crop by damaging the vines. Sometimes oil pots and other temperature-controlling devices are lit and placed throughout the vineyard to help combat any extremely cold temperatures.

The flowering (June) In early June the warmer temperatures encourage the vines to flower. At this critical stage the grower is hoping for warmer weather. Traditionally, harvest starts approximately one hundred days after flowering occurs. Soon after flowering, the petals drop, as tiny hard green grapes start to become visible.

Vineyard care (July) Vineyards are inspected, weeded, and sprayed, as weeds constantly compete with the grapevines for moisture. Unwanted vine growth is trimmed back so the vines can concentrate on producing fruit.

Véraison (August) The grapes now go through a stage that is known as *véraison*, or color change. It is at this point that the small green grapes take on their proper color, as dark grapes become dark and light grapes become light. With harvest around the corner, sugar, pH, and acid levels are monitored closely. If you were to taste one of the grapes at this stage, it would be very tart — a result of its high acid level. As the grapes spend more time in the sun, this acid will be converted into sugar and the grapes will become much sweeter. Too much rain at this stage may dilute the flavor and quality of the grapes.

Harvest preparation (mid-August through early September) Everyone is preparing for the harvest and praying for dry, sunny weather to insure a ripe and mature crop. Preparation includes checking and cleaning winemaking equipment, checking the sugar, acidity, and pH levels of the grapes, and scheduling which sections of the vineyards will be picked first, since certain sections will ripen sooner than others. Making sure the picking crew is available and properly equipped and instructed is of the utmost importance.

The year has now come full circle, and the harvest begins in early September.

CHECKING SUGAR LEVELS

I've now mentioned the task of checking the sugar level of grapes several times. This can be done three different ways. The first is to secure grape samples and bring them to a lab for testing. The second and most common method is done by field-testing right in the vineyard with an instrument called a *refractometer.* This is accomplished by opening a small hatch on the instrument and squeezing the juice from a grape onto the exposed glass lens. After the lens is closed, the refractometer is pointed at a light source (usually the sun), and a dark line will be highlighted on a numerical graph. The number correlated with the position of the line will give you the sugar level of the grape. This number also represents an estimate of the wine's alcoholic strength, since sugar is converted into alcohol during the fermentation process.

The final method was demonstrated for me during a vineyard visit with one of America's wine-making legends, Mike Grgich, at his Napa Valley winery. Mr. Grgich walked up to one of his grapevines, plucked a berry, and popped it into his mouth. After a few seconds he turned my way and said, "They are almost ready."

The Role of the Wine Maker/ Wine Caretaking

Too often wine makers take all the credit for transforming simple clusters of grapes into delicious offerings of fine wine, as if they possess supernatural powers or are the only ones who know the secrets of the vine. In actuality, nature provides grapes with all they need to turn into wine with little or no assistance.

Wine can basically make itself. This can happen when grapes that contain a high level of sugar are crushed or broken and the juice from the berries comes in contact with the yeast that is found naturally on the skins and stems of the grapes. This yeast acts as a catalyst to start the fermentation process, which, put simply, is the transformation of sugar into alcohol.

It is at this point that simple grape juice officially becomes wine. Granted, it will not be a very tasty beverage, but wine it will be. And while some of the tools of wine making may have changed over the centuries, the actual procedure of turning grape juice into grape wine has remained remarkably unchanged.

Although man did not invent wine making, it was through his interest and intervention that the process was refined into the craft it is today. On the subject of wine makers, the late Vincent Leflaive, of the great white Burgundy estate Domaine Leflaive, once said to me, "There are no wine makers, only wine caretakers."

Wine needs, and even demands, attention, care, gentle guidance, and occasional prodding to become wine of high quality, but it does not need a wizard, creator, or inventor. The wine maker's gentle attention, or sometimes nonattention, often makes the difference between mediocre wine and good wine, good wine and very good wine, and — occasionally — very good wine and great wine. The quality of the finished wine is, however, more often a reflection of the quality of the grapes used than of the wine maker's skills.

No matter how many ways we look at it, great wine is made first in the vineyards; it is enhanced, as well as protected, by the caring hands of the wine maker. I am in no way minimizing the role of the wine maker, as after all it is he or she who must make the decisions on important matters such as whether to use natural yeast or an inoculated strain (see chapter 5, "Wine Making"), the type of oak to be used for aging, how long the wine should be aged, and which grape types should be blended — to name just a few. These decisions will define the quality of the finished product. However, if you present a great chef with subpar ingredients, it is highly unlikely that he or she will be able to create a great dish, and wine makers should be viewed no differently.

The Role of the Vineyard Manager

When great wine is made in Europe, the owner of the vineyard receives the credit, and rightfully so, as his investment has led to the finished product. In the New World it is the wine maker who receives the accolades, and again rightfully so, as the wine maker makes the important decisions and assumes the responsibility for transforming grape juice into wine. You seldom hear, however, about the person who makes the major decisions about irrigation, fertilization, clones of grape types, pruning and vine training, whether to start the harvest or — equally important — whether to wait. That person is the vineyard manager, and one wrong decision on any of these matters can make the difference between a good wine and a great one.

We have already established the fact that great wine is made in the vineyard. It is the vineyard manager's job to deliver to the wine maker the best-quality grapes possible. Grape growing and vineyard management is a position that involves decision making throughout the entire year, as the grapevines and vineyard require constant attention. It is the vineyard manager who knows the different personalities of the vines — both good and bad — throughout the different sections of the vineyard. In a small winery a wine maker sometimes takes on the chores of the vineyard manager, in addition to his own wine-making duties. In most larger wineries the wine maker may be involved with the decisions that affect the harvest, but he is seldom involved with the vineyard chores. In each case it is the wise wine maker who keeps in touch with both the vineyard and the vineyard manager.

The Meaning and Importance of Vintage

Whenever wine is discussed, it's only a matter of time before the discussion turns to different vintages of wine. Vintage, known as *vendange* in France, pertains to the year that a wine's grapes were harvested. So, in effect, the grapes from the harvest of 1998 will produce wine from the vintage of 1998. Sometimes too much stock is put on a wine's vintage and sometimes not enough.

Vintage, as it pertains to wine grapes, is the culmination of an entire year's climatic conditions, including, but not limited to, the amount and timing of the sunshine, rain, heat, wind, and humidity that the grapes receive. Add to these variables vineyard tasks like fertilization, irrigation, and pruning and you can begin to understand just how unique a vintage can be. The combination of all of these factors will greatly influence the quality, price, and yield (production) of that vintage, resulting in what may later be described as a great, big, poor, or hot vintage.

The importance and effect of a vintage can vary greatly among the world's different wine-growing regions. Burgundy, France, for example, is home to the fickle Pinot Noir grape, and I know of no other grape that is more a reflection of its vintage than the overly sensitive Pinot Noir. If the vintage is poor in any red wine–producing commune in Burgundy, this will be reflected in the quality of its wines. It is in these poor or lesser vintages, however, that the quality-minded and skilled wine maker, who is provided with selective grapes, can actually improve the quality of the vintage and hence the finished wine.

In Bordeaux the quality of the vintage is also quite important, as proper ripening of the grapes varies from year to year and is always a cause for concern. Here the quality of a vintage is most often reflected in the wine's price, since there is always a higher premium for wine from a perceived great vintage than for wine from a lesser one. The vintages of 1990 and 1991 provide a good example of this price differential. Today the prices for the highly rated red Bordeaux vintage of 1990 are more than triple the prices of wines produced from the mediocre vintage of 1991.

Some wine regions are less affected by vintage variation, with the best example being California. Many areas of California are blessed with a climate that is quite consistent when it comes to ripening grapes. Because of this I often hear statements like "California doesn't have any bad or off vintages." This is true to some degree, but it should be noted that while the ripening of grapes is an important factor, it is not the only one. In fact, when overripening occurs, it is often considered a fault because wines made from overly ripe grapes are too high in alcohol. Bad vintages do occur in California, although not as often as in Bordeaux or Burgundy.

Another wine for which the quality of any single vintage is of less concern is nonvintage Champagne. While vintage-dated Champagne does exist, most Champagne is nonvintage. In its production it is the wine maker's skill at blending wines from many different vineyards and vintages that is most important. This is done so the Champagne houses can maintain and offer a consistent style of wine year after year, something that would be impossible if they worked with only a single vintage each year. The major benefit of producing nonvintage Champagne is the fact that any off year or poor vintage can be muted through the blending process by fortifying the poor vintage with wines from good vintages. It's interesting to note that it is not unusual for nonvintage Champagne to be just as good as — and sometimes even better than — more expensive vintage-dated bottlings.

Spain offers an extreme example of how the art of wine making and blending can actually eliminate vintage characteristics altogether. This is done in the production of Sherry through a unique and intricate system of blending many different vintages (many more vintages than used for nonvintage Champagne) through a wine-making process known as *solera*.

In Portugal the quality of the vintage can be obvious and confusing at the same time, since every year each of the Port houses decides on its own whether the vintage itself is worthy of being declared a vintage. If a house declares a wine to be vintage, it then produces a vintage-dated Port wine. If the quality does not meet the house's standards, then a vintage is not declared and the wine is used in producing nonvintage Ports — such as tawny Port — or in the house blend. It is always a bit confusing as well as controversial when in the same year some Port houses declare a vintage while others do not.

In conclusion, it is important to understand that vintage may play a varying role in defining the quality of different wines. While vintage is a very important piece of the puzzle of fine wine, it is still only one piece.

The Vintage Chart

A vintage chart is an organized compilation of different wines from different vintages paired with quality ratings assigned by the chart's author (see sample chart following). The ratings are most often numbers on a hundred-point scale. In this type of rating, a score of one hundred is the highest possible rating a wine can achieve. A ten-point scale is also frequently used, and with this system a rating of ten is the highest possible rating. Other rating symbols used are stars, letters, or clouds.

Although a vintage chart can be a quick and handy guide when selecting or ordering wine, it should never be considered a wine bible or the final word about the quality of any wine. Remember that each vintage chart is as different as the person writing it, and — more important — one single number or rating cannot be accurate for all the wines produced by all the different wine makers from all the different vineyards. I can only tell you that I have drunk many great wines from poor vintages and many poor wines from great ones. Remember, it is your palate. While guidance is always helpful, you alone must be the judge. Drink up and decide for yourself.

THE WINE ADVOCATE'S VINTAGE GUIDE 1970 - 1997® Date: 7/1/98

	REGIONS	1996	1995	1994	1993	1992	1991	1990	1989	1988	1987	1986	1985	1983	1982	1981	1980	1979	1978	1976	1975	1971	1970
Bordeaux	St. Julien/Pauillac St. Estephe	94T	93T	87T	85T	79E	75R	98T	90E	87T	82R	94T	90R	86R	98R	85R	78R	85R	87R	84R	89T	82R	87R
Bordeaux	Margaux	88T	88E	86T	85T	75E	74R	90E	86E	85E	76R	90T	86R	95R	86R	82R	79C	87R	87R	77R	78E	83R	85R
Bordeaux	Graves	86E	89E	89E	87T	75E	74R	90R	89E	89E	84R	89E	90R	89R	88R	84R	78C	88R	88R	71C	89T	86R	87R
Bordeaux	Pomerol	85E	92T	90T	88T	82R	58C	95E	93R	89T	85C	87T	88R	90R	96R	86R	79C	86R	84R	82R	94R	87R	90R
Bordeaux	St. Emilion	87T	88E	86T	84C	75R	59C	98T	88E	88E	74C	88E	87R	89R	94R	82R	72R	84R	84R	82R	85R	83R	85R
Bordeaux	Barsac / Sauternes	87E	85E	78E	70C	70C	70C	96T	90E	98T	70R	94T	85R	88T	75R	85R	85R	75R	75R	87R	90T	86R	84R
Burgundy	Côte de Nuits (Red)	92T	91T	84E	87T	78R	86T	92R	87R	86E	85R	74C	87R	85C	82C	72C	84C	77C	88C	86C	50C	87C	82C
Burgundy	Côte de Beaune (Red)	92T	90T	84E	87T	82R	72E	90R	88R	86R	79C	72C	87R	78C	80C	74C	78C	77C	86R	86C	50C	87C	82C
Burgundy	White	92E	93E	87R	72C	90R	70C	87R	92R	82R	79R	90R	89R	85C	88C	86C	75C	88C	88C	86C	65C	88C	83C
Rhône	North-Côte Rôtie Hermitage	86T	90T	88E	58C	78E	92E	92T	96E	92E	86E	84T	90R	89T	85R	75C	83R	87R	98E	82R	73C	84R	90R
Rhône	South-Châteauneuf du Pape	82R	92T	86T	85T	78R	65C	95E	96T	88R	60C	78C	88R	87R	70C	88R	77C	88R	97R	75C	60C	82C	88R
	Beaujolais	85R	87R	85C	80C	77C	88C	86C	92C	86C	85C	84C	87C	86C	75C	83C	60C	80C	84C	86C	—	—	—
	Alsace	86R	89R	93E	87R	85E	75E	93R	93R	86R	83R	82R	88R	93R	82C	86C	80C	84C	80C	90R	82C	90C	80C
	Loire Valley (White)	91E	88R	87R	86R	80R	75R	90R	92R	88R	82R	87R	88R	84C	84C	82C	72C	83C	85C	86C	—	—	—
	Champagne	91E	87E	N.V.	88E	N.V.	N.V.	96E	90R	88E	N.V.	89R	95R	84R	90R	84R	N.V.	88R	N.V.	90C	90R	90C	85C
Italy	Piedmont	92T	87C	77C	86E	74C	76E	96E	96E	90T	85E	78R	90R	75C	92R	80R	70C	86R	95T	67C	65C	90R	84R
Italy	Tuscany	78R	90E	85C	86T	72C	85T	90E	72C	89T	73R	84R	93R	80R	86R	82C	70C	75C	85C	60C	84R	88C	84C
	Germany	93T	87R	90R	87R	90R	85E	92E	90E	89R	82R	80R	85R	90R	80R	82R	65R	84R	72C	90R	85R	90R	80C
	Vintage Port	N.V.	N.V.	92T	N.V.	95E	90E	N.V.	N.V.	N.V.	N.V.	N.V.	95E	92E	86T	N.V.	84T	N.V.	83E	N.V.	82R	N.V.	90R
Spain	Rioja	85E	90E	90E	87E	85E	76E	87E	90E	87E	82E	82E	82R	74R	92R	92R	75R	79R	84R	86R	84R	74C	90R
Spain	Penedes	82E	89E	90E	87E	82E	74E	87E	88E	87E	88E	77R	85R	85R	87R	84R	85R	—	—	—	—	—	—
Aust	New So. Wales & Victoria	90E	87E	90E	87R	87R	89E	88E	88E	85E	87E	90E	86R	76R	83C	85C	88C	—	—	—	—	—	—
California-N. Coast	Cabernet Sauvignon	92T	90T	95E	93T	93E	94T	94E	84E	75E	90E	90R	90T	76C	86R	85R	87R	80R	92R	90T	85R	70C	92R
California-N. Coast	Chardonnay	87R	92R	88R	90C	92C	85C	90C	76C	89C	75C	90C	84C	85C	85C	86C	88C	83C	86C	80C	86C	82C	83C
California-N. Coast	Zinfandel	89E	87R	92R	90R	90R	91R	91R	83C	82C	90C	87C	88C	78C	80C	82C	82C	83C	86C	87C	80C	60C	96C
California-N. Coast	Pinot Noir	88R	88R	92R	88R	88R	86R	86R	85R	87R	86C	84R	86R	85C	84C	83C	85R	80C	84R	—	—	—	—
Ore	Pinot Noir	88C	76C	92E	89R	88R	87R	90R	86R	88R	72C	85C	87C	90C	84C	86C	86C	—	—	—	—	—	—
Wash	Cabernet Sauvignon	88T	86E	90T	87E	89E	85C	87E	92E	88E	90R	78R	86T	92R	78C	—	—	—	—	—	—	—	—

ABOUT VINTAGE CHARTS

This vintage chart should be regarded as a **very general** overall rating slanted in favor of what the finest producers were capable of producing in a particular viticultural region. Such charts are filled with exceptions to the rule … astonishingly good wines from skillful or lucky vintners in years rated mediocre, and thin, diluted, characterless wines from incompetent or greedy producers in great years.

KEY *(General Vintage Chart)*

90-100 = The Finest
80-89 = Above Average to Excellent
70-79 = Average
60-69 = Below Average
Below 60 = Appalling

Explanations of Symbols

C = Caution, too old or irregular in quality
E = Early maturing and accessible
T = Still Tannic Or Youthful
R = Ready to drink
NV = Non-Vintage
? = No Impression Yet Formed

COURTESY OF ROBERT M. PARKER JR'S. *THE WINE ADVOCATE*

5

WINE MAKING

Although I've spent a fair amount of time in different vineyards and wineries, it would be both foolish and wrong to present myself as a wine maker capable of making fine wine. I'm not a wine maker, but I'm quite familiar with the wine-making process, and as I wrote this chapter, I didn't hesitate to consult many of the fine wine makers I've come to know and respect. I've tried to make my account of wine making informative but not overly technical. Keep in mind, though, that the process of wine making can be, and often is, quite complex.

A partial list of basic wine-making terms and their meanings follows. While I will discuss and use these terms throughout this chapter, the reader will benefit by becoming familiar with them before proceeding.

Workers harvesting a cork tree in Portugal
COURTESY OF THE CORK QUALITY COUNCIL

Color and tannins are extracted during the fermentation process
COURTESY OF ROBERT MONDAVI WINERY

Important Wine-Making Terms (both still and sparkling wines)

Acidify To add an acid derived from natural fruit.

Cap A thick layer of grape skins and seeds that forms on top of fermenting wine.

Chaptalization The addition of sugar.

Crusher-destemmer A machine that removes the grapes from the stems while gently breaking open the grapes.

Fermentation A natural process that converts grape sugars into alcohol.

Filtration The clarification of a wine.

Fining A clarification and stabilization process that removes suspended solids from wine.

Fortification The addition of alcohol to a wine.

Free-run wine High-quality, free-flowing wine found under the cap of freshly fermented grapes. This wine is removed just prior to pressing.

Hopper A container that holds recently harvested grapes.

Inoculation The introduction of a controlled yeast to facilitate fermentation.

Malolactic fermentation A secondary (bacterial) fermentation that softens a wine's acidity.

Must The name given to grape juice, skins, and seeds once the grapes have been crushed.

Oak The preferred type of wood used for quality wine making.

Oxidation A chemical process that occurs when wine and grape juice are exposed to air.

pH A measure of a wine's combined or relative acidity. The lower the pH, the more overall acidity a wine has.

Pigeage The traditional method of pushing through the cap to extract color and tannin from the grape skins during fermentation.

Pomace Grape skins and seeds left at the bottom of a fermenting tank after the juice has been removed.

Pump over The modern version of *pigeage.* Here the juice from under the wine's cap is pumped back over the cap.

Press The equipment used to extract juice from pomace.

Pressing — first pressing Juice extracted from the first pressing of pomace.

Pressing — second pressing Juice extracted from the second pressing of pomace, always of a lesser quality than the yield from the first pressing.

Residual sugar The sugar that remains in wine after fermentation.

Sediment An undesired yet natural residue that sometimes settles out in wine.

Sulfur An antioxidant that is used in the wine-making process; also a byproduct of the wine-making process.

Tannin An organic compound found in the skins, seeds, and stems of grapes. Tannin is also found in wood barrels and containers.

Toasting A process in which the inside of a wooden wine barrel is slowly roasted over an open flame.

Triage A process by which undesirable or damaged grapes are sorted out.

Yeast The naturally occurring microorganism that converts sugar to alcohol through fermentation.

The Different Wine Types

TABLE WINES/STILL WINES

Any still, nonsparkling wine with an alcohol content of up to 14 percent is classified as a table wine under the United States labeling laws and tax code. A wine with an alcohol level above 14 percent and up to 24 percent must be classified either as a dessert wine or as a naturally occurring high-alcohol wine. A fortified wine with a similar level of alcohol may also be classified as a still wine.

SPARKLING WINES

The category of sparkling wines encompasses all wines that contain pressure. These occur when the wine is pressurized either through a natural process — carbon dioxide gas is trapped in the bottle in the production of Champagne — or artificially.

FORTIFIED WINES

Fortified wines are wines to which neutral grape brandy or alcohol has been added. This brandy may be added either to stop a wine's fermentation, rendering the wine sweet and in possession of natural residual sugar (as in the case of Port wine), or after fermentation for the purpose of increasing the wine's alcohol content (as is done with Spanish Sherries). Madeira, produced on the island of Madeira, and Marsala from Italy are other examples of fortified wines. The alcohol level for these wines ranges from 17 to 23 percent.

AROMATIZED WINES

Aromatized wines are flavored wines that are often fortified as well. The flavoring agents used in their production are usually extracts of different herbs, spices, or plants. Some commonly used flavorings include chamomile, orange peel, coriander, hyssop, and wormwood. The selected ingredients are blended together and added to a simple, neutral base wine. After the wine and the flavoring agents settle and integrate, the wine is filtered and released for sale.

Recipes for some of these wines blend combinations of many different flavorings. These recipes are often closely guarded and have been passed down from one generation to the next. The best-known example of an aromatized wine is Vermouth. Italy and France were the original producers, but America, Spain, and Portugal — among others — make good offerings as well. They are best enjoyed when fresh and served slightly chilled and are most often consumed as an aperitif. Alcohol levels for aromatized wines range from 17 to 20 percent.

The Ten Stages of Wine Making (table wines)

1. RECEIVING THE GRAPES (DARK AND LIGHT)

Once the grapes have been picked and transported to the winery, the process of wine making begins. This is what I call the passing of the torch, as the emphasis now switches from grape growing to wine making.

Most wineries prefer that all grape deliveries be made during the cool hours of the early morning. Heat and sun, once so vital in nurturing the grapes, can now cause disaster through premature oxidation of the fruit. Receiving cool grapes is so crucial that some wineries have gone to considerable expense to insure the good condition of their grapes. Sonoma-Cutrer Vineyards in Sonoma, California, for example, has created an expensive cooling tunnel for just this purpose.

Often grapes are sold to the winery from independent and contracted grape growers, and when this is the case, the first step after delivery is weighing the grapes. In most American wine regions, grapes are sold by the ton, and once the weight is determined and all the proper papers have been signed, the winery takes possession of the grapes. Any problem with the quality and condition of the grapes must be addressed at this point. Small amounts of sulfur are sometimes spread on the grapes as an antioxidant. This is most often done with white grapes, since oxidation will darken the color of the juice.

2. SORTING THE GRAPES (DARK AND LIGHT)

As soon as possible, the grapes are placed in a long, stainless-steel container called the *receiving hopper.* This is the last stage at which the winery has a chance to sort out any rotten fruit, leaves, or underripe fruit. The sorting procedure is done either by hand or with a long-pronged, rake-type apparatus.

3. THE CRUSHER-DESTEMMER (DARK AND LIGHT GRAPES)

Located at the bottom of the hopper is a large, long, stainless-steel auger that runs the entire length of the container. The auger rotates slowly and gently guides the grapes up an inclined shaft that leads to a machine called the *crusher-destemmer.* (Some newer wineries use a gentler alternative — a gravity-fed crusher-destemmer.) Once the grapes enter the crusher-destemmer, they move through a chamber that contains a rotating shaft with long, thin rods attached to it. These rods remove the grapes from their stems. The stems are automatically sent to a collecting bin and usually wind up in the vineyards as organic mulch.

Once detached from their stems, the grapes are gently crushed. The pressure used is enough to break the skins of the grapes, but not enough to break apart the seeds, which contain bitter and undesirable tannins. At this point the grapes begin to release their juice, which is collected in a holding tank. The destemmed and crushed grapes are now a gooey mixture that is called *grape must* or, simply, must. At this stage the road to making white wine diverges from the road to making red. The grapes intended for red wine are sent to be fermented and those for white are sent directly to the press.

4. YEAST SELECTION, CHAPTALIZATION, AND ACIDIFICATION (DARK GRAPES NOW, LIGHT GRAPES LATER)

The fresh must is now pumped directly into the fermenting tank. Fermenting tanks come in many different sizes and are usually made of stainless steel, although I have also seen tanks made of concrete, plastic, wood, tile, and glass. With the must in place the decision must be made to use either the wild natural yeast found on the grape skins or a safer, cultured, commercial yeast strain. Yeast acts as a catalyst to start the fermentation process that converts sugar from the must juice into alcohol and thus produces wine. Wild or natural yeast is unpredictable because there are both good and bad wild yeasts and no guarantee about which will show up. If the dominant wild yeast is a bad one, it can have a negative effect on the finished product. If you get a good one, there is a good chance that the finished wine will have a layer of complexity in both its aroma and its taste that it might not otherwise have.

Most wineries today decide in favor of the safer, more predictable cultivated yeast. Adding the yeast to the must is simple. If the wine maker has decided to use natural wild yeast, he does nothing. If he's chosen to use a commercial yeast strain, he simply measures the yeast, mixes it with a small sampling of the grape must, and then pours it into the fermenting tank in a process called *inoculation*.

Chaptalization, or the addition of sugar to the grape must, is usually performed just before or during the early stages of fermentation. This procedure is carried out only when a wine maker feels that the amount of natural sugar available in the must is insufficient to make a wine with the desired and legal amount of alcohol. It's a common perception that chaptalization is performed to make a wine taste sweeter, but this is untrue. Formulas have been devised that dictate the amount of sugar needed to achieve desired alcohol levels. While chaptalization is sometimes necessary, it is a procedure that most wine makers would prefer not to perform. It is always better to work with the grapes' natural sugars alone.

The addition of sugar is not legal in every wine-making region. It is legal and often necessary in the cooler wine regions of France, but it is illegal in the warmer climates of California, Italy, and Spain. Grapes grown in wine regions with warmer climates usually do not require chaptalization because the ripening of grapes in those regions is seldom a problem.

Sometimes grapes that contain too high a level of sugar will become deficient in acidity after fermentation. Remember that the higher the sugar level of a grape, the lower the acidity level, and vice versa. Wine made from grapes containing a high sugar level is often described as flabby or lifeless. Where legal (it is legal in California, but illegal in Bordeaux and Burgundy), a procedure called *acidification* may be carried out. This involves adding a natural fruit acid (most often tartaric) at the time of fermentation. When acid has been added to a wine, it can be called acidified.

5. PRIMARY ALCOHOLIC FERMENTATION (DARK GRAPES NOW, LIGHT GRAPES LATER)

When the grape must is in place and decisions have been made about yeast, chaptalization, and acidification, the fermentation process begins. Primary fermentation is a natural fermentation that starts when the sugar in the must comes in contact with yeast cells. This causes an aggressive action that transforms the sugar into ethyl alcohol. Carbon dioxide and heat are also produced and released as by-products.

Fermentation can start slowly but quickly heat up, becoming quite turbulent. If the fermentation process becomes too hot, it can strip the wine of many good components while introducing many negative ones. To keep this from happening, the wine maker tries to control the fermentation by controlling its temperature. Thousands of years ago the world's first wine makers combated this problem by burying fermentation containers underground to keep them cool. Today fermenting tanks are equipped with refrigerated bands that can be set and controlled by the modern, technologically equipped wine maker. Fermentation can last anywhere from a few days to a month, with one to two weeks being the average.

During the fermentation process (for most red wines) the grape skins and seeds rise to the top of the fermenting vat, forming a thick layer of solids on top of the fermenting must. This layer is called the *cap*, and in this cap lies the coloring matter that has to be extracted to give a wine its color. Tannin, which aids in a red wine's body and ageability, is also extracted from this cap. The color of a wine comes from the pigmentation found in grape skins. (The inside pulp of both light- and dark-colored grapes is light green.) This color matter is extracted when the heat of the fermentation process breaks down certain compounds and causes the skins to release the color pigments. To insure additional color extraction, red wines are often pumped over.

Pumping over is a procedure by which the wine under the cap is pumped up through a long, thick hose and redistributed on the top of the cap. The extreme force of the pumped must temporarily breaks open the cap, insuring that all the pumped must has passed through the thick, color-releasing cap. The amount and length of time for these pump-over sessions will depend on the vintage and the amount of tannin and color extraction that the wine maker desires. This procedure can also be done by hand through the use of a long plunger that is pushed down into the cap. This method is called *pigeage.*

Fermentation will stop either when all the sugar in the must has been converted into alcohol, rendering the wine dry, or when the alcohol level of the fermenting wine reaches approximately 16 percent. Yeast cannot survive these higher alcohol levels and will cease to function, thereby ending the fermentation.

6. THE PRESSING (DARK AND LIGHT GRAPES)

When fermentation has ended, the must has now officially become wine. The next stage is called the *pressing.* Just before the pressing, the free-flowing wine from below the cap is drained off. This wine is known as *free-run wine* and is usually of the highest quality. Sometimes free-run wine is kept separate, but most often it is blended. What remains at the bottom of the fermenting tank is the leftover grape solids and skins, called *pomace.*

The pomace is shoveled out of the fermenting tank and transported to the wine press.

There are many types of wine presses, from the old, medieval-looking, wooden screw type to the modern, inflatable bladder press. For the purposes of this book, I'll concentrate on the latter. The bladder press is a long, cylinderlike cage with a hatch that opens in the center. If you were to look inside this hatch, you would see a large, mainly hollow, empty cylinder that is made from stainless steel with small perforated holes throughout. Running the entire length of this cylinder is a long, collapsed, black rubber tube, which is called a *bladder*.

The pomace is placed into the press and distributed evenly throughout. Once the proper capacity has been reached, the hatch is closed and secured. At this point the weight of the pomace alone makes some of the juice drip through the perforated holes and collect in a holding bin. As the press begins its cycle, the cylinder containing the grape must slowly begins to turn. Next the collapsible bladder slowly inflates to a pressure level that has been preset by the wine maker. As the bladder inflates, it compacts the must against the walls of the press, and as this occurs, the juice begins to flow and is collected in the holding bin. Obviously the more pressure used, the more liquid will be extracted. If the pressure is too high, however, unwanted bitter tannins from the seeds and any small pieces of stem remaining in the must will be released into the wine.

Often there are two pressings: the first is always gentler, and the wine from it is always higher in quality. When all the pomace has been pressed, the extracted juice is transferred to either a stainless-steel container or an oak barrel to await the next stage. The leftover grape solids are either used to make a grape brandy or spread throughout the vineyards as organic mulch.

7. MALOLACTIC FERMENTATION (MOST DARK GRAPES, SELECT WHITE GRAPES)

Malolactic fermentation, known as ML in the wine trade, is not a mandatory process for all wines. In Latin the word *malic* means "apple," while *lactic* means "milk." Malic acid (apple) is a sharp, tart, crisp acidity, whereas lactic acid (milk) is softer and creamier. In effect, ML lowers the overall acidity and sensation of acidity of a wine.

The bacteria present in ML is a naturally occurring bacteria that is activated in springtime and transforms a wine's malic acid into lactic acid. This process, though natural, can be either induced or avoided by the wine maker. Almost all red wines go through this process, as they usually possess enough natural acidity to withstand this transformation without becoming too soft. With most white wines, however, ML is usually not recommended. Whites need to retain the higher acidity and fruitiness that is lost during ML. The exception to this rule is the Chardonnay grape, to which ML, in select cases, actually adds complexity and texture.

Malolactic fermentation can take place in oak barrels or stainless-steel tanks. Either choice, however, must be enclosed, so that the gases produced can be emitted without the introduction of a supply of fresh oxygen, thus avoiding any oxidation.

8. BARREL AGING

(See "The Oak Barrel" at the end of the chapter.)

A decision must now be made about barrel aging a wine. Many wines, especially white wines, require little if any barrel aging. If this is the case, the wine goes through a fining process, sometimes followed by filtration, and is then bottled.

9. CLARIFICATION/SETTLING/FINING/FILTERING

We are members of a society that expects purity in everything that is consumed. Most people would shudder at the thought of drinking a hazy liquid and would be even more repulsed by a liquid with particles floating in it. As a business that depends on satisfying the customer, the wine-making industry must give the consumer what he wants.

Clarification of wine is simply the removal of any particles or residue left in wine after it has gone through the different wine-making processes. Some examples of residue are dead yeast cells from the fermentation process, or small particles of grape skins, seeds, and stems, or even tiny pieces of wood from the wine barrels. Clarification can also remove the unfriendly bacteria that have ruined many a vat of wine.

Clarification can be done in many different ways, with some methods slow, some fast, some gentle, and some not so gentle. These different methods have caused much lively debate within the wine-making community, with some (usually the smaller wineries) feeling that a wine is stripped of color and complexity when certain clarification practices are employed and others (usually the larger commercial wineries) contending that the more aggressive clarification measures assure both the winery and the consumer a clear and consistent finished product.

Personally, I prefer the least aggressive methods of fining, with little or no filtration, as I believe the more natural the better. Wineries that forgo the practice of filtration often highlight this fact by printing the word *unfiltered* somewhere on the wine's label. The following description of the various methods of clarification begins with the least aggressive and ends with the most.

Racking Once again nature provides us with both an excellent and an inexpensive source of clarification — gravity. Given time, most of the solids found in a wine fall to the bottom of the container on their own, and the wine can be slowly and gently siphoned off (racked) without disturbing the fallen sediment. The downside to this method is also the result of the passage of time. Too much contact with oxygen can cause a wine's color to brown and gives oxidation, as well as an assortment of unwanted bacteria, a chance to gain a foothold.

Fining Fining is a process in which a fining agent — good examples are egg white, gelatin, or a specific type of clay called bentonite — is placed in the wine. These agents attract and collect any solids suspended in the wine, as they slowly descend to the bottom of the wine's container, leaving the wine above clear. Here again the wine must be gently siphoned off (racked). Fining can be done simultaneously with natural settling or racking.

Cooling If a winery has the capacity, it may choose to cool down the wine by lowering the temperature of the container. This process also helps any solids in the wine settle to the bottom.

Filtration Filtration is the most aggressive, quickest, and most thorough form of clarification; it is also the method that has the most critics. Filtration is usually performed by pumping the wine through different mediums such as microscopic pads or paper. Sometimes diatomaceous earth is used (the process is similar to that of a pool's filter). The desired amount of filtration can be selected by the wine maker through his choice of medium.

Another filtration device is the centrifuge. Spinning the wine at extremely high speeds sends off the larger, unwanted solids and leaves just the wine. This is considered very aggressive, and many feel it is harmful to the wine.

10. BOTTLING (DARK AND LIGHT GRAPES)

You may have thought we'd never get here, but yes, we've arrived at the end of the line — the bottling line, that is. It would be a shame to slip up here, after all the hard work and time that have already been invested.

Bottling facilities can vary greatly from winery to winery. Some very small wineries still bottle by hand, although this has become quite rare in these times of technology. The model I've chosen is an average-size California winery with a total production of, say, twenty to forty thousand cases of wine per year. As you will see, the bottling line works very efficiently with little help needed from man.

Bottling begins when the wine to be bottled is transferred to the bottling holding tank. The wine is then pumped from the bottling tank to the filler, where a final filtering of the wine often takes place. The filler has been calibrated to the size of the bottle to be filled. The bottles have all been cleaned, rinsed, and properly sterilized either before or right after being placed on the bottling line.

As the wine is run into a bottle through a feeding tube, a layer of carbon dioxide gas is injected at the last moment into the neck of the bottle. This gas is used to displace the oxygen remaining in the bottle's head space (the air space between the bottom of the cork and the wine). The wine bottle then travels to the corker, which inserts the cork into the neck of the bottle. The capsules are put on the bottles, and then the labels are applied. The bottles are then cased (usually by hand) and sent to a warehouse for storage and shipping.

Champagne and Sparkling Wines

Up until now I have been describing the production of still table wines only. Although there are different ways to produce sparkling wines, I will concentrate on the classic version known as *méthode champenoise*. *Méthode champenoise* is a set of wine-making guidelines that was developed and refined in France's Champagne region many years ago. In order to be called Champagne, all French Champagne must, by law, be produced from the approved grape types and adhere to these guidelines. Keep in mind that the sparkling wines produced everywhere else in the world are not entitled to be called Champagne. However, by using the classic grape types and following the traditions of *méthode champenoise*, wine makers may produce sparkling wines that possess some resemblance to Champagne.

DOM PÉRIGNON

It would be unthinkable to describe the process of making Champagne without first paying homage to a Benedictine monk named Pierre Pérignon, better known as Dom Pérignon. Considered the creator of Champagne, Dom Pérignon first discovered that wine stored in a closed bottle with sugar and yeast would, in time, become sparkling. "I'm drinking stars!" he exclaimed when he first indulged in a glass of this bubbly wine.

A master taster, Dom Pérignon was also the first to incorporate the blending of many different wines to produce the best Champagne. As if that weren't enough, he is also credited with being the first to pair strong glass bottles with the cork stopper. In recognition of Dom Pérignon's contributions to Champagne, the firm of Möet & Chandon honored him with a special prestige bottling bearing his name.

IMPORTANT CHAMPAGNE- AND SPARKLING WINE-MAKING TERMS

Cuvée The blend of different wines

Dégorgement A procedure used to remove sediment from bottles of Champagne and sparkling wines

Liqueur de tirage A mixture of sugar and yeast added to Champagnes and sparkling wines to start a second fermentation

Liqueur d'expédition A mixture of wine and sugar added to bottles of Champagne and sparkling wines before the final corking

Prise de mousse The process that gives wine its bubbles

Pupitres Slotted wooden frames that hold Champagne bottles

Racking Wine-making process in which wine is siphoned from one container to another to clarify it

***Riddling*/Remuage** The traditional method of collecting sediment in the neck of a closed bottle

MÉTHODE CHAMPENOISE

The production of Champagne and sparkling wine starts out in similar fashion to the production of still table wines. The grapes are picked, sorted, destemmed, crushed, and fermented. Similarities cease at this juncture, however. The chief goal in the production of fine Champagne is to create a house style and to be able to re-create that style consistently year after year. House style is the signature of the Champagne house, and a better house works very hard at maintaining its signature. Consistency can be difficult when working with a variable crop like grapes. After all, each vintage can be quite different from the last. The solution to this conundrum was found in the art of blending.

As I mentioned earlier, the blending of different wines for a consistent and better Champagne was first practiced in the seventeenth century by a Benedictine monk named Dom Pérignon. Today this fine art can take many decades to master, as it is not unusual for forty, fifty, or even sixty different wines to end up in a wine's final cuvée. Blending gives the Champagne house the flexibility it needs to provide its customers with a consistent-tasting wine every year, regardless of vintage variation.

The Champagne most produced is from a category called *nonvintage*. Nonvintage Champagnes can be blended from different vintages as well as different lots of wine. Vintage Champagne, on the other hand, may be blended from different lots, but it can come from only a single vintage. Once the proper blend is achieved, the wine is given a mixture of sugar and yeast called the *liqueur de tirage*, as it is bottled and sealed with a temporary cap. According to the procedures of *méthode champenoise*, once the wine is bottled, it must remain in the same bottle until it is consumed. The *liqueur de tirage* encourages the wine to start a second fermentation in the sealed bottle. This process is known as the *prise de mousse*, or the taking on of the sparkle. As we have previously learned, the fermentation process releases carbon dioxide as a by-product, and because this gas has no way to escape from the enclosed bottle, it slowly becomes incorporated into the wine. It is this trapped gas that creates the famous pop and effervescence, or bubbles, that have made Champagne so unique.

The wine is then stored in the calm and cool of the wine cave, anywhere from six months to three years, to mature. During this settling and aging period, the wine picks up additional complexities from being in constant contact with the residue of the yeast cells, which now take on the form of sediment. When this aging period has ended, the sediment that has formed in the bottle must be prepared for removal through a process called *riddling*.

Riddling, or *remuage*, as it is also called, is a slow, laborious procedure designed to collect all of the sediment at the neck of the bottle. Filtration would be much too disruptive to this delicate, and now carbon dioxide–integrated, wine. The bottles are placed neck first and horizontally into large, slotted, wooden A-frames called *pupitres*. As the wine rests, sediment begins to form on the side of the bottle. The person in charge of this process is called the *riddler*, and his job is to firmly grasp the back of each bottle (one at a time, of course), shake it gently, and return it to its former place in the *pupitres*. When he returns it, however, he places it at a slightly more elevated angle than before.

This procedure is repeated with each bottle many times over a period of months, and each time the bottle is returned to the *pupitres* at a slightly higher angle. This is done until the bottle appears almost upside down. An experienced riddler can riddle as many as thirty thousand bottles a day. The object of riddling is to slowly encourage the sediment to accumulate at the neck of the bottle in preparation for its removal at the next stage. Today machines have been designed for this labor-intensive chore. Many small, tradition-minded Champagne houses, however, still continue this time-honored practice.

When the riddling procedure is completed, the collected sediment must be removed in a way that will disturb the wine as little as possible. The procedure of choice for this task is called *dégorgement*. The first step in *dégorgement* is to chill the bottle to reduce the pressure that has built up from the trapped carbon dioxide gas. Next, the top portion of the bottle that contains the collected sediment is frozen in a saline solution. Once that portion of the bottle is frozen, the temporary cap is removed and the frozen plug of wine containing the sediment is expelled by the released pressure. With all of the sediment now evicted, a small amount of wine and sugar called the *liqueur d'expédition*, or final dosage, is added just before the permanent cork is inserted. The amount of sugar added in the final dosage will determine the Champagne's level of sweetness and its category. The wine is then prepared for additional aging or warehoused for shipping.

LA GRANDE DAME: CHAMPAGNE'S FIRST RIDDLER

The riddling process is believed to have been developed by a twenty-seven-year-old widow named Madame Clicquot. Affectionately — or, possibly, not so affectionately — she was called La Grande Dame by her employees at the Champagne cellars of Veuve Clicquot.

Clearing the wine of its sediments after the second fermentation was a difficult and wasteful task for all the Champagne houses. Quite often more of this magnificent but explosive wine would wind up on cellar floors than in bottles. A creative woman, Madame Clicquot tried many different procedures, all unsuccessful, to rid her wine of its sediment. History — with a fair dose of poetic license — reports that late one night, while resting in bed, Madame Clicquot conceived another idea. Not being a woman of patience, she jumped out of bed, summoned her servants, and instructed them to bring the long kitchen table down to the wine cellar. Next she sent for the carpenter, who was asleep at the time, and insisted he meet her immediately.

Down in the wine cellar, Madame Clicquot instructed the carpenter to carve out rows of holes at a precise angle in her kitchen table. The carpenter finished his work and was sent off, and Madame Clicquot proceeded to spend the rest of the night placing Champagne bottles in the angled holes. When she became confident that her idea would work, she invited in the cellar workers and instructed them in this new procedure.

La Grande Dame's idea was not immediately met with enthusiasm. Many of her employees chose to have a good laugh at her expense, the smart ones behind her back. Once implemented and given some time, however, this new process of riddling was obviously successful. Soon after, talk of this success traveled to the other Champagne houses, which quickly mimicked the new technology. The riddler now uses upright *pupitres* instead of a kitchen table, but his art has otherwise remained remarkably unchanged. Thank you, Madame Clicquot.

The Production of Sweet Wines

There are many types of sweet wines and many different methods used to produce them. The easiest and cheapest method of sweetening a wine is through the addition of a sweetener like sugar. While this does get the job done, its ease in production is quickly reflected in the wine's poor and unnatural quality. I call these types of wines "bubble-gum wines," and because the theme of this book is quality and value, I will not include them.

In the great sweet wine–making regions of France and Germany, any residual sugar (sugar left in wine after fermentation) must be natural sugar that comes from the grapes themselves. You may remember that chaptalization is the addition of sugar to a wine and that this process is, in fact, accepted in certain regions. The purpose of chaptalization, however, is to increase a wine's alcohol level during fermentation. Since the sugar added in the chaptalization process is transformed into alcohol, it has nothing to do with the creation of a sweet wine.

The most important ingredient in making a sweet wine is *natural* sugar; therefore starting out with grapes that contain a high level of grape sugar is essential. If you wish to make even sweeter wines, you must start with yet sweeter grapes.

Now I know you're saying to yourself that if sugar is transformed into alcohol during fermentation, wouldn't sweeter grapes simply produce higher levels of alcohol? That observation is accurate, but only up to an alcohol level of about 16 percent. At that point the alcohol kills off any remaining yeast and thereby halts the fermentation. The remaining, unfermented sugar becomes known as residual sugar, and the higher the level of residual sugar, the sweeter the wine.

Another way of stopping fermentation to preserve the grapes' natural sugar is to add alcohol to the must during fermentation. This addition will prematurely halt the fermentation and result in a sweet wine. Very cold temperature can also be used to halt the fermentation process, leaving the wine sweet. Another method is the use of what is called a *reserve wine*. A reserve wine is produced from unfermented, natural, sweet grape must. It can be added as a sweetening agent to a wine after fermentation.

THE NOBLE ROT

What single word could best describe the mood of a grape grower who has carefully and faithfully tended his vines all year long, only to find, just prior to harvest, that his grapes have been attacked by an unsightly mold? In a matter of days his once healthy-looking clusters of grapes have been transformed into moldy, shriveled-up raisins, hanging sadly on the vines. Chances are that if that grape grower is located in the Sauternes region of France, the Rhine and Mosel regions of Germany, or Hungary, the word that would best describe his mood would be elated.

How could he be happy? you ask. Because nature has just given him the most important ingredient needed to produce some of the most sought-after, expensive, complex, and deliciously sweet wines in the world. That ingredient is a mold called *Botrytis cinerea*. Also known as *pourriture noble* in France and *Edelfaule* in Germany, it is most affectionately called "the noble rot."

While almost all molds ruin wine grapes, the botrytis strain has the ability to greatly enhance them. When this particular mold forms on a grape, it punctures microscopic holes through the grape's skin in order to withdraw the nutrients it needs to survive. The grape's water content dissipates through these holes, causing shrinking and shriveling until the grape resembles a moldy raisin. What is left behind is a grape with an extremely high, concentrated level of sugar.

I said earlier that the best way to make a very sweet wine is to start with very sweet grapes. Here, as you can see, nature once again offers us the best recipe. Mother Nature, however, can sometimes be a fickle lady: what she generously offers with one hand, she can take back with the other. In this case, grapes that have been affected by the botrytis mold have an abundance of natural sugar but come with the price tag of minuscule yields. These tiny yields are the chief reason why the luscious wine made from these grapes is both rare and expensive. It can take the entire annual yield of six to eight grapevines to produce a single bottle, while under normal grape-growing conditions, one grapevine alone usually yields three to four bottles of wine.

The development of the botrytis mold in a vineyard is far from automatic. It can occur only in a select few of the world's wine regions and only when the climatic conditions needed for its development are ideal. These conditions include a cycle of cool, damp evenings, along with misty, mold-inducing mornings, followed by rain and then long, warm, dry afternoons. For the best possible results, the grapes must already be fully developed before botrytis sets in. Even when botrytis does develop, it does so indiscriminately, as some vines will have it while others will not. Sometimes the mold affects only a portion of a grape cluster, leaving the remaining grapes unaffected. Because of this inconsistency, these grapes must be hand-picked, and the process requires many passes through the vineyard. The botrytis mold is instrumental in the production of the great sweet wines of Sauternes in Bordeaux, the rare and delicious Essencia from Hungary, and the great, late-harvest wines of Germany. Canada, California, and even parts of New York State have also had some success with this type of wine.

Offering complex and exotic aromas of honey and apricots, complemented by a finish and viscosity that seem to last forever, wines produced from this noble nectar have the ability to age for many decades. To my mind they provide the taster with an experience that is always worth seeking out.

The Production of Rosé Wines

Rosé wines, commonly called *blush wines,* can be made two different ways. The first and easiest method is by the addition of red wine. In such an application, the color of the finished wine is controlled by the amount of red wine added. The more traditional method involves crushing red grapes and permitting the grape juice only limited contact with the red grape skins. (Remember that the coloring matter for all wines lies in the grape skins.) Using this procedure, the wine maker controls the depth of color by regulating the length of time the juice is left in contact with the red grape skins. Once the desired color is achieved, the juice is simply separated from the skins.

Rosé wines usually contain a certain amount of sweetness, which is one of the reasons so many wine-consuming beginners find them attractive and easy to drink. The amount of sweetness in the finished wine is controlled by the wine maker's decision about when to stop the fermentation process. The sooner it is stopped, the sweeter the wine will be. When left alone during fermentation, most wines continue fermenting until all of the grapes' sugars have been converted into alcohol, rendering the finished wine dry. Generally speaking, rosé wines benefit very little from aging. Their charms are shown at best advantage when the wines are young and chilled.

The Cork

Natural cork has been the preferred closure for sealing wine bottles for centuries. Cork offers a tight seal that allows slow evaporation and oxidation, and no other substance — natural or man-made — has proved to do a better job. The highest-quality cork is produced from the cork oak tree *(Quercus suber)* found primarily in Portugal and Spain. With a life span of over three hundred years, the cork oak tree is ready to be harvested once it has reached roughly fifty years of age. During the warm summer months, workers go into the groves with long-handled axes and strip the trees of both bark and cork. The desired cork is located just below the surface of the bark. These stripped sections of cork are then cleaned, boiled, and punched out into their more recognizable finished form. Once harvested, the cork oak tree requires approximately ten years to replenish its bark and cork before it can be harvested again.

Cork closures are not without drawbacks. The life span of even the best-quality cork becomes questionable after twenty to twenty-five years. Longer corks have been proven to offer some benefit for long-term aging. Fortunately, most wines for which cork closures are used are unaffected, as they are consumed long before cork failure becomes an issue. The collector, retailer, or restaurant that holds wine for many years should monitor corks and recork bottles if necessary.

The other drawback to the use of corks is the occasional faulty or unsterilized cork, which can ruin a wine's aroma and taste. A wine suffering from a bad cork is described as a corked or corky wine. There has been some experimentation with plastic corks, especially in California; however, most wineries still prefer the cork closure. Until the wine industry finds a better alternative to cork and a willingness to use it, the occasional corked wine will remain one of those unfortunate things wine drinkers must tolerate.

The Oak Barrel

If only one image were to be used as an international symbol for wine, what would it be? A grape cluster? A neatly terraced hillside vineyard? How about a wine bottle? While these are all good choices and would do just fine, to my mind the one, universal image that defines wine is the wooden wine barrel.

The wine barrel is the most popular prop used for winery logos, labels, marketing photos, and even business cards. What is most fascinating about the popularity of this image is that less than 5 percent of all the wine produced in the world has spent any time at all in a wine barrel. The vast majority of the world's wines are simple, inexpensive, everyday drinking wines that are released for sale immediately after they are produced. Most of these wines would benefit little, if at all, by barrel aging. In fact, barrel aging could even have a negative effect on these wines because it could overpower and mask the simple, fruity charm that made them popular in the first place. On the other hand, a wooden wine cask, when properly incorporated into the production of certain types of wines, often adds a fine layer of complexity and flavor in both a wine's aromas and its tastes — a complexity and flavor that would be unachievable without its use. Oak aging also softens and matures a wine over time through its slow evaporation process. Following is a list of the major grape types that have been known to benefit when aged properly in wine barrels.

White Grape Types

- Chardonnay
- Sauvignon Blanc
- Sémillon
- Viura

Red Grape Types

- Cabernet Sauvignon
- Merlot

Pinot Noir
Tempranillo
Syrah/Shiraz
Grenache
Nebbiolo
Sangiovese
Zinfandel

Many different types of wood have been used to make wine barrels. None, however, have had the success of oak. The most sought-after oak is French oak, grown in select French forests. Limousin, Nevers, Troncais, and Allier are the most popular types of French oak and are named after the districts they are from. American oak has become popular recently for red wines, although it has been used for red wines in Spain for over a century. Each type of oak possesses its own flavor profile and aging rate (the amount of wine that evaporates through the wood of the wine barrel) and is selected by the wine maker accordingly.

An oak barrel may also go through a process called *toasting,* by which the inside of the barrel is slowly roasted over an open flame to give additional flavor to the wine. If a barrel is to be toasted, it can be ordered with a light, medium, or heavy toast, depending on the amount of time the wood is exposed to the flame. Each toasting level imparts different flavors and nuances to the finished wine. Wine barrels and tanks come in many different sizes and are used for fermentation as well as aging.

Barrel aging adds to the cost of a wine, since this type of aging can last many months to many years, depending on the wine. It also adds to the chores the winery must perform — most notably, refilling each barrel to the proper level after evaporation, a process known as *topping off.* The extra time barrel aging requires can interrupt the all-important cash flow.

On the subject of cash, should you choose to incorporate French oak barrels into your wine-making program, bring your checkbook. The cost of a 225-liter French oak wine barrel, as of this writing, is over $600. That is quite a lot of money for a barrel that, in most cases, is useless after three to four years of use. There has been some limited success in experiments in which oak chips or large blocks of oak have been placed in wine in order to extract the flavors of an oak barrel without the major capital outlay of purchasing one.

6

THE GRAPE VARIETALS

Knowing the basic characteristics of different grape types *(varietals)* will help you isolate and identify wines you might like and distinguish them from the ones you might not. This can save both time and money when you buy new wines as well as help prepare your palate for wines possessing new and different flavors.

In this chapter I will focus on the many different grape types that are common in fine wine making. I will discuss the individual characteristics of each varietal along with its basic flavor profile. Listed with each type will be the wine regions that have had the most tradition and success with it, as well as some of the newer regions that have had recent success. While there are too many grape types to list them all, I have divided the important ones into two groups. In the first, "Major Grape Types," I will describe the most important grape varieties used in wine making today. In the second, "Other Grape Types," I will focus on less popular grape varietals or the grapes that often play a supporting role in the making of fine wine. The ageability of certain grape types will be explained first.

Aging Scale

To understand the following scale, you must first understand what aging — as it pertains to wine — means. Ageability should be considered a virtue only if the process improves the wine. Most wines will benefit to some degree from a little aging — say, a year or so — because after the turbulent wine-making process, a little settling time has a positive effect on a wine. However, the majority of the world's wines do not improve after this settling period. With most wines there is little, if any, benefit to the consumer who waits.

A better-quality wine is another story, since type of wine, grapes used, methods of production, and vintage year all play critical roles in a wine's potential to improve with time. Many top wines can age for years — even decades. Remember, however, that the perception of improvement depends on the personal preferences and experience of the person doing the tasting. There is no perfect time to drink any particular bottle of wine. The scale that follows is my general guide and is based solely on my own experience and judgment. Please use it with this in mind.

None — Should be consumed within six to twelve months of release
Little — One to two years of age
Moderate — Two to four years of age
Good — Four to seven years of age
Very good — Seven to ten years of age
Excellent — Ten to twenty years of age
Exceptional — Twenty to thirty years of age
Extraordinary — Above thirty years of age

Major White Grape Types

CHARDONNAY (char-da-nay)

Also known as Pinot Chardonnay

Most famous areas of production Burgundy, Champagne, Chablis; California.

White grape cluster
COURTESY OF ROBERT MONDAVI WINERY

Other good areas of production Australia; United States; Italy; Argentina; Spain.

The Chardonnay grape is the most famous white grape and responsible for producing the greatest, as well as the most expensive, dry white wines in the world. The great white wines of Burgundy and Chablis, as well as the popular California Chardonnays, are all produced exclusively from this grape. Chardonnay is also the only white grape used in the production of Champagne. Because of its popularity and adaptability to many different climates and soils, the Chardonnay grape has become one of the most widely planted varietals around the world.

Preferred climate Cool.

Preferred soil Limestone, chalk.

Flavor profile Chardonnay can be produced in many different styles and has a definite affinity for being aged and fermented in French oak barrels. Flavors range from apple and pear to more tropical fruits, depending on where the wine is made. The versatile Chardonnay offers a full spectrum of styles, from simple, clean, and crisp to buttery, toasty, complex, and creamy. Although a number of Chardonnays are produced in a sweet style, tradition demands that Chardonnay be made dry.

Aging potential Moderate to excellent.

SAUVIGNON BLANC (sew-vin-yon blawnk)

Also known as Fumé Blanc

Most famous areas of production Bordeaux and Loire, France; New Zealand.

Other good areas of production United States; Italy; South Africa.

Sauvignon Blanc possesses a split personality. In its first persona it is most famous for producing the dry, crisp, and smoky-style wines of Pouilly-Fumé and Sancerre. In its second it's much sweeter. When blended with the Sémillon grape, Sauvignon Blanc becomes a partner in creating the lusciously sweet and long-lived white wines from the Bordeaux region of France called Sauternes. This combination also produces a dry version known as white Graves. Recently, New Zealand, with a climate that is well suited for the production of dry Sauvignon Blanc, has received much attention for its excellent offerings of this grape.

Preferred climate Cool.

Preferred soil Gravelly, alluvial stone.

Flavor profile A wine drinker's wine, the dry version of Sauvignon Blanc offers aromas that have been described as racy, grassy, weedy, smoky, slatey, and steely. Sauvignon Blanc is at its best when very dry and crisp. Marrying well with wood, Sauvignon Blanc can be a moderate aging wine.

Aging potential Little to good.

RIESLING (rees-ling)

Also known as Johannisberg Riesling or white Riesling

Most famous areas of production Germany; Alsace, France.

Other good areas of production Austria; United States.

Considered by many to be the greatest white wine grape, Riesling has a reputation for being sweet, yet dry wines of excellent quality can also be produced from the Riesling grape. Generally the noble Riesling is made in a sweet style in Germany — the Riesling grape is Germany's finest — and California and produced in a drier style when made in Alsace, France. Wherever it is produced, when Riesling is made in a late-harvest style, it is quite capable of being one of the finest and longest-aging sweet wines made anywhere.

Preferred climate Cool.

Preferred soil Varied.

Flavor profile Riesling offers crisp acidity with scents of peaches, pears, apricots, and oranges that give it a very distinct and attractive fresh floral aroma. Contact with new oak barrels is quite unusual, as the flavor of wood does not marry well with the delicacy of this grape. Made dry, semidry, sweet, and extremely sweet. When dry and semisweet, Riesling is elegant, with a light to medium body. When made in the sweet style, it becomes creamy and thick and possesses a long and deliciously sweet viscous finish that is framed by firm acidity. Firm acidity is a trademark of this grape.

Aging potential Little to extraordinary. Depending on production methods, grape sources, and level of ripeness, Riesling can be made to be consumed immediately or to last for decades.

SÉMILLON (sem-e-yon)

Most famous areas of production Bordeaux, France; Australia.

Other good areas of production United States.

Sémillon is best known for its blending qualities with Sauvignon Blanc in the production of Sauternes, a lusciously sweet white wine from Bordeaux, France. Sémillon is susceptible to the botrytis mold that is necessary to produce Sauternes. Australia has also made some excellent dessert wines with this grape. Sémillon is also blended with Sauvignon Blanc in the production of dry white wines, white Graves from Bordeaux, for example.

Preferred climate Cool.

Preferred soil Alluvial stone.

Flavor profile Sémillon is a thick-skinned, low-acid grape that offers aromas of peaches and apricots that are intensified in the sweeter versions of wine made from this grape. When affected with the botrytis mold, Sémillon will also have honey aromas.

Aging potential Good to excellent.

GEWÜRZTRAMINER (ga-vurtz-tra-me-ner)

Most famous areas of production Alsace, France; Germany.

Other good areas of production United States; Italy; New Zealand.

The German word *Gewürz* means "spice," and *spicy* seems to be the word most commonly used when describing this grape's strong aromatics. Like the Riesling, this varietal has performed best when produced on German and French soils. Usually the German version of this wine is sweeter. Gewürztraminer produces a small crop that is early ripening.

Preferred climate Cool.

Preferred soil Varied.

Flavor profile Gewürztraminer is a low-acid grape, which gives the wine made from it a soft texture. This wine is also known for its full and spicy aroma. Gewürztraminer seldom sees oak during the wine-making process, as freshness of flavors is essential. Gewürztraminer is also made in a very sweet, late-harvest style. On the palate, Gewürztraminer offers a high level of viscosity.

Aging potential Little to very good (sweet wines tend to age better than dry).

CHENIN BLANC (shen-in blawnk)

Most famous areas of production Loire, France.

Other good areas of production United States.

Chenin Blanc is quite a versatile grape, with its best offerings coming from France. It can be made in a variety of different styles ranging from the simple and easy-drinking house wine (such as many of the Chenin Blancs from California) to the more complex French versions of Vouvray and Savennières that offer more mineral and nutty flavors with extremely high acidity. Vouvray can also be produced in both sweet and semisweet styles that have the ability to age for decades.

Preferred climate Cool.

Preferred soil Chalky soils; limestone.

Flavor profile Chenin Blanc has high acidity and is very crisp when produced in the dry style, with a light to medium body and delicate fruit aromas of melon, citrus, and mineral. When produced in the sweet style, Chenin Blanc maintains its high acidity, but this characteristic is much less obvious, as the sugar tends to mask it. When it is sweet, Chenin Blanc also often develops a much more rounded and thicker mouth feel. Often a slightly green tint highlights this wine's color.

Aging potential Little when produced in California and moderate to excellent when produced in both dry and sweet styles in France.

PINOT GRIS (pee-no gre)

Also known as Tokay-Pinot Gris (Alsace, France), Pinot Grigio (Italy), Rulander (Germany)

Most famous areas of production Italy; Alsace, France.

Other good areas of production Oregon; Germany.

Probably best known for the popular Pinot Grigio wine made in Italy. The Pinot d'Tokai version is its best example. Oregon has of late produced some very good examples of this varietal as well.

Preferred climate Cool.

Preferred soil Varied.

Flavor profile Pinot Gris is a relatively simple, clean, and refreshing wine with a slightly nutty aroma and good acidity. While the more popular Italian version is light-bodied with little complexity, the Alsatian version offers more dimension and depth.

Aging potential Little to moderate.

Other White Grape Types

FRANCE

Aligoté (al-e-go-tay) Minor white grape of decreasing importance in Burgundy. Produces a simple wine with good acidity and refreshing but uncomplex fruit flavor. Bottled as Bourgogne Aligoté and quite often a good value. Aligoté is the original wine used in the making of a Kir, which consists of white wine and a little crème de cassis.

Marsanne (mar-sahn) Grown in the Rhône Valley, this grape produces a medium-bodied, fruity wine.

Muscadet (mus-ka-day) Muscadet, also known as Melon, is the name of the grape as well as the name of the wine. This grape is grown in the Loire region of France and produces a crisp, lean, fresh wine with occasional yeasty overtones. It is best consumed well chilled and upon release.

Pinot Blanc (pee-no blawnk) Grown with good success in Alsace; permitted, though not often seen, in Burgundy. Grown with less complexity in Italy and California. Pinot Blanc has been called a poor man's Chardonnay, because it can be made in a style that is similar yet less complex.

Viognier (vee-own-ni-ay) At its best in Condrieu or the rare Château Grillet from the southern Rhône. It produces a very low-yielding crop; hence it is usually expensive. Exotic and fragrant, with hints of citrus and melon. The alluring aromas of this grape are complemented by its full and rich body.

GERMANY

Scheurebe (sha-rue-bay) A cross between the Riesling and the Silvaner grapes, Scheurebe produces flavorful, sweet wines with an aroma of fresh peaches and apricots.

Silvaner (sil-van-er) Produces a light, simple, short-lived wine.

Müller Thurgau (mule-er thur-gow) A low-acid cross between the Riesling and the Silvaner.

GREECE

Retsina (rett-see-na) This is a style of wine making rather than a particular grape. Retsina has a unique resin flavor that is the result of an old custom of sealing the barrels with a resined pitch.

HUNGARY

Tokaj (toe-kye) Made from the Furmint grape, this is one of the finest and most age-worthy sweet wines produced in the world. Always rare and expensive and quite lusciously sweet and complex.

ITALY

Cortese (kor-tay-zay) Cultivated in Italy, the Cortese grape produces light and simple wines with little distinction.

Garganega (gar-ga-nay-ga) Blended along with the Trebbiano grape to produce Soave, a light, simple, fresh wine.

Moscato (mus-scot-o) There are many varieties of this grape, which is also known as Muscat. Most of the wines made from it are in a sweet style, and all possess fresh floral aromas. It is also used in the production of Italy's most famous sparkling wine, Asti Spumante.

Trebbiano (tre-be-on-oh) Cultivated in Italy, the Trebbiano grape — on its own — produces a wine with little personality. It is the white varietal that is used as a blending grape for the traditional versions of Italy's red Chianti wines. It is thought to be the same grape as the Ugni Blanc, which is used in the production of Armagnac and Cognac from France.

Verdicchio (ver-deek-e-o) Produces light, simple, short-lived wines.

SPAIN

Albariño (al-bah-re-nyo) Small, low-yielding grape, best cultivated in the Galicia region of Spain. Thought to be a relative of the German Reisling grape, Albariño produces very pleasant, aromatic, dry wines that are best when consumed early.

Palomino (pal-o-me-no) Used for the production of Spain's unique, dry Sherry.

Pedro Ximénez (pay-dro m-e-nez) Also known as P.X., this Spanish grape is at its best when produced in the vineyards of Jerez and used for sweet and cream Sherry.

Viura (ve-your-ah) Also known as Macabeo, Viura is the major grape used in making Spain's white Rioja and one of the three grapes used in the production of the Spanish sparkling wine Cava.

SWITZERLAND

Chasselas (chas-ah-las) Also known as the Fendant or Gutedel, Chasselas produces a good yet simple, low-acid wine.

Major Red Grape Types

CABERNET SAUVIGNON (cab-er-nay sew-vin-yonn)

Most famous areas of production Bordeaux, France; California.

Other good areas of production Spain; Italy; Chile; Washington State.

Cabernet Sauvignon is to red wine what the Chardonnay grape is to white. It is the chief grape used in producing most of the world's most famous and expensive red wines from Bordeaux, France. Time and again, wines with high proportions of this grape type — Château Lafite and Château Latour, for example — fetch the highest prices at wine auctions. On the domestic front, it is the success of Cabernet Sauvignon in California that has brought worldwide attention and recognition to the United States. Quite adaptable to many different regions, Cabernet Sauvignon is now widely planted around the world.

Preferred climate Warm, temperate.

Red grape cluster

Preferred soil Nonfertile, alluvial, gravelly, sandy loam.

Flavor profile Black cherry, currants, cassis, and bell pepper are some of the trademark aromas of this great grape. Cabernet Sauvignon is deeply colored and capable of great weight and structure. This grape type is greatly enhanced when aged in oak barrels (French as well as American). Cabernet Sauvignon is produced in a variety of different styles, from a soft and flavorful version, which is meant to be consumed upon release, to the classic hard, tannic, and unyielding style that may require decades to open up.

Aging potential Good to excellent.

PINOT NOIR (pee-no no-r)

Most famous areas of production Burgundy, France.

Other good areas of production California; Oregon.

Pinot Noir is the grape that offers the greatest challenge to wine makers. It is inconsistent, delicate, fickle, and — oh, yes! — capable of producing some of the greatest, most elegant, most sought-after wines that have ever been produced anywhere. It is also capable of producing a very light, lean, almost colorless, insipid wine. The attraction and problem with Pinot Noir is that when it is good it is oh-so-good, but when it is bad it is oh-so-bad. Unfortunately, great Pinot Noir is rare and usually expensive, with its best examples coming from the Côte de Beaune and Côte de Nuits regions of Burgundy. Domestically, California and, more recently, Oregon have had some success with this noble grape as well. This varietal does benefit greatly from French-oak aging.

Preferred climate Likes long, cool growing seasons.

Preferred soil Limestone.

Flavor profile When good, Pinot Noir has the aromas of strawberries, dampened soil, fresh berries, cherries, and is slightly barnyardy, with a fair to medium extraction of tannin. The color range is light to medium red. Purple hues are also common when the wine is young. Pinot Noir, when good, possesses a long, seductive, silky mouth feel that is hard to duplicate with any other grape type. When bad, it is thin, green, simple, and quite unimpressive. Pinot Noir is a grape type that can often disappoint its taster.

Aging potential Little to very good.

MERLOT (mer-low)

Most famous area of production Bordeaux, France.

Other good areas of production California; Washington State; Long Island; Chile; South Africa; Italy.

Traditionally Merlot has built its reputation on being one of the major grapes used in the production of red Bordeaux. While Cabernet Sauvignon receives most of the credit in the production of Bordeaux, in fact, Merlot is quite often the significant other. The wines of Pomerol and St.-Émilion (also Bordeaux wines) are quite often made chiefly with Merlot. Château Pétrus, one of the rarest and most expensive wines in the world, is almost always made exclusively from this noble grape. Since the early 1990s, however, Merlot has become the darling of the wine world, with California once again leading the charge. Unfortunately, with all of this new demand for Merlot, many mediocre offerings have been produced.

Preferred climate Cool.

Preferred soil Nonfertile, alluvial, gravelly, sandy loam.

Flavor profile By itself, Merlot is softer, smoother, less tannic, and less acidic than Cabernet Sauvignon. It can be deeply colored, and it is quite often described as perfumy, round, and mellow, yet it can be quite firm when young. When part of a blend, Merlot adds a dimension of softness along with smooth textures, while retaining its attractive perfume.

Aging potential Moderate to excellent.

CABERNET FRANC (kab-ber-nay frawnk)

Most famous area of production Bordeaux, France.

Other good areas of production Loire, France; California; South Africa.

Cabernet Franc has been called the poor man's Cabernet Sauvignon, yet it is an important and consistent part of the blend in the production of most red Bordeaux. In rare instances, Cabernet Franc can produce a world-class wine on its own, and nowhere is this more evident than in the delicious red Bordeaux wines of the famous St.-Émilion estate Château Ausone. In the Loire region of France this varietal produces lovely yet less complex, fruity wines such as Chinon. Most recently, California has had moderate success producing this varietal on its own.

Preferred climate Varied; prefers cool climates.

Preferred soil Limestone and clay.

Flavor profile In Bordeaux, Cabernet Franc is less intense and complex than Cabernet Sauvignon, with some aromatics and high acidity. In the Loire, Cabernet Franc has fresh young raspberry and black currant aromas. The color range is light to medium. Cabernet Franc has some aging ability.

Aging potential Little to very good.

SYRAH (se-rah)

Also known as Shiraz (sha-raz)

Most famous area of production Rhône Valley, France; Australia.

Other good areas of production California; Washington State; South Africa.

There is more Shiraz under vine in Australia than in any other wine region in the world. If you have experienced some of the successful offerings of this varietal, you understand why this is so. Australia may very well offer the best value for this grape as well. The other major quality producer is France (once again), where this grape is called Syrah. The northern Rhône is home to the vineyards of Côte Rôtie and Hermitage, where Syrah performs its best magic, while making up the majority of the blend used in producing these wines.

Preferred climate Warm regions.

Preferred soil Varied alluvial.

Flavor profile Australian Shiraz is often spicy, with scents of different herbs and violets, and is medium to deeply colored. It has a very good tannin structure that acts as a good foundation for its thick rich fruit, which often results in a smooth, long finish. Shiraz can be made in an approachable style, yet its greatest effort requires some time to soften. The French version has traditionally been more massive and rustic, but modern winemaking practices seem to have softened this strong varietal by bringing its thick, plummy, violety, and sometimes smoky fruit to the forefront without eliminating its sheer power. Although not all wine purists are happy with this stylistic change, most consumers are.

Aging potential Good to excellent.

GRENACHE (gren-osh)

Also known as Garnacha Tinta in Spain

Most famous areas of production Rhône Valley, France; Spain.

Other good areas of production California; Australia.

The lightly colored Grenache is best known for its contributions in the southern Rhône, where, along with Syrah, Cinsaut, and other grape types, it is used as part of the blend of France's famous red Châteauneuf-du-Pape wine. In Spain it is called Garnacha, and it is again used as a blending grape, this time in the production of the red wines of Rioja. Grenache is also enjoyed when made into a rosé wine such as those from Tavel and Provence in France or the Navarra region of Spain.

Preferred climate Very warm.

Preferred soil Alluvial.

Flavor profile As a rosé, Grenache is served chilled and provides an enjoyable, refreshing, light, raspberry-flavored wine that offers little complexity or aging ability. When blended in the making of Châteauneuf-du-Pape, the light-colored Grenache is used for its alcoholic strength and its simple charm, which provides an additional layer of complexity.

Aging potential Moderate to very good when part of a blend; little to moderate when on its own.

GAMAY (gam-may)

Most famous area of production Beaujolais region of Burgundy, France.

Gamay may produce the easiest-drinking wines made in all of France. While it is grown throughout many regions of France, its best expression comes from the granite soils of Beaujolais. Most Beaujolais wines go through a process called *carbonic maceration,* in which the berries are fermented whole in an effort to preserve as much of the grapes' natural freshness and fruitiness as possible.

Preferred climate Cool.

Preferred soil Granite; clay.

Flavor profile Gamay produces refreshing, light-colored, light-bodied wines with scents of light cherry, strawberry, and fresh grape juice. Serving this wine slightly chilled preserves the essence of its simple fruit flavors. When made from the higher-rated Cru vineyard sites in Beaujolais, it can possess more color, structure, and textures, and it can have a bit more aging ability. Beaujolais Nouveau, which is France's first vintage wine released each year and is used as a marketing tool, offers little complexity and no aging ability. To this writer it is little more than a watered-down acidic fruit juice with a little alcohol.

Aging potential Little to moderate.

TEMPRANILLO (tem-pra-knee-lo)

Also known as Tinto Fino, Tinto del País, and Cencibel

Most famous area of production Spain.

The Tempranillo varietal is the most important red grape used in Spain's most famous red wine region, Rioja. Rioja Reservas and Gran Reservas are usually produced with a majority of this grape. It has also enjoyed much success in the Ribera del Duero region, as Tempranillo does seem to favor cooler climates. Tempranillo is indigenous to Spain, and little experimentation has been done with it outside the country despite its quality and success.

Preferred climate Cool and temperate.

Preferred soil Varied.

Flavor profile The Tempranillo varietal is capable of producing wines of great elegance and finesse. Despite its soft and gentle nature, Tempranillo blends very well with oak (especially with American oak) and can be produced to age amazingly well. Flavors of cherry and light strawberry when young give way to more complex aromas of chocolate, caramel, and even crème brûlée when aged in wood. One of the best sensations in wine tasting is often described as a silky finish, and when Rioja is done well, it is capable of fitting that description to perfection.

Aging potential Depending on its classification, little to excellent.

NEBBIOLO (neb-e-o-lo)

Most famous area of production Piedmont, Italy.

Italy's famous Barolo, Barbaresco, and Gattinara are all made from this great grape. Considering Nebbiolo's proven ability to produce great wines, it is curious that it has not been cultivated to any serious degree anywhere outside its native Italy. The thick-skinned late ripening Nebbiolo has proven to be Italy's most age-worthy red grape.

Preferred climate Temperate, warm.

Preferred soil Varied.

Flavor profile At its best in the production of Barolo, Nebbiolo is very deeply colored, massive, and tannic, with thick scents of tar, leather, and truffles that often require years to emerge. Aged Barolos are a good reason to cellar wines, as they are usually worth the wait.

Aging potential Good to excellent.

SANGIOVESE (san-jo-vay-zay)

Also known as Sangioveto and Brunello

Most famous area of production Tuscany, Italy.

Other good areas of production California.

One of Italy's most planted (and consumed) grapes, Sangiovese wears many different hats. It is responsible for Italy's best-known and most traditional wine, Chianti. Certain producers have broken rank and tradition by blending different amounts of Cabernet Sauvignon, Merlot, and Cabernet Franc with and without the traditional Sangiovese grape, thus creating new wines that have become known as the "Super Tuscans." Some examples are Tignanello, Solaia, Sassicaia, Concerto, and Masseto.

Preferred climate Warm, temperate.

Preferred soil Varied.

Flavor profile The late-ripening Sangiovese grape is capable of producing many different styles of wine. It is a lightly colored grape with good acidity and a medium tannin base. Aromas of soft cherry are complemented by a full assortment of different herbs. The body of this wine can be light and gentle — as in the simpler, traditional Chiantis — or silky, sleek, and racy — as in the new wave of Super Tuscan wines.

Aging potential Moderate to very good.

ZINFANDEL (zin-fan-del)

Most famous area of production California.

Is Zinfandel California's native grape? No, yet nobody does it better. Zinfandel is an excellent, consistent, and versatile producer. Ridge Vineyards, under the direction of Paul Draper, one of America's premier wine makers, made a statement with stylish bottlings of this grape twenty years ago that still define the benchmark. Maybe it's time for other wine regions around the world to emulate an American wine.

Preferred climate Varied.

Preferred soil Varied.

Flavor profile Zinfandel has the aromas of fresh crushed berries — both blue and black — and a smooth texture, when done well. Zinfandel can be made in many different styles, from the now famous white Zinfandel (most occasional wine drinkers don't realize that the Zinfandel is a red grape) to the sweet, late-harvest, high-alcohol style. In my mind Zinfandel is best when made like a Cabernet Sauvignon and thus the recipient of the best of both worlds — it has the structure and complexity of the Cabernet and the freshness and texture of the luscious Zinfandel. When aged (seven to ten years), this varietal sheds some of its Zinfandel qualities and more closely resembles an aged Cabernet Sauvignon.

Aging potential Moderate to very good.

Other Red Grape Types

FRANCE

Alicante Bouschet (al-e-kan-tay boo-shay) French hybrid of little distinction other than its deep color; used mainly for blending.

Petit Verdot (puh-tea ver-dough) A minor blending grape of decreasing importance in Bordeaux.

Malbec (mal-bek) The principal red grape of Cahors; also grown in the Loire and a minor blending grape in Bordeaux. This grape has good color and tannins.

Pinot Meunier (pee-no muhn-yee) Most widely planted of the three grapes used in Champagne. Major part of many blends of nonvintage Champagne; said to be a cousin of the more noble Pinot Noir.

Cinsault/Cinsaut (sin-sew) Grown in the southern Rhône and Provence. One of the grape varietals used in the blending of Châteauneuf-du-Pape. Low in tannin, with good acidity and little color.

Mourvèdre (more-ved-dra) Grown in the southern Rhône and Bandol, this varietal produces a thick, full, alcoholic wine that requires time to come around. Used in the production of Châteauneuf-du-Pape.

ITALY

Amarone (am-ah-rhone-ay) A style of Valpolicella made from select parts of the grape clusters. Produces full, rich, ripe, and sweet wines that can age extremely well.

Barbera (bar-bear-uh) Native to Italy, the Barbera grape is widely planted there. Quality depends on yield, as the wines made from smaller crops are much more serious and complex. Wines have good acidity and color and are easy to drink and enjoy.

Dolcetto (dole-chet-to) Chiefly grown in the Piedmont region of Italy, this dark-colored wine is packed with easy, perfumed, up-front fruit. Best when consumed at two to four years of age.

Grignolino (gree-nyo-lean-no) A very good grape that often has orange highlights. It is light with high acidity and is used for rosé wines.

Valpolicella (val-pol-lo-chella) Famous red wine from northern Italy that is made from the Corvina, Rondinella, and Molinara grapes, which produce light, fruity wines for early consumption.

Super Tuscans A term used to describe newly developed wines from the traditional region of Chianti that often feature nontraditional grape types, mostly Cabernet Sauvignon and Merlot. Some examples are Tignanello, Sassicaia, Solaia, and Terrabianco.

SOUTH AFRICA

Pinotage (pee-no-taj) A cross between Pinot Noir and Cinsaut, it has had some success.

SPAIN

Graciano (graz-e-ahn-o) High-quality, low-yielding grape used as a blending grape in the production of Rioja.

Manzuelo (man-zway-lo) Also known as Cariñena, Manzuela, or Carignan (in France). Used as a blending grape in the production of Rioja.

Which Wine, Which Grape

Many wines produced in the United States and Australia, as well as in other emerging wine regions worldwide, are named from the majority grape type used in their production. Most European wines, on the other hand, are named after the region where they are made. "Which Wine, Which Grape" is meant to give you a quick reference to which grape types certain European wines are made from (and provides the correct pronunciation), in order to help you make an educated selection when ordering a wine with which you are unfamiliar. Following is a list of some well-known wines and wine regions and the grapes used in the production of the wines.

FRANCE—WHITE WINES

Burgundy The grape used in the production of virtually all French white Burgundy (over 99 percent) is Chardonnay. Listed here are most of the major white wine–producing communes of Burgundy. When you come across these wines in either a restaurant or the retail environment, keep in mind that they are almost always wines made exclusively from the Chardonnay grape.

Bâtard-Montrachet (bah-tar mohn-rah-shay)
Beaujolais Blanc (bow-joe-lay blawnk)
Bienvenues Bâtard Montrachet (bee-en-vah-new bah-tar mohn-rah-shay)
Blagny (blahn-yee)
Chablis (shab-lee)
Chassagne-Montrachet (sha-sahn mohn-rah-shay)
Chevalier-Montrachet (shev-al-yay mohn-rah-shay)
Corton-Charlemagne (core-tuhn shar-luh-main)
Criots Bâtard Montrachet (cree-o bah-tar mohn-rah-shay)
Mâcon (mah kahn)
Mercurey Blanc (mer-cure-ray blawnk)
Meursault (mure-so)
Montagny (maun-tan-yee)
Monthélie (mawn-tay-lee)
Montrachet/Le Montrachet (mohn-rah-shay)
Nuits-St.-Georges Blanc (nwee-san-george blawnk)
Pernand-Vergelesses Blanc (pair-non vair-ja-less blawnk)
Pouilly-Fuissé (poo-yee fwee-say)
Puligny Montrachet (pool-een-yee mon-rah-shay)
Rully (roo-yee)
St.-Aubin (sahn-oh-banh)
St.-Véran (sahn-vah-rahn)

Champagne (sham-pon-ya) Chardonnay is the only major white wine grape permitted in the production of Champagne. It is usually blended with the other two grape types that are permitted — Pinot Noir and Pinot Meunier — both of which are red grapes. When Champagne is produced from 100 percent Chardonnay, it is termed *blanc de blancs*.

Other grape types Wines made exclusively from the Chenin Blanc grape:

Vouvray (vouv-ray)
Savennières (sav-ven-yair)

Wines made exclusively from the Sauvignon Blanc/Fumé Blanc grape:

Sancerre (sahn-sair)
Pouilly-Fumé (poo-yee foo-may)
Menetou-Salon (men-e-to sal-ohn)

Wines made from a blend of the Sauvignon Blanc and Sémillon grapes (Muscadelle is also added for Sauternes and Barsac):

Graves (grahv)
Sauternes (saw-turnz)
Barsac (bar-sack)

Wines made exclusively from the Viognier grape:

Condrieu (cawn-dree-ew)
Château Grillet (cha-toe gree-ay)

Wines made exclusively from the Muscat (Melon) grape:

Beaumes de Venise (bome duh ven-neese)

Wines made exclusively from the Muscadet grape:

Muscadet (mus-kah-day)

FRANCE—RED WINES

Burgundy The grape used in the production of all French red Burgundy is the Pinot Noir. Listed here are most of the major red wine–producing communes of Burgundy. When you come across these wines in either a restaurant or the retail environment, remember that they are made from 100 percent Pinot Noir.

Aloxe-Corton (ahl-uhx core-tuhn)
Auxey Duresses (oak-say dew-ress)
Beaune (bone)
Bonnes-Mares (baun-marr)
Chambertin (sham-bear-tin)
Chambolle-Musigny (sham-boll mooz-een-e)

Chassagne-Montrachet (sha-sahn mohn-rah-shay)
Chorey-les-Beaune (shor-ray lay bone)
Clos de Vougeot (clo duh voo-zho)
Corton (core-tuhn)
Echézeaux (esh-shay-zo)
Fixin (feex-san)
Gevrey-Chambertin (jev-ray sham-bear-tin)
Morey-St.-Denis (mor-ray sahn duh-nee)
Monthélie (mawn-tay-lee)
Musigny (mooz-een-yee)
Nuits-St.-Georges (nwee-sahn-George)
Pommard (po-mar)
Santenay (sahn-ten-nay)
Savigny-lès-Beaune (sav-een-yee lay bone)
Volnay (vowl-nay)
Vosne-Romanée (vone ro-man-nay)

Bordeaux Red Bordeaux can be made from Cabernet Sauvignon, Merlot, Cabernet Franc, Malbec, and Petit Verdot. It can be made entirely of one type, but it is more commonly a blend of the five. The final blend is usually a reflection of the vineyards, the region, and the vintage. Cabernet Sauvignon and Merlot are the two most widely used grape types in Bordeaux. Listed here are the major red wine–producing communes of Bordeaux, along with the grape types used in descending order of importance.

Pauillac Cabernet Sauvignon, Merlot, Cabernet Franc, Malbec, Petit Verdot
St.-Julien Cabernet Sauvignon, Merlot, Cabernet Franc, Malbec, Petit Verdot
Graves Cabernet Sauvignon, Merlot, Cabernet Franc, Malbec, Petit Verdot
Margaux Cabernet Sauvignon, Merlot, Cabernet Franc
St.-Émilion Merlot, Cabernet Sauvignon, Cabernet Franc, Malbec, Petit Verdot
St.-Estèphe Cabernet Sauvignon, Merlot, Cabernet Franc, Malbec, Petit Verdot
Pomerol Merlot, Cabernet Sauvignon, Cabernet Franc, Malbec, Petit Verdot

Wines made from the Gamay grape:

Beaujolais

ITALY — RED WINES

Wines made exclusively from the Nebbiolo grape:

Barbaresco (bar-ba-ress-co)
Barolo (ba-roll-lo)
Ghemme (ghemm)
Grumello (grew-mell-o)
Inferno (in-fair-no)
Sassella (sas-sell-ah)
Spanna (spahn-na)
Gattinara (got-tee-nar-rah)

Wines made exclusively from, or from a majority of, the Sangiovese grape:

Chianti (key-ahn-tee)
Brunello (brew-nel-lo)
Select Super Tuscan wines

Wines made from a majority of the Cabernet Sauvignon grape:

Select Super Tuscan wines

Wines made from a majority of the Merlot grape:

Select Super Tuscan wines

SPAIN — RED WINES

The traditional red wines of Rioja can be made exclusively from, or from a blend of, the following grape varietals (in order of importance and use): Tempranillo, Garnacha, Graciano, Manzuelo.

The red wines of Ribera del Duero can be made exclusively from, or from a blend of, the following grape varietals: Tempranillo (also known as Tinta del País), Garnacha, and — in certain regions — Cabernet Sauvignon, Merlot, Malbec.

PART TWO

The Wine Regions

France, Germany, Spain, Italy, the United States, Chile, New Zealand, Hungary, Australia, Austria, Portugal, Madeira, Argentina, South Africa — the list of wine-producing countries goes on and on. Each country is steeped in its own wine-making traditions, wines, and history, and each deserves its own chapter. But in writing any entry-level book, one has to observe some limits, and a book on wine is no different.

Choosing which countries to include was not as difficult as deciding how much space to allot to each one. France, the most important and greatest wine-making country, receives the lion's share of attention. A solid knowledge of French wines will provide a strong foundation for anyone interested in wine. The second country I have concentrated on is the United States, especially California. Through dedication and the use of modern technology, the American wine industry has raised wine making worldwide to a higher level. Concentrating on these two countries meant compromising on the other major wine countries — most notably, Italy, Spain, and Germany — while ignoring others altogether. It has not been my intention to showcase the wines of one country at the expense of others or to create false impressions of wine superiority. I have simply tried to provide the information I felt was essential for the wine novice. Three chapters follow, the first focusing on the United States; the second on France; and the third on Germany, Italy, New Zealand, Chile, South Africa, Australia, and Spain.

Vineyard in winter

COURTESY OF WASHINGTON STATE WINE COMMISSION

7

THE UNITED STATES

America is a young wine-producing nation, especially when compared with the wine-making communities of the Old World. In European wine cellars, where wines older than the United States can still be found, wine history and traditions are spoken of in terms of centuries. America's serious wine-making tradition is only decades old.

Although America's wine history is not nearly as long or as illustrious as Europe's, it can be traced back several centuries. Possibly the earliest recorded reference to wild grape-bearing vines in America can be found in the sixteenth-century records of the Italian explorer Giovanni da Verrazano. While exploring the southern region (now North Carolina) in 1524, Verrazano noted, "There are many vines growing naturally here." The vines Verrazano saw were most likely America's native *Vitis labrusca* species, a prolific yet inferior species when compared with the *Vitis vinifera* types found in Europe. Over the next few centuries early American settlers familiar with wine and wine making would try their hands at producing wine from the vines in this new land. While their hard work was often rewarded with a sizable crop of fruit, the wines produced were not of the same quality as the wines of Europe.

America's First Wine Connoisseur: Thomas Jefferson

Thomas Jefferson was one of America's earliest and strongest advocates for quality American wine. From 1785 to 1789 Jefferson served as the U.S. minister to France, where he is said to have developed a taste for fine wine. Jefferson became obsessed with the fact that great wine was not being produced in America. After much frustration with wines produced from native vines, Jefferson imported European vines to be planted in vineyards that lay east of the Rockies. His hopes of re-creating the great wines of Europe were dashed when, after they were planted, the vines became sickly and died.

There are two possible explanations for Jefferson's failed attempts. The first is his choice of inappropriate vineyard sites in areas of extreme hot and cold temperatures, and the second is the possibility that the then unknown phylloxera plant louse (see chapter 4, "The Vineyard and the Vintage") attacked and killed the vines' root systems. Jefferson, thinking the problem lay in the soil, went so far as to import European soil in what became his final failed attempt at viticulture.

A Brief History

Vitis vinifera grapevines (European grapevines) were first planted in America in the late eighteenth century when Jesuit missionaries brought cuttings of the Mission grape into the Baja region of California. This Mission grape was a descendant of a Spanish variety that is said to have been planted in Mexico around 1542 by Cortés, conqueror of Mexico. After the Jesuits were expelled from Mexico in 1767, the Franciscans arrived. They gradually moved up the coast, establishing a chain of missions that ran from Mexico to Sonoma. As they traveled north, the Franciscans planted the Mission grape and produced more and more wine. Today the Mission grape has been replaced by many others, but it can still be found in parts of California.

Today wine is produced in more than half of America's fifty states. Most of the wine production takes place in four areas. The first and by far most important area — in terms of both quality and quantity — is California. The second in terms of quality is the Pacific Northwest, which is followed by the eastern seaboard and, finally, the southern and midwestern states. The areas this chapter will concentrate on are California and the Pacific Northwest, the two wine-producing regions considered America's finest.

American Wine and Labeling Laws

Wine laws, rules, and labeling guidelines are approved and enforced by the U.S. federal government's Bureau of Alcohol, Tobacco, and Firearms, known as the BATF. In 1983 specific viticulture areas throughout America were recognized by the BATF as American Viticulture Areas (AVAs), of which today there are over a hundred. The main function of an AVA is to set distinct boundaries based on climate, soils, and topography. No doubt the AVA was modeled after France's Appellation d'Origine Contrôlée as well as Italy's Denominazione di Origine Controllata. Unlike these two wine-governing bodies, though, the AVA has not up to this point included under its guidelines any restrictions on which grape varietals may be planted in any particular area or what maximum grape yields can be. I suspect that at some point in the future restrictions of this sort may well be added. Following is a list of the major requirements for the labeling of American wines.

- If a wine's label includes the name of any single grape type — Chardonnay or Merlot, for example — the wine must contain a minimum of 75 percent of the named grape. The exception to this rule is Oregon, where, except for Cabernet Sauvignon, varietally labeled wines have been regulated by the state to contain a minimum of 90 percent of the named grape type. If the label names an American Viticulture Area such as Santa Cruz or Sonoma, a minimum of 85 percent of the grapes used must come from that AVA.

- The winery and region of origin must appear on the label. A region is listed when grapes from two or more states are used in a wine's production. If a state's name appears on a label, 100 percent of the grapes must come from that state. If a county name is listed (Napa Valley or Santa Barbara, for example), a minimum of 75 percent of the grapes used must come from that county.

- Vintage dating is defined by the BATF as follows: If a year or vintage date appears on a wine's label, a minimum of 95 percent of the grapes used in producing that bottle or container of wine must be from grapes harvested in that year.

- Certain health warnings are mandatory on American wine labels. The consumer must be advised of the presence of any additives such as sulfites and of the possible danger of alcohol consumption for pregnant women. Such warnings are not necessary on wines that are to be shipped outside of the United States.

READING AMERICAN WINE LABELS

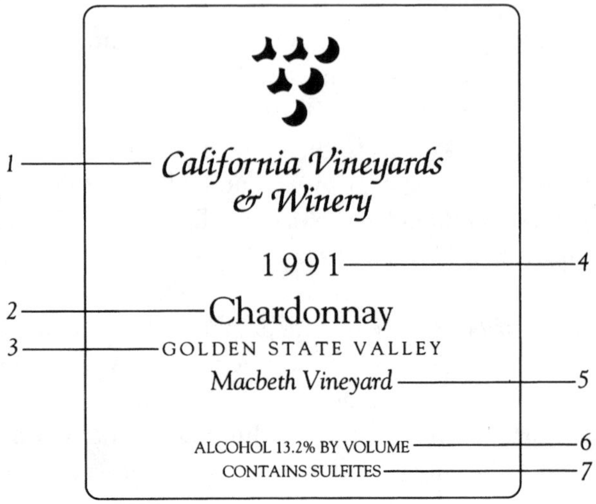

1. Brand/Producer name. *This is the name chosen by the bottler.*

2. Type of wine. *This may be varietal, generic, or proprietary. Varietal wines must be made from 75 percent of the variety.*

3. Place of origin. *This is the geographical growing area. To state "California," 100 percent of the grapes used must be grown within the state; to use a county name, 75 percent of the grapes must come from that county; and to use an AVA (a federally approved viticultural area) 85 percent of the grapes must come from the defined area.*

4. Vintage. *This is the year the grapes were grown. Wines must contain a minimum of 95 percent of the stated vintage.*

5. Individual vineyard. *A minimum of 95 percent of the grapes must have come from the named vineyard.*

6. Alcohol content. *Wines designated as "Table Wine" (7 to 14 percent) are not required to show alcohol content. However, if a wine exceeds 14 percent, the label must show that.*

7. Sulfite statement. *Sulfur dioxide is a natural by-product of wine making, and has been used for centuries as a preservative in virtually all wines. Federal law now requires the statement on the label that the wine contains sulfites.*

COURTESY OF SONOMA COUNTY WINERIES ASSOCIATION

OTHER TYPES OF WINE LABELS

There are two other types of wine labels that you may encounter when purchasing wine: generic and proprietary. The makers of generic wines borrow famous, recognizable wine names like Chablis, Sauternes, or Burgundy and label their wines as such. This kind of label often confuses and even tricks the consumer into purchasing a wine that has nothing in common with the name on its label. Generic wines, which are usually inexpensive jug wines, are most often mass-produced. Some examples are Mountain Chablis by Paul Masson or Inglenook Burgundy.

A proprietary name is a name that has been trademarked by a winery or company, thus securing for the company exclusive rights to the name. Marketing strategies to the contrary, a proprietary name is no indication of a wine's quality. Some examples of proprietary wines of high quality are Insignia by Joseph Phelps Winery or Opus One of the Robert Mondavi Winery, both from Napa Valley, California. Night Train and Thunderbird are wines of considerably less refinement but are also examples of proprietary labeling.

California

When we think of American wine we almost immediately think of California. Most of our nation's greatest wines have been — and most likely will continue to be — produced from grapes grown there. California can be further described with an even bolder statement. No wine-making community in the history of wine has had such an impact on fine wine making in such a short time as California. Although wineries such as Buena Vista, Martini, Wente, Beringer, Inglenook, Christian Brothers, and Krug have been in operation for over a century, California gained its reputation for producing quality wines much more recently.

It was only after the end of Prohibition in 1933 that quality wine and California were first linked together. During the 1940s, 1950s, and 1960s the vast majority of California's wines were still, for the most part, of a rather simple nature, the product of unproved soils, poor wine-making techniques, and unsuitable grape varieties. As a result, Californian wines were never mentioned in the same breath with the great wines of the established vineyards of France, Italy, Spain, or Germany. All this was about to change, however, through the inspiring efforts and dedication of a new generation of wineries, among them Beaulieu Vineyard, Martin Ray Vineyards, Ridge Vineyards, Robert Mondavi Winery, Hanzell Winery, and Heitz Wine Cellars. Legendary wine makers André Tchelistcheff, Joseph Heitz, Robert Mondavi, Mike Grgich, and Martin Ray are clearly among the most important wine-making visionaries who, through hard work and a deep respect and love of both wine and the land that produced it, laid a strong foundation for America's future generations of wine makers. These wine makers were motivated to produce the best possible wines — not the most wine, not the easiest, and certainly not the cheapest. While many wine makers contributed to this explosive era of quality wine, three merit special attention.

ANDRÉ TCHELISTCHEFF: BEAULIEU VINEYARD (NAPA VALLEY)

True greatness can occur in any field, from sports to music to science to wine making, but it has always been rare. In the field of wine there are wine makers who through hard work, dedication, sacrifice, and pride have flirted with greatness. There are even those who — for a moment or two — have achieved it. True greatness, however, must be sustained, and when it occurs, it is obvious, seamless, natural.

André Tchelistcheff was a great wine maker, America's greatest. Born in Russia, the son of the chief justice of the Russian imperial court, André was exposed to intelligent, analytical minds from an early age. Upon graduation from the military academy of Kiev, he migrated to Yugoslavia and later studied agricultural technology in Czechoslovakia. He then furthered his education at the Institute of National Agronomy in Paris and studied alcoholic fermentation and microbiology at the Institute Pasteur. It was in Paris during 1937 that André met Georges de Latour, the owner of Beaulieu Vineyard, who lured him to California.

During his four-decade career at B.V., Tchelistcheff raised the standard for California wine and wine makers by example. He believed strongly in the importance of microclimates and lectured about the importance of planting the right grape in the appropriate region and climate. It was André, along with Louis Martini (Martini Winery), who first urged the planting of Chardonnay and Pinot Noir in Napa's Carneros region (a common practice today). Although he was capable of producing many different types of wine, it was no secret that throughout his career Cabernet Sauvignon was his priority. His bottlings of Georges de Latour Private Reserve were considered for decades California's benchmark for the type.

Today's common practice of aging red wines in small oak barrels (American oak) was brought to the attention of wine makers as a result of Tchelistcheff's experiments at B.V., as was his early belief in the use of cold fermentation for white wines and malolactic fermentation for red wines. Beaulieu Vineyard and André Tchelistcheff will always be linked, but as early as 1947 André was also a respected consultant to many top wineries. Joseph Heitz, Mike Grgich, and B.V.'s current wine maker, Joel Aiken, all either were trained by André or consulted him.

Tchelistcheff officially retired from B.V. in 1973, but he was not one to take retirement in a leisurely fashion. He started his own consulting firm, working with up-and-coming California wineries such as Jordan and Neibaum-Coppola (owned by Francis Ford Coppola), as well as with more established wineries like Sonoma's Buena Vista Winery. André's special talents soon crossed state lines when he headed north to serve as a consultant to Oregon's Erath Winery and Washington State's Château Ste. Michelle and Columbia Crest Winery. André was especially instrumental in the rebirth of Washington State's wine industry. Sadly, André Tchelistcheff died at the youthful age of ninety-two in 1994, but his achievements, talents, dedication, sense of humor, and passion will continue to shape and influence the way wine is made, cultivated, thought of, and enjoyed.

ROBERT MONDAVI: THE ROBERT MONDAVI WINERY (NAPA VALLEY)

There are few true visionaries in life, just as there are only a handful of natural promoters. Robert Mondavi has been both in the American wine industry. Robert's parents, Cesare and Rosa Mondavi, emigrated from Italy in 1910, and he was born in 1913. Upon moving to California, Cesare became involved in shipping California wine grapes to fellow émigrés, and after numerous trips to California he decided to set up a business in Lodi that would specialize in grapes from the Central and Napa Valleys. This innocent move was the seed that would soon develop into the Robert Mondavi Winery empire.

Robert became involved in the wine business, and in 1943 he convinced his father to acquire the Charles Krug Winery with its hundred acres of vineyards. He was certain great wines could be made there, and from 1950 into the 1960s he tirelessly experimented and innovated in all phases of grape growing and wine making. In 1966 Robert left the Charles Krug Winery and erected the Robert Mondavi Winery on Highway 29 in Oakville. It was at this site that his hard work and constant dedication soon brought California wines into the international arena.

Most often praised for his brilliant marketing abilities, Robert Mondavi was a talented and capable wine maker. He was the first Napa Valley vintner to use cold fermentation extensively. He also popularized previously unpopular wines such as Chenin Blanc by producing slightly sweeter versions. And while today everyone is familiar with the term *Fumé Blanc,* it was Robert Mondavi who coined the term in 1966 in a marketing and wine-making coup that brought worldwide attention to the unpopular Sauvignon Blanc grape and the wines made from it. In 1979 California's first joint wine-making venture with a French château (Château Mouton-Rothschild) was released under the name Opus One.

In his quest to produce world-class wines, Robert Mondavi was always willing to share his ideas and the results of his experiments with his wine-making neighbors. Because of his unselfish and genuine love for wine and country, Robert Mondavi has become one of the world's most recognized and respected wine personalities. During the mid-1960s and 1970s, the Mondavi Winery became a sacred learning ground for many new up-and-coming California wine makers, with Warren Winiarski of Stag's Leap Wine Cellars, Zelma Long of Simi Winery, and Mike Grgich of Grgich Hills as three examples from an extensive and impressive list.

JOSEPH HEITZ: HEITZ WINE CELLARS (NAPA VALLEY)

If Robert Mondavi was the visionary for the wine industry, Joseph Heitz was its master craftsman. After working at Beaulieu Vineyard as André Tchelistcheff's understudy for seven years, Heitz decided it was time to go out on his own. Well schooled in oenology at the University of California at Davis, Joe had both a technical and a practical training that few wine makers had at the time. In addition, when he purchased the tiny Heitz Wine Cellars in 1961, Joe brought to it something that no other California winery had — his will.

Joseph Heitz was simply the most determined, hardworking, and, yes, opinionated wine maker in the country. To this day I believe that if ever there was a wine maker who could improve a wine simply by staring at it, that wine maker was Joe Heitz. While many in the industry took unkindly to his hard line and his opinions, he was just being honest, and Joe Heitz was simply more honest than most.

One fact that can't be argued was Heitz's unparalleled success as a wine maker. Part of the great success of Heitz Cellars' Cabernet Sauvignons was Joe's keen eye for procuring top-quality grapes. This ability soon led to the wine industry's most celebrated combination of wine maker (Joe Heitz) and grape source (Napa's Martha's Vineyard, owned by Tom and Martha May). Joe Heitz's wine-making talents, his belief in harvesting as late in the season as possible, and Martha's Vineyard grapes have produced America's finest examples of Cabernet Sauvignon. The quality of the 1968, 1969, and 1970 vintages of Heitz Wine Cellars' Martha's Vineyard Cabernet Sauvignon clearly proved to everyone that California was indeed capable of producing world-class Cabernet Sauvignon. If there were any doubts remaining, the great back-to-back vintages of 1973 and 1974 made believers of all skeptics.

The success of Heitz Wine Cellars paved the way for today's small boutique wineries and emphasized the importance of specific vineyard sites and microclimates. Heitz must also be credited with raising the image of

California wines by defying California's practice of pricing wines lower than the finest French red Bordeaux wines. He believed that if it's in the bottle, they'll pay for it. They did pay, and they literally stood in long lines on hot days for the privilege.

Today Heitz Wine Cellars' Cabernet Sauvignons continue to be among the world's most sought-after wines at auctions. Heitz Cellars produces other fine wines from Chardonnay, Grignolino, and Zinfandel grapes. However, Cabernet Sauvignon from designated vineyards such as Bella Oaks, Trailside, and Martha's Vineyard continues to be the house specialty.

CALIFORNIA'S DEFINING MOMENT: THE PARIS WINE TASTING OF 1976

After a string of very good to excellent vintages in the late 1960s and early 1970s, those familiar with the best California wines were becoming confident that California was capable of producing world-class wines. But wine making was a craft that had been developed and refined on European soil, and it was hard to imagine that the new wines from America would ever be welcome on the same platform where the world's established wine elite had stood alone and unchallenged for centuries. With the California wine industry ripe for a defining moment, it was soon delivered — quite unintentionally — by a respected Parisian wineshop owner, an Englishman named Steven Spurrier.

Having experienced the quality of select California wines, Spurrier thought it would be interesting to set up a blind wine tasting (a tasting at which the participants do not know the identities of the wines served) with some of the most respected French wine experts. The tasting was to include famous French red Bordeaux and white Burgundy along with offerings of California Chardonnay (the same grape used for white Burgundy) and Cabernet Sauvignon (the predominant grape used for most red Bordeaux wine). Spurrier's original intention was to demonstrate the differences between the two wine-making regions. The wine tasting was to be part education and part curiosity. While Spurrier did not present the tasting as a competition between David (California) and Goliath (France), the international media portrayed it in just that fashion.

When the votes were collected and the final scores tallied, to everyone's shock the unimaginable had taken place. The titanic reputation of French wine was dealt a stunning blow as the California wines placed first in both red and white categories. What was perceived as even more damaging and embarrassing was the fact that the voting panel was exclusively French. The results of this historic tasting, now known as "the Paris Tasting," immediately brought California's wines out of Europe's shadow and into the international limelight as the up-and-coming wines of the future.

The rankings of the top five red and the top five white wines follow:

The Paris Tasting Results: Red Wines

First	Stag's Leap Wine Cellars Napa Valley Cabernet Sauvignon 1973*
Second	Château Mouton-Rothschild — Pauillac — 1970
Third	Château Haut-Brion — Graves — 1970
Fourth	Château Montrose — St.-Estèphe — 1970
Fifth	Ridge Vineyards Monte Bello — Santa Cruz Cabernet Sauvignon 1971*

The Paris Tasting Results: White wines

First	Château Montelena Chardonnay — Napa Valley — 1973*
Second	Meursault Charmes, Domaine Roulet — 1973
Third	Chalone Vineyard's Chardonnay — Monterey — 1974*
Fourth	Spring Mountain Chardonnay — Napa Valley — 1973*
Fifth	Beaune "Clos des Mouches" Domaine Drouhin — 1973

To this day there are wine professionals who dispute the importance of the Paris Tasting of 1976. I believe, however, that although it was intended as an innocuous exercise, it proved to be a defining moment in California's, as well as America's, wine history.

Today California is recognized as one of the great wine-producing regions of the world. As a leader in both wine-making technology and vineyard management, California rose quickly to world-class status and made both traditional and emerging wine communities pause and take notice. Although there are many reasons for this success, I will only discuss the two most important.

First, much of California is blessed with a natural climate for farming and viticulture. While many other grape-growing regions around the world — including France — struggle to ripen their grapes, most of California, with its predictable sunshine, rarely has any trouble doing so. Frost that can devastate a region year after year can, for the most part, be managed. Even nature's schedule of rain in California seems to agree with the natural cycles of grape growing. California also possesses many different

*California wines.

geographic landscapes that provide unique pockets of microclimates and soil variations.

The second reason for California's quick rise was its unparalleled embrace of technology. For decades — even centuries — European wine-making practices evolved very little. The grandfather taught the father, who in turn taught the son. The son adhered to the advice of his elders, and for the most part that was that. In truth, the advice that was handed down was fine-tuned very slowly through trial and error over many generations, resulting in an understanding of the vineyards that technology could never supply.

Many professionals — myself included — feel strongly that the best wines ever produced came from technologically untrained wine makers. Be that as it may, technology has an upside that is difficult to ignore. Nowhere is this more obvious than in the fermentation process, in which spotless stainless-steel fermenting tanks of various sizes have been replacing time-honored yet less controllable large wooden vats. The addition of highly cultivated and predictable yeast prior to fermentation has also helped remove some of the surprises (both good and bad) that wild, natural yeast has been known to create.

There are many other areas into which technology has been introduced, from mechanical harvesters to synthetic corks, and it is not surprising that, for the most part, California has led the charge. While many wine-making communities around the world have accused California of embracing technology too quickly, it's amusing to note how quickly these communities adopt this new technology when it proves successful.

CLIMATIC ZONES

The University of California at Davis (UC Davis) has long been associated with the California wine industry. Many of the world's best-known wine makers, including Christian Moueix of Château Pétrus in Bordeaux, studied oenology and wine making at Davis. For decades it has been involved in studies of the grapevine and its adaptation to the soils and climates of California.

One of Davis's major studies involved heat summation and has led to the classification of five climatic zones or regions that can be found around the world. One practical application of this study has been to match each climatic zone with the grape types best suited to that zone. The classification of these five regions was determined by figuring the total daily mean temperatures above 50 degrees Fahrenheit from April 1 through October 31 (the grape-growing season). For example, if the average mean temperature for ten consecutive days is 62 degrees, the total heat summation for those ten days is (62–50 = 12) x 10 = 120 degree days. If we take that same mean temperature of 62 degrees and calculate it from April 1 through October 31 (214 days), the total heat summation is (62–50 = 12) x 214 = 2,568 degree days. If you match this total to the chart that follows, you will find that the tested location is classified as a zone 2 location, and the grape types best suited to it are Cabernet Sauvignon, Merlot, and Sauvignon Blanc. Knowing which zone is best suited for each grape type can save a grape grower both money and time when deciding which grape to plant in a particular vineyard. The most suitable growing zones for the production of wine grapes are zones 1, 2, and 3. My only criticism of this system is that other important factors like soil, drainage, and rainfall are not included.

CALIFORNIA WINE REGIONS

California can be divided into five main wine-producing areas: the North Coast, the Central Valley, the Central Coast, the Sierra foothills, and the South Coast. Clearly the most important in terms of producing quality wine, the North Coast and the Central Coast are the chief focus of this chapter. The least important wine-producing area is California's South Coast. What follows is an outline of these five regions, including the individual wine districts (or AVAs) of each.

The Five Climatic Zones (Coolest to Hottest)

Zone 1 Requires a total of 2,500 degree days or less and is best suited for Chardonnay, Pinot Noir, Riesling, and Gewürztraminer.

Zone 2 Requires a total of 2,501 to 3,000 degree days and is best suited to Cabernet Sauvignon, Merlot, and Sauvignon Blanc.

Zone 3 Requires a total of 3,001 to 3,500 degree days and is best suited to Zinfandel, Barbera, Syrah, Cabernet Sauvignon, and Gamay.

Zone 4 Requires a total of 3,501 to 4,000 degree days and is best suited for Thompson Seedless and Malvasia.

Zone 5 Requires a total of 4,000 degree days or more and is best suited for Thompson Seedless and assorted dessert table grapes.

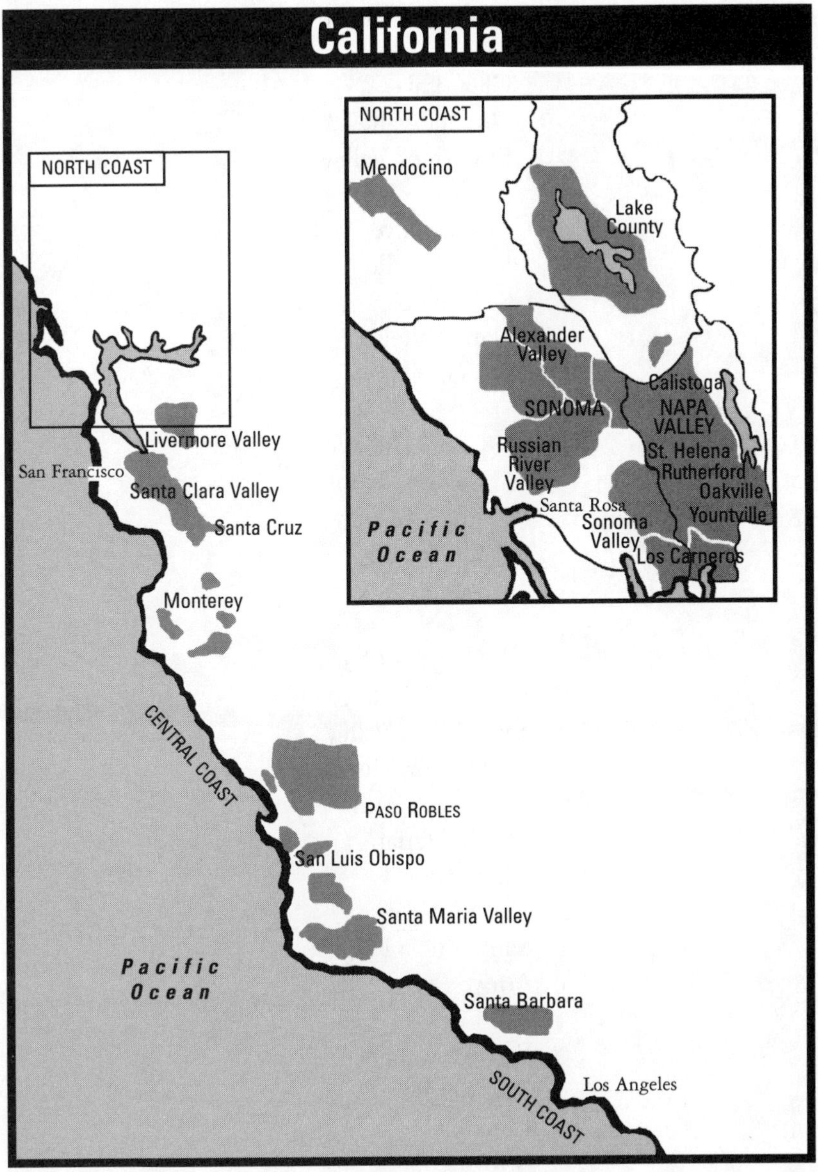
California
NORTH COAST
Mendocino
Lake County
Alexander Valley
SONOMA
Russian River Valley
Santa Rosa
Sonoma Valley
Calistoga
NAPA VALLEY
St. Helena
Rutherford
Oakville
Yountville
Los Carneros
Pacific Ocean
NORTH COAST
Livermore Valley
San Francisco
Santa Clara Valley
Santa Cruz
Monterey
CENTRAL COAST
Paso Robles
San Luis Obispo
Santa Maria Valley
Pacific Ocean
Santa Barbara
Los Angeles
SOUTH COAST

North Coast

Mendocino
Clear Lake
Guenoc Valley
Dry Creek Valley
Alexander Valley
Russian River Valley
Knights Valley
Sonoma County
Napa Valley
Los Carneros

Central Valley

Solano County
Suisun Valley
Clarksburg
Lodi

Central Coast

Livermore Valley
Santa Clara Valley
Santa Cruz Mountains
Monterey County
Mount Harlan
Chalone
Carmel Valley
Santa Lucia Highlands
Arroyo Seco
San Lucas
York Mountain
Paso Robles
Edna Valley
Arroyo Grande
Santa Maria Valley
Santa Ynez Valley

Sierra Foothills

El Dorado
California Shenandoah Valley
Fiddletown

South Coast
Temecula
San Pasqual Valley

THE NORTH COAST

The North Coast begins in the Carneros district of the Napa Valley and runs north to Mendocino. It is from the North Coast districts that most of California's quality wine is produced. Within the North Coast counties, however, there are dramatic differences in climate, drainage, and soil composition. So much variation leads to the production of a diverse selection of wines and wine styles.

One of the most important and interesting factors affecting the North Coast vineyards is their proximity to the cooling fog that runs off the San Francisco Bay and spills over the coast every day in the summer. This fog offers the vineyards a cooling influence that protects and preserves the grapes' precious acidity. The fact that the vineyards of Napa, Sonoma, and Carneros produce most of the North Coast's best fruit and are the closest to, as well as the most influenced by, this fog is no coincidence. The vineyards farther north — for example, Mendocino — are much less influenced by the cool moisture, and as a result they are considerably warmer.

The Napa Valley I've already said that when the subject of American wines is broached, we automatically think of California. It is equally true that when we think of California wines, we think first of Napa Valley. The Indian translation of Napa is "Land of Plenty," and fur trapper George Yount clearly recognized the potential of the valley's fertile soils when he settled there in 1831. With Yount came cuttings of the Mission grape from General Vallejo's vineyards in Sonoma, cuttings he soon cultivated. In the late 1850s other settlers began experimenting with planting the more classic European grape types imported from Europe.

The Indians named Napa well; it is still known as a land of plenty, but today chiefly for wine. Napa Valley, located approximately fifty miles north of San Francisco, has been called one of the most concentrated, continuous stretches of quality grape-growing land in the world. It's hard to believe that this reputation belongs to a stretch of land that runs a mere thirty miles in length and ranges between one and five miles wide.

To understand just how small the Napa Valley is, imagine this: Two Napa Valleys could fit neatly within the borders of the Champagne district of France. Small as it is, though, should you ever drive down its now famous and undersize Highway 29, just how sacred this ground is will immediately become obvious. You will see that Highway 29 is California's Champs Élysée of wine, as one by one you pass the famous wine names of Mondavi, Beaulieu Vineyard, Inglenook, Beringer, and Grgich Hills, to name just a few. The Silverado Trail, only a mile or so east of Highway 29, runs parallel for most of the valley. While taking this route does not offer as complete a perspective of the Napa Valley as Highway 29 does, it provides good insight into the topography of the valley. Clos du Val, Stag's Leap Wine Cellars, Joseph Phelps, Heitz Wine Cellars, Silverado, and Duckhorn are some of the top wineries with Silverado Trail addresses. Should you be a little more adventurous, explore the many roads throughout the valley that lead to an assortment of mountain vineyards and wineries such as Togni, Mayacamas, Mount Veeder, and Dalla Valle. Be careful if you consume wine at mountain wineries, however, as navigating down these steep and dangerous hills is always a little more difficult than driving up.

Most wine consumers think of the Napa Valley as one large winegrowing region, but the Napa Valley actually comprises many different individual wine regions and subregions. If a region or subregion has special microclimates, soil composition, or other strong individual characteristics, it can apply for its own appellation. Some examples of appellations within the Napa Valley are Carneros, Mount Veeder, Oakville, Rutherford, St. Helena, Spring Mountain, Howell Mountain, Stag's Leap District, Atlas Peak District, and Wild Horse Valley. To be approved as a separate appellation or AVA, each region must define itself as being different from other regions and must be able to display individual characteristics in its finished wine. Napa's southernmost vineyards are located in the cool Carneros district, which borders the Mayacamas mountain range. Napa's northernmost vineyards are located in the much warmer district of Calistoga.

Napa Valley grape types. Earlier I described the five climatic zone classifications developed by UC Davis. The Napa Valley is quite diverse in its climates and offers examples of three of the five climatic zones. Zone 1, the coolest, can be found from Carneros to Yountville. Pinot Noir, Chardonnay, and Riesling perform best in this zone. Riesling, however, is not widely planted, because Chardonnay and Pinot Noir offer the grape grower a much higher level of profit and prestige. The ten-mile stretch from Yountville to St. Helena is classified as zone 2 and is slightly warmer. The Cabernet Sauvignon, Merlot, and Sauvignon Blanc varietals are well suited to it. From St. Helena to Calistoga the valley warms up to zone 3, where Zinfandel, Syrah, Cabernet Sauvignon, and Merlot can be cultivated. It should be remembered that these classifications are general guides and are not to be viewed as absolutes. Rainfall is approximately twenty-six to thirty inches per year, although the summer months are usually dry. Frost can be a problem, especially in the cooler districts of Carneros and Yountville, where oil cans and large windmill-type fans are used quite successfully as methods of frost management.

Soils. The Napa Valley enjoys a host of different soil types: sandy loam, clay, volcanic ash, rocky knolls, and alluvial fans. Poor drainage and fertile soils are found throughout much of the valley floor, and thus it is easy for the vines to overproduce. The inclined hillside vineyards with good drainage are better suited for lower yields, as well as to supply helpful stress for the vines.

Napa Valley easy pick wineries. Today there are hundreds of Napa Valley wineries producing thousands of different wines. While having so many different choices may be the democratic way, it also creates confusion if your goal is simply to purchase a good bottle of wine at a fair price. The prices of Napa Valley wines, like those of most other quality wines, have soared over the past five years, making good-value wines harder to find. Following is a list of four Napa Valley wineries whose wines are easy to find and which have consistently produced some of California's best values.

- *Beaulieu Vineyard.* Dollar for dollar, B.V. has produced California's best red wine values for the important entry-level wine consumer. Cabernet Sauvignon is produced at different price points, from Coastal, to Rutherford, to the winery's top-of-the-line Georges de Latour Private Reserve Bottling (California's first reserve bottling, produced since 1936). B.V. also produces quality Pinot Noir from the Carneros region. A consistent product and value, the Reserve of this type has gotten pricey of late. While B.V. has long been considered a red wine house, it has made considerable strides in raising the quality of its white wine portfolio, especially Chardonnay. Buy B.V. wines with confidence and enjoy.

- *Markham Vineyards.* Markham Vineyards provides consistently good-value wine in the intermediate price level. Merlot is the house specialty, although good Chardonnay and Sauvignon Blanc are also made. Good distribution and solid production make Markham a safe choice with an excellent track record.

- *The Joseph Phelps Winery.* The Joseph Phelps Winery produces so many different styles of wine so well that it is hard to pick out a house specialty. Be it the delicious Sémillon, late-harvest Riesling, Chardonnay, crisp Sauvignon Blanc, Cabernet Sauvignon, or Merlot, no winery does as much as well. Within the Phelps portfolio is the Vin du Mistral program, an ambitious project that specializes in Rhône-style, Syrah-, Viognier-, and Grenache-based wines. At the top end, the winery's flagship proprietary Bordeaux blend known as Insignia (California's first *meritage* — that is, blended — wine) remains one of the state's best examples.

- *Franciscan Estates.* Franciscan Estates represents a family of different wineries kept remarkably individual by offering different pricing, regions of origin, wine-making practices, labeling, and marketing. Listed within this group are Estancia, Franciscan Oakville Estate, Mount Veeder, and Quintessa. There is also a Chilean label in the portfolio known as Veramonte. With the exception of Quintessa, which is the superpremium, superpriced showcase wine of the group and has yet to establish a track record, all represent value, availability, consistency, and very high quality for their respective price levels. Be confident when purchasing wines from this group because they seldom disappoint.

Recommended Napa Valley Wineries

Acacia
Beaulieu Vineyard*
Beringer
Cakebread Cellars
Carneros Creek Winery*
Caymus Vineyards
Château Montelena
Clos du Val Winery
Dalla Valle Vineyards
Domaine Chandon*
Dominus
Duckhorn Vineyards
Dunn Vineyards
Etude
Far Niente
Franciscan Estate*
Freemark Abbey*
Frog's Leap
Grgich Hills
Groth Vineyards
Guenoc*
Harlan Estate
Heitz Wine Cellars
Inglenook*
Louis Martini*
Markham Vineyards*
Mayacamas Vineyards
Mount Veeder
Newton Vineyards
Niebaum-Coppola Winery
Opus One
Philip Togni Vineyard
Pine Ridge Winery
Robert Mondavi Winery
Saintsbury
Schramsberg
Shafer Vineyards
Silverado Vineyards*
Silver Oak Cellars
Spottswoode
Stag's Leap Wine Cellars
Stag's Leap Winery
Steltzner
Stonegate Winery
Stony Hill Winery
Swanson Vineyards
Terraces
Trefethen*

Joseph Phelps Winery*
Kent Rasmussen
Long Vineyards
Turley
Z. D. Winery

Sonoma County While the Napa Valley receives most of the attention for producing California's fine wines, many believe that Sonoma County, located west of Napa, is California's significant other. It's hard to disregard this notion, since Sonoma has produced quality wine even longer than Napa has. The town of Sonoma was founded as a Franciscan mission around 1830 and was soon put to the vine by a Hungarian immigrant named Agoston Haraszthy. Haraszthy, who has been called "the father of California wines," imported thousands of European grape cuttings and planted them at his Sonoma property in 1856. This property became known as Buena Vista and remains as vineyards to this day.

Sonoma County starts just north of San Francisco and has a flavor very different from that of the Napa Valley. Unlike Napa's vineyards with their continuous, back-to-back concentration, Sonoma's wineries and vineyards are much more spread out. Sonoma County supports other forms of agriculture in addition to viticulture and appears more intimate and approachable. Buena Vista, Sebastiani, Italian Swiss Colony, Foppiano Wine Company, and Korbel & Bros. are some of Sonoma's oldest wineries.

As was the case in Napa, Sonoma enjoyed a burst of new growth in wineries after Prohibition, especially during the 1960s and 1970s. Some examples are Hanzell, Château St. Jean, Matanzas Creek, Simi, Jordan, Sonoma-Cutrer, and Kistler. Sonoma's wineries have been the originators of many new ideas and concepts in the California wine industry — Château St. Jean Winery's work with botrytised dessert wines from the Riesling grape, for example, or the Sonoma-Cutrer Winery's dedication to producing only one type of wine (Chardonnay) from individually designated vineyards. Of all Sonoma's contributions to the new era in California wine making, however, none has had the impact of the discovery (or, to be more accurate, the rediscovery) of the French oak barrel by Hanzell Winery's late owner, James D. Zellerbach.

James D. Zellerbach: Hanzell Winery. James Zellerbach, a former ambassador to Italy, was an experienced taster who was quite an admirer of France's red Burgundy wines, made from the Pinot Noir grape. He especially fancied the Grand Cru wines of Clos de Vougeot. So impressed was Zellerbach with Clos de Vougeot that when he constructed his own Sonoma winery it was in Clos de Vougeot's image. In his quest to produce wines comparable in quality to red Burgundy, Zellerbach tried to mimic

*Good-value wineries.

the wine-making practices of Clos de Vougeot as closely as possible. He imported both grapevines and wine-making tools from Burgundy. Then Zellerbach borrowed one more article that almost immediately brought the quality of California wines to the next level: the French Burgundy oak barrel. When Zellerbach first released his Burgundy barrel-aged wines under the Hanzell label, other California wine makers — as well as the fast-paced California wine industry — stopped, tasted, sighed, and immediately incorporated the use of French barrels in their own wine-making practices. This increase in quality was soon taken a step too far when many wine makers adopted the philosophy of "the more wood, the better the wine." This led to a decade (the late 1970s) of overoaked, hard, unfriendly wines in which the amount of wood in the wine was showcased instead of the complexity that wood could add. Happily, in time common sense and cost prevailed (French barrels cost over $600 each), and the excessive use of oak began to give way to more appropriate and balanced levels.

Sonoma County viticulture areas. Bordering San Pablo Bay to the south, the Pacific Ocean to the west, and Napa Valley to the east, Sonoma, like Napa, is greatly influenced by its proximity to water. Carneros, which is located partially in Sonoma and partially in Napa, is Sonoma County's southernmost vineyard area. To the north, the Alexander Valley is home to the region's northernmost vineyards. Between Carneros and the Alexander Valley are other individual grape-growing areas, including Sonoma Mountain, Sonoma Valley, Sonoma Coast, Russian River, Green Valley, Chalk Hill, Knights Valley, and Dry Creek. Each of these individual sites has its own climatic makeup and soil composition, giving Sonoma County many unique grape-growing possibilities.

Recommended Sonoma County Wineries

Alexander Valley Vineyards*
Arrowood Vineyards
Benziger Winery
Buena Vista Winery*
Carmenet
Chalk Hill Estate
Château Souverain*
Cotturri
De Loach Vineyards
Dry Creek Vineyards*
Ferrari-Carano Vineyards
Fisher Vineyards
Gloria Ferrer
Lambert Bridge*
Laurel Glen Vineyard
Marimar Torres Estates
Mark West Vineyards*
Martinelli
Matanzas Creek
Merry Edwards Winery
Paul Hobbs
Peter Michael Winery
Ravenswood*
Robert Stemmler Winery
Rochioli Vineyards
Rosenblum Cellars

Hanzell Winery	Kitler
Hartford Court Winery	Sebastiani Vineyards
Iron Horse Vineyards	Sonoma-Cutrer
J. Fritz Winery	St. Francis Winery*
Jordan Vineyard and Winery	Williams & Selyem

Mendocino Mendocino is the northernmost vineyard area of the North Coast wine areas. It is also the warmest. Within Mendocino lie four individual AVAs (south to north): McDowell Valley, Cole Ranch, Anderson Valley, and Potter Valley. Anderson Valley is the coolest of the four and has had good success as a quality source of grapes for sparkling wines. So much is thought of the Anderson Valley that Roederer and Pommery, two fine French Champagne houses, have invested here and are producing traditional-method sparkling wines under the Roederer Estate and Scharffenberger labels, respectively. The warmer vineyards of Mendocino are well sited for hearty red wine production, such as Cabernet Sauvignon, Zinfandel, and Syrah, along with other Rhône varietals. Fetzer Vineyards and Parducci are two of the better-known and -valued wineries of Mendocino.

Recommended Mendocino Wineries

Fetzer*	McDowell Valley Vineyards
Fife Vineyards	Parducci*
Hidden Cellars	Scharffenberger
Jepson Vineyards	

CENTRAL COAST

While California's Central Coast may not possess the panache and name recognition of the well-known North Coast region, it is clearly capable of producing some of the state's best wines. Stretching from San Francisco to Santa Barbara, the Central Coast has twenty-four AVAs. Following is a brief description of select Central Coast counties.

Livermore Valley Fifteen miles long and ten miles wide, the Livermore Valley has produced wine for over a hundred years and is one of California's oldest AVAs. It is located just east of the San Francisco Bay in Alameda. Cool and foggy mornings that give way to long, warm afternoons create a fine environment for grape growing, while deep rocky soils provide good drainage. The predominant red grape types cultivated are

*Good-value wineries.

Cabernet Sauvignon and Merlot; Sauvignon Blanc, Sémillon, and Chardonnay produce the majority of the whites. Wente is by far the largest and best-known winery of the Livermore Valley and produces an assortment of reasonably priced, well-made wines. Many decades ago it was Wente that first labeled and released a wine as Chardonnay. Wente must also be credited with being a loyal holdout against the temptations of selling its precious land for urban development in the region.

Santa Cruz County For more than a decade I had an annual California wine trip ritual. I would fly out of Newark International Airport nonstop to San Francisco, adjust my watch, rent a car, and drive an hour north to the Napa and Sonoma wine country. Each day I would visit five or six wineries, tasting eight to fifteen wines at each stop. After eight or nine days I would pack up my bags and return home.

Back at The River Café early in 1982 I received a call from Mario Daniele, New York's original and leading purveyor of fine California wines. Daniele is the person who single-handedly selected California's best wineries and introduced them to New York City — to the world, for that matter. "Joe," he said, "I'm glad you're in. I'd like to come for lunch with the owner of Mount Eden Vineyards. I think you should taste her wines."

Now Mario didn't often call with a request of this sort, so I of course agreed. He arrived with Ellie Patterson, part owner of Mount Eden and wife of its wine maker, Jeffrey. With her she brought bottles of Mount Eden Estate Chardonnay 1978 and 1980 and Pinot Noir Estate 1980. After some polite introductions, Ellie told me how little wine was produced from Mount Eden's estate vineyards and how old mountain vineyards produce only tiny yields — often less than a ton per acre. Now I've heard this pitch before and prepared myself before asking the price. Ellie then said to me, "I can tell from your wine list that you enjoy fine wine. So why don't we just taste the wines first."

"Done," I said.

Ten minutes later I was trying to buy New York's entire allocation. These wines were simply the best examples of California Chardonnay and Pinot Noir that I had ever tasted. Unfortunately for me, Mario Daniele is an honorable man; while he was, as always, quite fair, he could not give me the entire allocation.

This brief tasting greatly altered my California ritual. No longer would I land in San Francisco and activate the automatic pilot for Napa and Sonoma. On my next trip I went south, headed for Mount Eden's homeland, the Santa Cruz Mountains in Santa Clara. Ridge Vineyards was my first stop, and the trip up the mountain would have pleased most Extreme sports enthusiasts. When I finally navigated my way to Ridge Vineyards, I was at an altitude of over two thousand feet. I was greeted graciously by Paul Draper, my host. "We don't get too many visitors up here," he said.

"I wonder how many make it back down," I replied.

At Ridge Vineyards we tasted multiple vintages of Monte Bello Cabernet Sauvignon, and as with my earlier experiences with Mount Eden's Chardonnay and Pinot Noir, I was quite impressed. As I was about to leave Ridge, I asked Paul Draper for directions to Mount Eden Vineyards (the original Martin Ray Vineyards). He brought me to a clearing, pointed, and said, "It's right over there, around that bend." It was on this trip "around the bend" that I began to understand why there are so few visitors to this part of California's wine country: it took me well over an hour to reach Mount Eden Vineyards. In Napa an hour is enough time to drive up and down the entire valley, passing dozens of wineries. The quality of these select Santa Cruz Mountains wineries, however, makes the trip well worth the time.

Because of urban development in Santa Clara and the Santa Cruz Mountains, there are precious few remaining vineyards. As a result, wineries often purchase fruit from different sources to supplement their production. In the case of Ridge Vineyards, additional Cabernet and Zinfandel are purchased from different regions, and in the case of Mount Eden, additional Chardonnay and Pinot Noir are purchased. Yields in the remaining mountainous vineyards are tiny, owing in part to infertile shale soils and hillside plantings. These tiny yields can often result in stunning, concentrated, complex wines. Unfortunately, low yields also create hefty price tags as well as limited availability.

Recommended Santa Cruz Wineries

Bonny Doon	Mount Eden Vineyards
Cinnabar	Ridge Vineyards
David Bruce	Santa Cruz Mountain Winery

Monterey County Three hours south of Santa Cruz we come to beautiful Monterey County. Of late, Monterey has become one of California's most expansive sites for the planting of new vineyards, especially Chardonnay vines. Within Monterey County smaller wine appellations exist — Chalone, Carmel Valley, and Arroyo Seco, for example. The primary grape-growing district, however, lies in the warm Salinas Valley. Referred to as "the salad bowl," the Salinas Valley, with its deep, rich, fertile soil and its hot, dry climate, has become home to vast, flat vineyards. It also supports tons and tons of lettuce, broccoli, and artichokes. Its salad bowl reputation may be more than just words, as an unpleasant aroma, often described as vegetal or stewed, seems to work its way into some of the region's wine, especially Cabernet Sauvignon and Merlot.

As a whole, Monterey is a warm region with minimal rainfall, and many wineries need or choose to irrigate. Chardonnay, Pinot Noir, Pinot Blanc, and Riesling are the grapes that have shown the most promise. While the Salinas Valley would have a hard time boasting about the suitability of its soil for wine grape production, treasured and rare limestone soils can be found at extremely high altitudes within the Gabilan Range below Pinnacles National Monument. It is here that some of the region's best wines are made. Chalone Vineyards and Calera are both located in this vicinity.

The county's most famous winery has been Chalone Vineyard, and although quality has been inconsistent, Chalone Vineyard is always capable of producing stellar Pinot Noir and Chardonnay, as well as California's best Pinot Blanc. Calera Vineyards specializes in Pinot Noir and produces tiny amounts of a white Rhône varietal called Viognier. Talbott Winery also deserves special mention for producing top-quality Chardonnay consistently. While the wines of Chalone, Calera, and Talbott are usually expensive and hard to find, J. Lohr Winery and Morgan Winery offer very good wines at more palatable prices, especially for Chardonnay and Pinot Noir. Jekel Winery produces a reasonable, consistent, slightly sweet Riesling as well.

Recommended Monterey Wineries

Boyer Winery
Chalone Vineyard
Durney Vineyards
Estancia*
Jekel Vineyards*
J. Lohr*
Morgan Winery*
San Saba
Talbott Vineyards

Following is a list of other Central Coast wine regions that have also been producing quality wines.

Additional Central Coast AVAs

Arroyo Grande
Edna Valley
Paso Robles
Santa Barbara
Santa Clara
Santa Lucia Highlands
Santa Maria Valley
Santa Ynez Valley

*Good-value wineries.

Oregon

Directly above California lies the beautiful state of Oregon, bordered by breathtaking mountains and surreal coastlines. Although wine has been produced in Oregon for over a century, its modern era of wine began in the late 1950s. One of the new wineries was Hillcrest Vineyards, founded in 1959 by Richard Sommer. During the late 1970s and the 1980s, many other new wineries were founded, particularly in the Willamette Valley. Some of Oregon's pioneering wine makers during this early and important developmental stage were Dick Ponzi of Ponzi Winery, David Lett of Eyrie Vineyards, and Dick Erath of Knudsen Erath, known now as Erath Winery. Some other more recent, important wine makers on the scene include Russ Raney, the talented wine maker of the tiny Evesham Wood Winery, and Mike Etzel of Beaux Frères Winery.

A defining moment for Oregon's wine industry that validated the generally favorable perceptions of the region occurred in 1979 when famous French Burgundy *négociant* Joseph Drouhin purchased and developed a winery in Willamette dedicated to the production of top-flight Pinot Noir (his specialty) and called Domaine Drouhin Oregon. Another example of foreign interest in Oregon was the purchase (also in 1979) of eighty acres by the French Champagne firm Laurent-Perrier. The growth of wineries continued steadily throughout the 1990s, as evidenced by the fact that the number of wineries increased from 54 in 1987 to 120 in 1997. Today the state of Oregon ranks second only to California for the number of its wineries and ranks fourth in total wine production behind California, Washington State, and New York State.

There are four major wine-producing appellations in Oregon, with three located in the western part of the state. The largest, most planted, and most important is the Willamette Valley, which further breaks down into northern and southern Willamette. Willamette vineyards enjoy wet winters, dry summers, and long, cool autumn days. When this climate is coupled with the region's deep, well-drained soils, ideal growing conditions are created for Pinot Noir, Pinot Gris, and Riesling. The vineyards of southern Willamette are slightly warmer, with more clay and loam in their soil composition.

The Umpqua region is south of Willamette and is typically warm and dry. Here the confluence of the Cascade Mountains and the Pacific Coast creates massive thermals that can cause quick evening cooling. The climatic conditions of the Umpqua are similar to those of Bordeaux, and as in Bordeaux, Cabernet and Merlot are the Umpqua region's best-suited varietals. Farther south is the southernmost wine-producing region of the state, called the Rouge region. Warmer still, the Rouge region specializes in Cabernet Sauvignon and Merlot, although Chardonnay, Pinot Noir, and Sauvignon Blanc are planted as well.

East of the Willamette region, extending well into Washington State, lies the Eastern Oregon/Columbia/Walla Walla wine region. Its hot, dry, desertlike climate is supported by only six inches of rain, and thus irrigation is required in most vineyards. The major varietals planted in the sandy and silty soils of this region are predominately Cabernet Sauvignon, Merlot, Riesling, and Chardonnay.

Oregon's wine-labeling laws are the strictest in the country and require that varietal-labeled wines be produced entirely in the region stated and contain a minimum of 90 percent of the stated grape. The lone exception to this rule is Cabernet Sauvignon, which must have a minimum of 75 percent.

Oregon is serious red wine country, with a production ratio of 62/38 red to white wine. Of all the red varietals planted, Pinot Noir is clearly the king. Almost 40 percent of Oregon's entire wine acreage is planted with this varietal. Merlot and Cabernet Sauvignon are also planted, but Oregon's reputation as a great wine-producing state will either succeed or fail on Pinot Noir and Oregon's climatic abilities to ripen it. (Watch out for those wine makers who overoak many of the more delicate Pinot Noirs.) In fact, Oregon is billed as America's premier region for growing Pinot Noir, owing in part to a climate similar to that of France's Burgundy region (the land of Pinot Noir's greatest success) and in part to some near great yet inconsistent success with this fickle grape. This ranks the grape growers of Oregon as among America's most adventurous, as even in Burgundy consistent quality from the Pinot Noir grape is a yearly struggle.

What is consistent about Oregon's Pinot Noirs is their prices, which can be outrageously high, especially for many of the so-called special or reserve blends. Quality, well-priced Pinot Noir is available; however, a little effort may be required to seek it out. Oak Knoll Winery, for example, offers some good-quality, fairly priced Pinots in their portfolio.

Pinot Gris, Chardonnay, and Riesling are the most planted white grapes in the region, with Pinot Gris showing the most promise at becoming the region's sleeping giant for white wines. Some successful offerings produced by Argyle Winery indicate that sparkling wine production may also prove suitable to parts of Oregon.

Recommended Oregon Wineries

Adelsheim Vineyards
Archery Summit
Argyle Winery*
Beaux Frères
Bethel Heights
Domaine Drouhin Oregon
Domaine Serene Vineyards
Erath Vineyards
Evesham Wood Winery
Eyrie Vineyards*
Fiddlehead Cellars
King Estate Winery*
Oak Knoll Winery*
Panther Creek Cellars
Ponzi Vineyards
Rex Hill Winery
Sokol Blosser*
St. Innocent
Tualatin
Willamette Valley Vineyards*
Yamhill Valley Vineyards

Washington State

Washington State is quietly becoming America's rising star in the production of fine wines. The number of wineries has more than quadrupled from nineteen in 1981 to nearly a hundred today. While grapevines have been grown in the region since the 1800s, they were the *Vitis labrusca* species. It wasn't until decades after Prohibition that *vinifera* was planted and given a chance.

Today, after California, Washington State produces more *Vitis vinifera* table wine than any other state. The per capita consumption of wine is also high (no wonder Seattle doesn't mind all that rain!) at twelve liters, ranking it fourth overall in the country. The best news is that when the wine-drinking public discovers the high value/quality ratio that these wines offer, there is plenty of land for vineyard expansion, a fact that should keep the prices reasonable. White wine production accounts for 60 percent of total production. The highest quality I have encountered in this state, however, has been in its red wines, especially Cabernet Sauvignon, Merlot, and Syrah.

The Cascade Mountain Range divides the state into two distinct climate zones. West of the Cascades is Washington's newest and smallest (thirty-five acres) AVA, Puget Sound. Here it is cool, wet, and less suited to *vinifera* grape growing. East of the Cascades lie three of Washington State's AVA areas: the Columbia Valley, the Yakima Valley, and the Walla Walla Valley. The massive, warm, well-drained basin of the Columbia Valley is ideal for grape growing and accounts for more than 95 percent of the state's wine grapes. Sharing the same latitude as the Bordeaux and Bur-

*Good-value wineries.

gundy regions of France, vineyards east of the Cascades enjoy long summer days averaging seventeen hours of sunlight a day. This permits the grapes to ripen slowly and results in properly matured fruit. Cool evenings preserve the grapes' acid levels. Rainfall is minimal (as low as six to eight inches per year), creating the need for controlled irrigation.

The soil base is an infertile sandy loam and volcanic with good to very good drainage. These soils are unfriendly terrain to the vine-destroying phylloxera louse, and as a result most vines do not need to be grafted to resistant rootstock. The major grape varietals planted are Merlot, Cabernet Sauvignon, Cabernet Franc, Lemberger, and Syrah for red wine and Chardonnay, Chenin Blanc, Riesling, Sauvignon Blanc, Sémillon, and Gewürztraminer for the whites. The best reds are dry, as are the majority of the white wines, although several sweet whites, especially Riesling and Chenin Blanc, have also been successful.

The showcase winery of the region in terms of both beauty and dedication has been Château Ste. Michelle in Woodinville. What the Mondavi Winery did for the recognition of California wines, Château Ste. Michelle has done for Washington State. In 1967 American Wine Growers began experimenting with *Vitis vinifera* grapevines with the guidance of America's most influential and talented wine maker, André Tchelistcheff. In 1973 the United States Tobacco Company purchased American Wine Growers and infused the company with capital, marking a new era for Château Ste. Michelle. With the construction of a beautiful state-of-the-art wine-making facility in 1976, the stage was set for the Washington State wine industry.

Columbia Crest is the sister winery of Château Ste. Michelle and produces very good wines at very fair prices. Two other important, though much smaller, wineries are Columbia Winery (not to be confused with Columbia Crest), guided by Master of Wine David Lake, and the tiny Leonetti Cellars run by Gary Figgins. Lake and Figgins are two of the state's most prolific wine makers, consistently producing world-class Cabernet Sauvignon and Merlot. Leonetti Cellar's Cabernet Sauvignons and Merlots are produced in such tiny amounts that they have become among America's most sought-after wines. They may well be the state's most expensive. David Lake has been called one of the most important wine makers in America. His track record and talents back this up, especially in regard to Cabernet Sauvignon, Merlot, and Syrah. After tasting different vintages of Syrah at the winery some years ago, I came to the conclusion that Syrah may well be Washington State's diamond-in-the-rough wine varietal. Other top wineries include Quilceda Creek (whose gifted owner/wine maker, Alex Golitzin, is the nephew of the late André Tchelistcheff), L'École No. 41, and Woodward Canyon.

Because many of these wineries have minuscule production, procuring their wines may be difficult as well as expensive. However, they do represent the state's best wines. For value, availability, and quality, Hogue Cellars, Château Ste. Michelle, and Columbia Crest offer entire lines of very good wines, both red and white.

One glaring oddity about many Washington State wineries is the fact that they do not own vineyards and must purchase their fruit. This is fine when long-term contracts have been signed, but inconsistencies in house styles are bound to become evident when a winery continually changes its grape source. I am happy to report that as of this writing there is a growing trend toward vineyard ownership. This is important, because only when vineyards are owned, controlled, understood, and lived in can the potential of their fruit be fully realized.

Recommended Washington State Wineries

Andrew Will Cellars
Canoe Ridge Vineyard
Château Ste. Michelle*
Columbia Crest*
Columbia Winery
Covey Run
Hogue Cellars*
L'École No. 41 Winery
Leonetti Cellar
McCrea Cellars
Quilceda Creek
Waterbrook Winery*
Woodward Canyon Winery

New York State

New York has set the standard for many of the world's important industries. Be it fashion, music, food, theater, art, or sports, New York has almost always been a step ahead of everyone else. Internationally, in fact, few place names carry the cachet of New York.

The New York I'm talking about, of course, is New York City, a place that is never out of touch with important developments. New York State, however, is another matter altogether. I've lived here all my life and have yet to understand why the wine industry has been so slow to improve, why New York State wines have yet to be given a chance to live up to their potential.

*Good value wineries.

There is a long tradition of wine making and grape growing in New York State. The soils and climates within the state's three major grape-growing regions — the Hudson Valley, the Finger Lakes, and Long Island — are certainly diverse. In fact, New York State is rated second in the country for total grape acreage and second in total wine production. Many of the grapes grown, however, are Concord grapes, the *labrusca* grape responsible for most grape jellies, and are used for the production of grape juice. Most of the grapes grown for the production of wine are also of the lesser *Vitis labrusca* species, and while interesting wines can be produced from native varietals such as Niagara, Seyval, and Chardonel, they will never reach the heights of quality of *vinifera* grape types like Chardonnay, Merlot, Zinfandel, and Sauvignon Blanc. Many wineries are just not willing to make the switch, while many others seem perfectly content to produce wine from the native grape types and sell them locally.

What is frustrating is the fact that quality wine can be and is produced in New York State. Dr. Konstantin Frank was one of the first to try this when he and former Veuve Clicquot French Champagne master Charles Fournier planted *vinifera* vines in the Finger Lakes region in 1953. I have tasted fine examples of five- and ten-year-old Rieslings produced by Dr. Frank that would make any region proud.

Today there are other wineries producing fine wine in New York State. Long Island currently cultivates the highest proportion of *Vitis vinifera* vines in the state and, as a result, produces most of the state's best wines. Lenz Winery, Palmer, and Hargrave are three consistent examples of such wineries. Incidentally, Hargrave was the first winery on Long Island to dedicate to *vinifera* vines, and Eric Fry, the talented wine maker at Lenz, trained at California's famous Jordan Winery in Sonoma when André Tchelistcheff was its consultant and worked at Dr. Frank's winery in the Finger Lakes.

The Hudson Valley AVA also offers good wine-making examples like Benmarl and Millbrook Winery. Riverview Winery's Tim Biancalana produces fine sparkling wines that prove high quality is obtainable when the right grapes are grown on the right sites.

The New York State wine region would benefit greatly if it adopted a unified approach in the pursuit of quality wine or if a leader emerged, someone to do for New York what Robert Mondavi did for California or what Château Ste. Michelle Winery did for Washington State. Sadly, until attitudes are adjusted and vineyards are replanted, New York State — with the exception of a few dedicated wineries — will most likely continue to flounder into the millennium.

Recommended New York State Wineries

LONG ISLAND

Bridgehampton Winery	Lenz
Hargrave Vineyard	Palmer

HUDSON VALLEY

Benmarl Vineyards	Rivendell
Millbrook Winery	Riverview Winery

THE FINGER LAKES

Dr. Frank's Vinifera Wine Cellars	Hunts County Winery
Fox Run Vineyards	Knapp Winery
Glenora	Lakewood Winery
Hermann J. Wiemer	Wagner Vineyards

8

FRANCE

There is no question that in terms of quality the greatest wine-producing country has been, and continues to be, France. No other country sets the benchmark for so many different wine types. The best sparkling wines I have ever tasted have been French Champagnes, as well as the best Cabernet Sauvignon, Merlot, Cabernet Franc (red Bordeaux), Chardonnay (white Burgundy), Pinot Noir (red Burgundy), Sauvignon Blanc (Sancerre and Pouilly-Fumé), Chenin Blanc (wines of the Loire), dessert wines (Sauternes), Gamay (Beaujolais), and Syrah and Grenache (Côtes du Rhône). And add to this list the best (and only true) Cognacs and Armagnacs.

How can one country produce so much great wine? One reason is that France has been making top-quality wines longer than any other country and has more experience in fine wine making and grape growing. Another factor is the intimate bond that exists between many French wine makers and their vineyards, something that cannot be taught and can be acquired only after many years of close personal contact with the soil. France's soil and its wine makers' understanding of that soil are believed to be reflected in the finished wine and are the chief reasons French wines are often superior. France is also blessed with a multitude of different climates and microclimates that have proven over the centuries to be highly compatible with the cultivation of certain noble grape types. It is hard to argue with this success, as French wines are the standard by which other wine regions measure their own success. I have repeatedly heard wine makers in other countries brag about how their current wines taste as good as French wines.

Not all is perfect on the French wine scene, however. Lately there have been some alarming compromises in quality as a result of overproduction, most notably in Burgundy. With increased worldwide demand and blank checks being written for untasted wines from new and inexperienced emerging markets, many top French châteaus and domaines have given in to higher production from their vineyards. And higher production almost always translates into lower-quality wine. We can only hope that clear thinking and pride will prevail and such temptations will be kept in check.

Steeped in its own traditions, France was initially slow to apply modern learning to wine making and grape growing. This is now changing as each new and younger generation of French wine makers explores the benefits of modern technology. While this change of direction has led to a better understanding of the scientific process, many traditionalists feel that as it becomes easy and safe to rely on technology, wines are becoming more international in style and less individualized. Looking to the future the French wine industry will begin the new millennium exactly where it has been sitting comfortably for the last millennium — on top of the mountain. This time around, however, there will be much more competition and new challenges from revitalized traditional regions like Italy, Spain, and Germany, as well as from new and emerging regions like Australia, New Zealand, and the United States. I feel quite strongly that no one can out-French the French. But if the strong demand for French wines encourages overproduction while prices continue to soar — a result of the euphoria that the game of supply and demand creates — the French wine industry, if it isn't careful, may very well out-French itself.

French Wine Classifications

In France there are four classifications of wine. In ascending order of quality, they are as follows: Vins de Table, Vins de Pays, AO VDQS (Appella-

---

Vielles Vignes (old vines) at Château Beaucastel
COURTESY OF VINEYARD BRANDS

tion d'Origine Vins Délimités de Qualité Supérieure), and AOC (Appellation d'Origine Contrôlée). Each classification has its own set of restrictions, as sketched out here:

Vins de Table

- Wines labeled Vins de Table must have an alcohol content of no less than 8.5 or 9 percent (depending on the area of production) and no more than 15 percent.
- If the wines are of French origin, they can be called Vin de Table Français.
- This classification of wine is often sold under a trade name and is most often a blended wine meant to be consistent in style and quality year after year.

Vins de Pays

- Wines labeled Vins de Pays represent the best wines of the Vins de Table classification. Unlike Vins de Table wines, a Vins de Pays wine can list its origin on the label.
- Vins de Pays wines can be produced only from specific, delimited areas.
- Vins de Pays wines must have a minimum alcohol level of 10 percent by volume in Mediterranean regions and 9.5 percent in all other regions.
- Each of these wines must be tasted and approved for appropriate characteristics for its type by the Office National Interprofessional des Vins (ONIVIN).

AO VDQS

- Wines of this classification are strictly regulated and monitored by the Institut National des Appellations d'Origine (INAO).
- The name or appellation of the wine must be listed.
- The words "Appellation d'Origine Vins Délimités de Qualité Supérieure" must be located on the label below the wine's name.
- Once certain conditions stipulated by the Ministry of Agriculture have been met, these wines receive a seal of approval that is displayed on the wine's label. Some of these stipulations cover alcohol content, approved grape varieties, maximum yield requirements, and specific vinification and cultivation methods. As with Vins de Pays wines, AO wines must also be passed by a tasting panel.

AOC

- AOC wines, or Appellation Contrôlée wines, represent France's highest-quality classification of wine. The term *Appellation Contrôlée*, as well as the name of the appellation (Bordeaux, Burgundy, Champagne, and so on), must appear on the label of all AOC wines. Soil, grape varieties, yields, alcohol levels, vine densities, pruning, and other variables are all officially regulated.
- After being tasted and approved, an AOC wine receives a certificate of approval issued by the INAO, which entitles the wine maker to market the wine under the name of its appellation.

Major Wine Regions

Famous wine regions are located throughout France. Champagne represents the country's coolest and northernmost vineyards, Languedoc Roussillon the warmest and southernmost. Bordering Germany on the east is the picturesque region of Alsace, and to the west lies the Loire. In between

READING FRENCH WINE LABELS

1. The wine is a product of France.
2. The region in which the wine was produced — for example, Burgundy, Bordeaux, Champagne.
3. The appellation for which the wine qualifies: AOC (Appellation d'Origine Contrôlée), VDQS (Vins Délimités de Qualité Supérieure), Vin de Pays, or Vin de Table.
4. The name and address of the shipper, except in the case of Champagne where, usually, the Champagne house (brand) is also the shipper.
5. The name and address of the importer.
6. The alcoholic percentage by volume.
7. The net contents of the bottle.

The following is optional information that may appear on the label:

8. Vintage.
9. Brand name or château name.
10. "Estate bottled," "Château bottled," or similar phrase.

COURTESY OF FOOD AND WINES FROM FRANCE, INC./SOPEXA

these points lie the world's most copied and envied wine regions: Bordeaux, Burgundy, Chablis, Beaujolais, and the Rhône Valley. Keep in mind that most French wines are named and labeled after the region they are from and not after the grapes that are used to produce them.

French Wine Bottles and Shapes

Many of the different wine regions throughout France use wine bottles of different shapes, colors, and sizes according to regional and traditional practices. In some areas the bottle used is governed by law, while other ar-

French bottle shapes

COURTESY OF FOOD AND WINES FROM FRANCE, INC./SOPEXA

eas are guided more by tradition. Above is a French bottle reference chart you may find useful.

Champagne

The Champagne region is a ninety-minute drive northeast of Paris. It is the only location that can legally call its sparkling wines Champagne. (Champagne wine making and the guidelines that govern it are discussed in detail in chapter 5, "Wine Making.") Champagne is also France's coolest and northernmost wine appellation. The uniqueness of French Champagne was created through a combination of climate, grape types, production methods, and — most of all — its much envied, rich chalk soils. This chalk is solid and pure white, and carved from it are miles of underground passageways used to store millions of bottles of Champagne that are being aged. The entire Champagne region covers an area of over twenty-five thousand hectares, with most of its vineyards located around the two major towns of Reims and Épernay. Champagne's vineyards are rated on a hundred-point scale. Wines produced from vineyards (communes) rated at 100 percent can be called Grand Cru, while wines produced from vineyards rated between 90 and 99 percent can be called Premier Cru. While the Champagne region is known for wine that has bubbles in it, still wines are also produced. Coteaux Champenois produces both red and white wines from the permitted grape types. They are simple, fruity, pleasant wines that are best consumed when young. Rosé des Riceys, a lovely, still rosé wine, is also produced in small quantities.

Permitted Grape Varieties
Chardonnay (white grape)
Pinot Noir (red grape)
Pinot Meunier (red grape)

CHAMPAGNE STYLES

Nonvintage Nonvintage Champagne is a blended wine with no vintage date on the label. More nonvintage Champagne is produced and sold than any other category of Champagne. The purpose of nonvintage is to develop a house style. A consistent Champagne, without any vintage characteristics, can be offered to the consumer each year. These wines often represent Champagne's best values.

Vintage Vintage Champagne is produced from a single vintage and often develops characteristics reflecting that vintage. It is produced only in very good and excellent vintages and is always more expensive than nonvintage Champagne.

Tête de cuvée/Prestige Wines in this category represent the best a Champagne house has to offer. These are almost always produced as vintage wines and are always expensive. Some examples of tête de cuvée Champagnes are Moët's Dom Pérignon, Roederer's Cristal, Bollinger R.D., and Clicquot's La Grande Dame.

Blanc de blancs When a Champagne is produced entirely from Chardonnay grapes, it is labeled blanc de blancs. Wines of this classification are usually quite refined and elegant, reflecting the Chardonnay grape. Blancs de blancs can be produced as nonvintage, vintage, tête de cuvée, or crémant.

SWEETNESS LEVELS OF CHAMPAGNE

To accommodate many different foods, tastes, and applications, Champagnes are produced at several different levels of sweetness. The desired level of sweetness is obtained by adding precise amounts of sugar just before the final corking of the bottle. Following is a list of terms that will help you select the appropriate Champagne (ranging from driest to sweetest).

Type	*Residual Sugar Level*
extra brut, brut savage, ultra brut (bone dry)	less than 0.6%
brut (most popular and most produced)	less than 1.5%
extra dry (dry)	between 1.2 and 2%
sec (slightly sweet)	between 1.7 and 3.5%
demi-sec (sweet)	between 3.3 and 5%
doux (very sweet)	no less than 5%

Recommended Champagne Producers

Pol Roger
Billecart Salmon
Louis Roederer
Charbaut
Charles Heidsieck
Bollinger
Krug
Perrier-Jouët
Moët & Chandon (vintage bottlings)
Laurent Perrier
Salon
Drappier
Lanson
Mercier
Taittinger
Heidsieck & Co.
Veuve Clicquot Ponsardin

ENJOYING CHAMPAGNE

From the classic toast or roast through dessert, Champagne made in different styles can be enjoyed throughout the entire meal. Refreshing as an aperitif, perfect with many types of appetizers, and quite capable of holding its own with most desserts, Champagne is a most versatile wine. When I celebrate I offer my guests Champagne, as no other wine is quite as festive.

Champagne is best served quite chilled and in a tall, thin, fluted glass. It is done a disservice when served in those wide, flat, catering-house glasses, which dissipate the wine's effervescence in no time. Once opened, Champagne has a short shelf life and should be consumed fairly soon, although special caps are sold that help it keep a little longer. Champagne is ready for consumption upon release and offers little reward for being aged further. So buy, chill, drink, and enjoy.

Alsace

Located in northeastern France, Alsace is nestled comfortably between the foothills of the Vosges Mountains and the Rhine River. A peacefulness surrounds this picturesque region, and time seems to move just a little bit slower here than in the rest of the world. The wine-producing area of Alsace is a strip roughly seventy miles long, with a width that varies between one and two miles. The Rhine River is not the only thing that Alsace shares with Germany, as many of the same grape varietals (almost exclusively white) are planted and excel in both countries. Unlike German wines, which are predominantly low in alcohol and sweet, most Alsatian wines are dry. Alsace has a very dry climate with summers that are prolonged, giving the grapes a long slow period in which to ripen and become physiologically mature. Almost all of Alsace's wines are unblended (the exceptions are Pinot d'Alsace, Edelzwicker, and the sparkling Crémant d'Alsace) and are labeled by the grape variety the wine has been made from (100 percent). This practice is different from that of most French wine regions, where wines are named after the areas they come from.

White still wines are the main focus when discussing the wines of Alsace, although small amounts of red Pinot Noir and the aforementioned sparkling Crémant d'Alsace are produced. The Riesling is the region's most famous and successful grape type, although Pinot Gris, Gewürztraminer, and Pinot Blanc all share the ability to produce very good to great wine. Depending on the harvest, wines can be produced in many different styles, from the aromatically dry (most common) to the much sweeter classifications known as Vendanges Tardives (late harvest) and Sélection de Grains Nobles (selection of noble grapes), also called S.G.N. These sweet wines can rival the world's best and most expensive of this type. The best vineyards in Alsace are rated Grand Cru and can be listed on the wine's label along with either the Alsace or the Alsace Grand Cru appellation. Alsatian wine labels sometimes also include the name of the wine's district of origin — Riquewihr or Mittelwihr, for example. The wines of Alsace must by law be bottled in their region of production and only in Alsace's tall, thin, fluted wine bottles.

Permitted Grape Varieties	*Soil Compositions*
Gewürztraminer (white)	Wide-ranging: chalk
Pinot Gris (known as Tokay d'Alsace) (white)	marl, sand, stone,
Riesling (white)	alluvium, granite
Sylvaner (white)	rock
Muscat d'Alsace (white)	
Chardonnay (white)	
Pinot Noir (red)	

Recommended Alsatian Producers

Léon Beyer	Dopff et Irion
Domaine Weinbach	Hugel et Fils
Trimbach	Domaines Viticoles Schlumbergers
Domaine Zind-Humbrecht	Willm
Charles Schleret	

ENJOYING ALSATIAN WINES

It would be difficult not to enjoy Alsatian wines, as they offer so many different pleasures. Many professionals feel that Alsatian wines are the world's most food-friendly grouping of white wines. Ready for consumption upon release, most of these wines require little cellaring, although some — when selected carefully — can improve for years. One of the reasons for the early readiness of these wines is that since their appeal is found in their delicate and fresh expression of fruit, few spend any time in new oak barrels. The dry versions of Sylvaner and Pinot Gris are perfect aperitif wines. Riesling, Alsace's most versatile wine, can be enjoyed as an aperitif as well, but it also goes quite nicely with a host of different foods, including most fresh seafood, shellfish, fowl, and hams. Dry or slightly sweet Gewürztraminer is one of the few wines that match well with spicy and flavorful foods like sausage or Chinese food. A sweet Alsatian wine can either complement dessert or be dessert, and it is also a wonderful digestive. Dollar for dollar, the wines of Alsace represent France's best white wine values. Serve chilled in small, frequently poured amounts.

Burgundy/Bourgogne

Burgundy is one of the world's finest and oldest red and white wine districts. Unfortunately, far too often the good name of Burgundy has been borrowed to describe and sell inferior wines from inferior wine regions. Remember: Burgundy is a geographic location in France, and only wines from this location are entitled to be called Burgundy. There are many different districts and communes within the whole of Burgundy, each with its own traditions, flavors, and specialties. The wine districts of Burgundy start up north with Chablis, pick up again south of Dijon in the Côte de Nuits, continue south through the Côte de Beaune, Chalonnaise, and Mâconnais, and end with the district of Beaujolais. I will discuss these districts shortly, but before we proceed, we should look at some basic information.

BURGUNDY GRAPE TYPES

For the most part, the grape types used in the production of Burgundy wine are almost exclusively Chardonnay for white and Pinot Noir for red. The exception to this is Beaujolais, where Gamay is the most cultivated grape. Other grape types are permitted, although they are seldom seen — for example, the white Aligoté and the red Gamay.

APPELLATIONS

There are five levels of Appellation d'Origine Contrôlée in Burgundy. The regional appellation is the least restrictive, and its wines would simply be called Bourgogne, or Bourgogne Aligoté if produced from the Aligoté grape. These wines are simple and pleasant and offer good, everyday value and quality. The second level is the subregional appellation that offers a general location such as Bourgogne Hautes Côtes de Nuits. A step above wines with the Bourgogne appellation, these wines often offer slightly better quality at a slightly higher cost.

The Village appellation is next, and wines with this appellation make up the majority of wines produced in Burgundy. These wines are named after the village or commune they are from. Some examples are wines labeled Appellation Puligny-Montrachet Contrôlée or Appellation Vosne-Romanée Contrôlée. Wines at this level should represent a significant qualitative leap and should reflect the characteristics of the named village

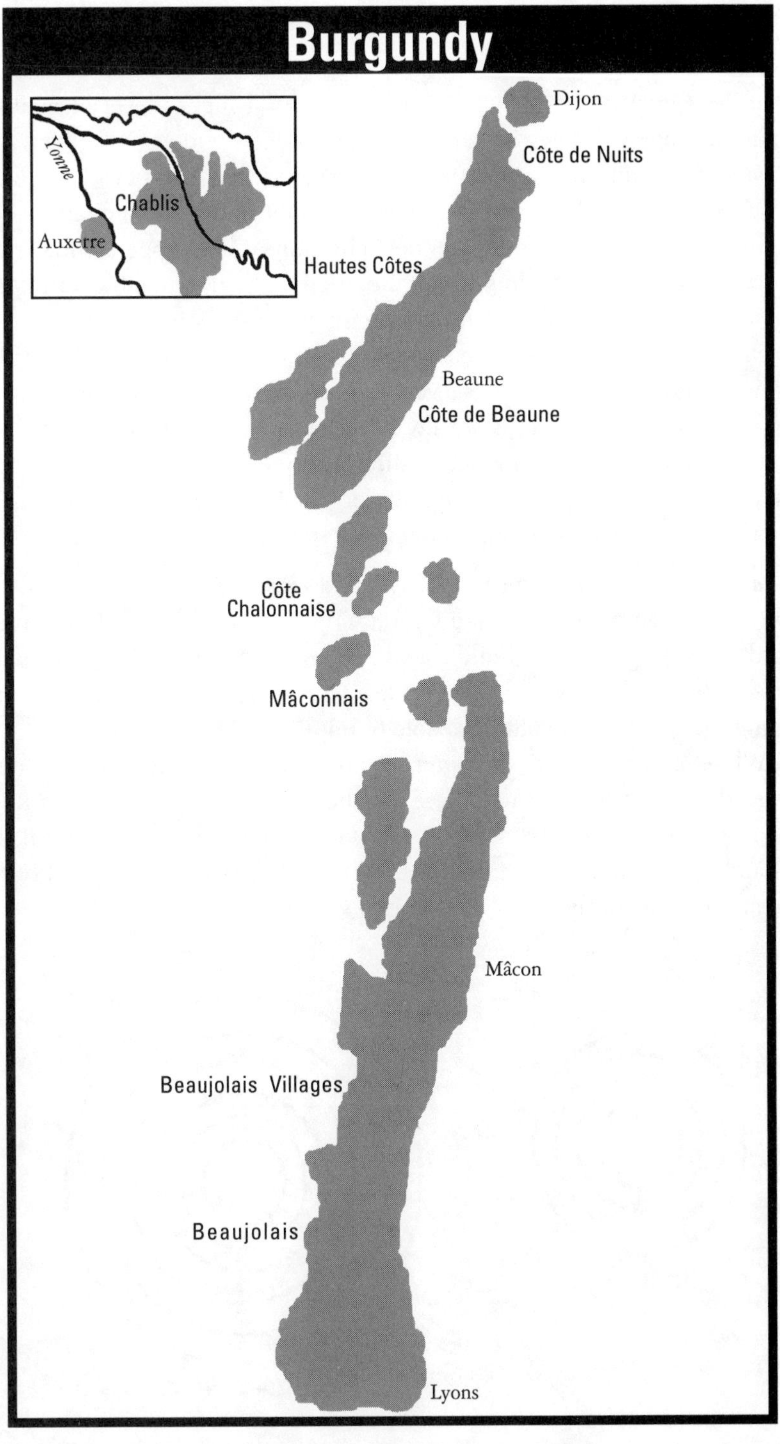
Burgundy
Yonne
Chablis
Auxerre
Dijon
Côte de Nuits
Hautes Côtes
Beaune
Côte de Beaune
Côte Chalonnaise
Mâconnais
Mâcon
Beaujolais Villages
Beaujolais
Lyons

or commune in the finished wine. These wines are much more expensive than wines at the previous two levels.

Premier Cru Vineyards that are considered of a higher level of quality than the typical Village vineyards have been rated Premier Cru. The term *Premier Cru* and the name of the vineyard are listed on the wine's label. Two examples are Puligny-Montrachet Premier Cru Les Combettes and Volnay Premier Cru Clos des Chênes. There are Village appellation wines on which the name of a vineyard is also listed, but only when the term *Premier Cru* appears is the wine from a Premier Cru vineyard.

Premiers Crus wines can be expensive and are often rare as well. These wines should possess a higher level of quality than those with the Village appellation; however, this is not always the case. Higher-rated vineyards do not automatically make higher-quality wine. Too often growers become lazy and unmotivated about producing the best possible wine, since they've already been granted Premier Cru status.

Grand Cru The rarest, most selective, and most expensive wines of Burgundy are from vineyards rated Grand Cru. It is from Grands Crus vineyards that Burgundy has built a worldwide reputation for its many great wines. Both red and white Grands Crus wines also benefit the most from being aged, as they are often capable of improving for decades.

While most producers, or *domaines*, do produce the best possible wines from these sacred vineyards, there are those who choose to catch a free ride on the reputations of others who are more dedicated. As great as Grands Crus wines can be, the possibility of disappointment can also be great. Buy selectively.

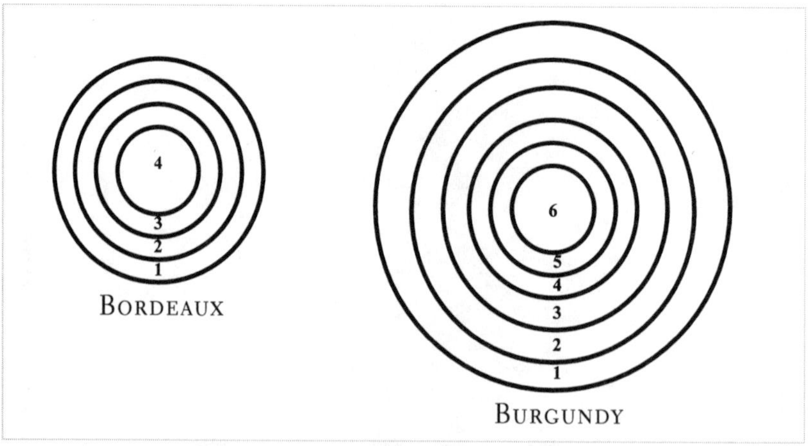

The Inner Circle

The inner circle The standard archery target is a group of concentric, colored circles. These circles get progressively smaller and smaller, and the closer to the center (the smallest circle) an arrow lands, the better the shot. The French wine appellation system can be compared to an archery target. The larger, outer circle represents the largest wine appellation (France), and with each smaller circle the origin of the wine becomes more defined. In theory, the more defined the origin of the wine, the better it is. While quality can never be guaranteed from the inner circles, higher prices most certainly can.

Bordeaux Wine

1. France
2. Bordeaux
3. Pauillsac
4. Château Latour

Burgundy Wine

1. France
2. Burgundy
3. Côte d'Or
4. Côte de Beaune
5. Meursault
6. Meursault Charmes

THE BURGUNDY *NÉGOCIANT*

In the French wine trade a *négociant* is a wine merchant or shipper. The role of a *négociant* is very important, and in Burgundy there is more than one type of *négociant*. The most common *négociant* is one who buys wines from different properties or estates (usually small growers with limited wine-making facilities), blends them together to create a desired style, and then labels them under his own label. The *négociant-éleveur,* on the other hand, is involved with the complete wine-making process. He often selects the grapes and makes the wine, as well as cellaring, aging, bottling, and releasing it. A *négociant* is free to purchase grapes (or wine) from different sources each year and is not bound to any one vineyard for any longer than his contract specifies.

It is common for a *négociant* to sell wines from many different communes. The prices of *négociant* wines are usually lower, and the wines are easier to find. The downside is that singular vineyard expressions are often lost, as the wines are most often a blend of many. Today many *négociants* enjoy the best of both worlds. They are purchasing their own vineyard land to provide quality and continuity, while they continue the practice of choosing the best available grapes and wines from independent sources.

Partial Listing of Well-Known Burgundy Négociants

Bouchard Père et Fils	Boisset
Faiveley	Verget
Louis Jadot	J. Moreau & Fils
Joseph Drouhin	Jafflin
Louis Latour	Louis Carillon
Leroy	J. J. Vincent

WHY BURGUNDY IS HARD TO DESCRIBE

You may be thinking that after twenty years in the wine business, and after tasting thousands of wines from the different communes of Burgundy, I should be able to provide an accurate flavor profile for each commune's wines. Add to my résumé the fact that I have visited the vineyards of Burgundy on many occasions and have spent more time discussing these wines with professionals — including the wine makers themselves — than I have spent on the wines of any other region. Your expectation that I can give you accurate descriptions of the wines of Burgundy should be quite high. Ah, but Burgundy is not like the other fine wine regions. Anyone who thinks he can offer anyone else a simple one-size-fits-all description of even a single commune of Burgundy would be fooling himself and performing a disservice to his audience.

My overriding goal in writing this book is to simplify wine. Burgundy, however, is far from simple. Entire vineyards owned by one grower are rare. Instead Burgundy's vineyards have multiple owners, each of whom may own parcels of land in a number of vineyards. This is in part owing to inheritance laws that constantly divided and subdivided the vineyards among hundreds of new and different owners and wine makers. Each new owner and wine maker brings a unique sense of direction and commitment, as well as individual abilities and resources. The end result, of course, only compounds the inconsistencies and confusion of Burgundy wine.

Let me offer an example. In Bordeaux there is only one Château Latour and only one Château Certan-de-May. This makes deciding whether you like the wines of a particular château quite simple. If you do not like the wines of, say, Château La Mission-Haut-Brion, you can at least walk away knowing that you don't like the wines of Château La Mission-Haut-Brion.

In Burgundy, where in any given vintage there can be fifty or more different Clos de Vougeots or dozens of different wines labeled Gevrey-Chambertin, Chassagne-Montrachet, or Meursault Charmes, it is not so easy to be so conclusive. In Burgundy you need a much more intimate knowledge of the individual grower or *négociant*, a knowledge that can take years to acquire.

The wines of Burgundy are quite personal. How one experiences them can be likened to the way one experiences color. Take red, for example. Is red one color? Does everyone see red the same way? Can anyone describe the depth, shades, or hues of red in one way that is accurate for everyone? Of course not. Do all artists (wine makers) use colors the same way? What about shading? How about the effect the light source has when you look at a painting or color? Don't things appear differently when viewed in sunlight as opposed to fluorescent lighting or moonlight? Haven't we all bought something — a carpet, wallpaper, paint, clothes — only to discover that what we chose looked different when we got it home? This is what it is like trying to pin down the wines of Burgundy.

In Bordeaux wine makers also have the benefit of blending together several different grape types, a practice that alone affords the wine maker and château much needed vintage flexibility. This is not the case in Burgundy, where different grape types are never blended. The Burgundians live and die on the strength of Pinot Noir for red wine and Chardonnay for white. Pinot Noir is capable of producing great wines. However, it is much less reliably consistent when compared with the sturdy Cabernet Sauvignon and Merlot of Bordeaux. Pinot Noir is also much more subject to the wine maker and his skills, which adds another layer of variation to the equation.

I have been fooled, surprised, disappointed, elated, and humbled by Burgundy far too often to even try to offer definitive descriptions of its wines. On the following pages, however, I offer a basic overview of each commune and its characteristics. Please keep in mind that these are only my basic guidelines. I urge you to remember that in all the confusion also lies the beauty of Burgundy wine. It is a handcrafted wine that must be experienced, tasted, and personalized by you, the taster, because — as with love — no one can do it for you.

Chablis

Chablis is one of the most recognized white wine names in the world. Unfortunately, because of its fame, wineries all over the world have borrowed its name to describe what are chiefly inferior white wines that have nothing to do with the real thing. Only the white wines of Chablis, the wine region located between Paris and Dijon, are entitled to be called Chablis. Unlike the other sections of Burgundy that are almost contiguous to one another, Chablis is separated from the Côte d'Or by seventy-five miles.

Chablis produces white wine almost exclusively from the Chardonnay grape, although Aligoté is also grown. The climate is cool in these vineyards, Burgundy's northernmost. Because of this cool, northern location, the Chardonnay grape does not fully ripen each year and frost is a major threat and problem. These two factors make both the price and the availability of Chablis very volatile. The soil is chalk and marl based and produces a delicious, bone-dry white wine, high in natural acidity. The refreshing flavor profile of the green-tinged Chablis wine is often described as flinty. In the past Chablis wines were made with little influence of new oak; however, today's trend to "fatten" them up has gained momentum against the wishes of traditionalists.

There are four quality levels of Chablis. Appellation Grand Cru Chablis is the finest, rarest, most age-worthy, and most expensive of the group and must be produced from one of the seven Grands Crus vineyards located in Chablis. Chablis Premier Cru is the next level of quality, and 25 percent of all Chablis is of this level. There are over thirty Premiers Crus vineyards. The simple Chablis appellation is next and accounts for the majority of all Chablis produced. Wines of this level are approachable sooner and often represent a good value. Petit Chablis is the lowest quality level, the least expensive, and rarely seen outside of France. Following is a list of the seven Grands Crus vineyards as well as some of the top Premiers Crus vineyards.

Grands Crus Vineyards	*Top Premiers Crus Vineyards*
Bougros	La Fourchaume
Blanchot	Montée de Tonnerre
Les Clos	Mont de Milieu
Grenouilles	Vaillons
Les Preuses	
Valmur	
Vaudésir	

Recommended Chablis Producers

Jean Dauvissat	Servin
Rene Dauvissat	Joseph Drouhin
Raveneau	Defaix
Fevre	Jean Collet
Guy Robin	Louis Michel

ENJOYING CHABLIS

When I want a crisp, refreshing, racy, mouthwatering wine, I think Chablis. Many feel that Chablis can be a bit too lemony tart, but I find that quality palate cleansing. Grand Cru and Premier Cru Chablis benefit with some time in the cellar for proper settling and better integration. Chablis AOC is usually ready to drink when purchased and makes an excellent first-course wine, especially when served with shellfish or smoked salmon. Chill well and pour generously.

Côte d'Or

Côte d'Or can be translated as "the Golden Slope," and the cost of some of the wines produced within its boundaries gives new meaning to the term. It is from this golden slope that Burgundy's — maybe France's and possibly the world's — greatest wines are produced. What is simple about the Côte d'Or is that there are only two grapes of importance here: the red Pinot Noir and the white Chardonnay. One must remember that while Chardonnay and Pinot Noir are today two of the most recognized grape types in the world, they got their start in the Côte d'Or. Simply put, the best and most envied Chardonnay and Pinot Noir are from this region.

The Côte d'Or is divided into two parts. The first to the north is the Côte de Nuits, which begins just south of Dijon and extends to the town of Nuits-St.-Georges. The wine communes of importance in the Côte de Nuits are (north to south) Marsannay, Fixin, Gevrey-Chambertin, Morey-St.-Denis, Chambolle-Musigny, Vougeot, Flagey-Echézeaux, Vosne-Romanée, and Nuits-St.-Georges. The Côte de Nuits is predominantly a red wine–producing region with a variety of different soils that are a combination of chalk and powdery clay.

To the south of Nuits-St.-Georges, and extending to the Côte Chalonnaise, is the Côte de Beaune. Here are found the wine-making communes of Ladoix, Pernand-Vergelesses, Aloxe-Corton, Savigny-lès-Beaune, Chorey-lès-Beaune, Beaune, Pommard, Volnay, Meursault, Monthélie, St.-Romain, Auxey-Duresses, Puligny-Montrachet, St.-Aubin, Chassagne-Montrachet, and Santenay. In the Côte de Beaune there is a better balance between white and red wines than in the Côte de Nuits; however, most of its greatest wines are white.

Soil varies throughout the Côte de Beaune from pebbly light clay and chalk, to redder iron-rich soils, to marl and chalk. On my trips to Burgundy I observed firsthand how drastically and suddenly the soil can change. On one trip, for example, standing in the vineyards of Louis Latour's *monopole* Corton-Grancey (a Grand Cru vineyard in Corton), I could easily see that the soil was heavy, deep red, and seemingly quite fertile. Here the vineyards were planted with the Pinot Noir grape. Just a short walk up the hill, however, the soil changed dramatically, with the topsoil becoming much finer, lighter, and powdery. In these vineyards centuries of grape growing have shown that the Chardonnay grape will perform the best magic. And that it does, in the form of a Grand Cru white wine called Corton-Charlemagne.

I explained earlier how a vineyard that has proven over time superior to surrounding vineyards of the same commune can be rated as either a Premier Cru or a Grand Cru vineyard. As a testament to the quality of the Côte d'Or, it is interesting to note that while Premiers Crus vineyards can be found in most of Burgundy's communes, the small and elite group of Burgundy's Grands Crus wines are found only in the Côte d'Or. And if we further dissect the Grands Crus wines of the Côte d'Or, we discover that, with the exception of Aloxe-Corton, the Côte de Nuits houses all red grape Grands Crus vineyards, while the white Grands Crus are exclusively in the Côte de Beaune.

Following is a brief tour of the major wine communes of the Côte d'Or.

1. CÔTE DE NUITS

Marsannay South of Dijon, Marsannay represents the first important wine commune of the Côte de Nuits. It received its own appellation in 1986 for its red, white, and rosé wines. Before 1986 the wines of Marsannay were sold as Bourgogne. While traditionally known for its fine rosé wines produced from the Pinot Noir, Marsannay has lately become more involved in making red wines. The red wines of Marsannay are well colored and fruity and can be well structured. There are no Premiers Crus or Grands Crus vineyards in Marsannay, and its wines can be a very good value. Domaine Bruno Clair is Marsannay's best-known producer.

Fixin South of Marsannay we come to the commune of Fixin. The majority of the wine produced is red, from the Pinot Noir grape, of course. There are five Premiers Crus vineyards and no Grands Crus sites. The red wines are earthy, fairly tannic, and robust, with few complexities. The whites are seldom exported. *Recommended producers:* Faiveley, Berthaut, Gelin.

Gevrey-Chambertin The finest stretch of Pinot Noir–producing vineyards begins south of Fixin with the commune of Gevrey-Chambertin. One of

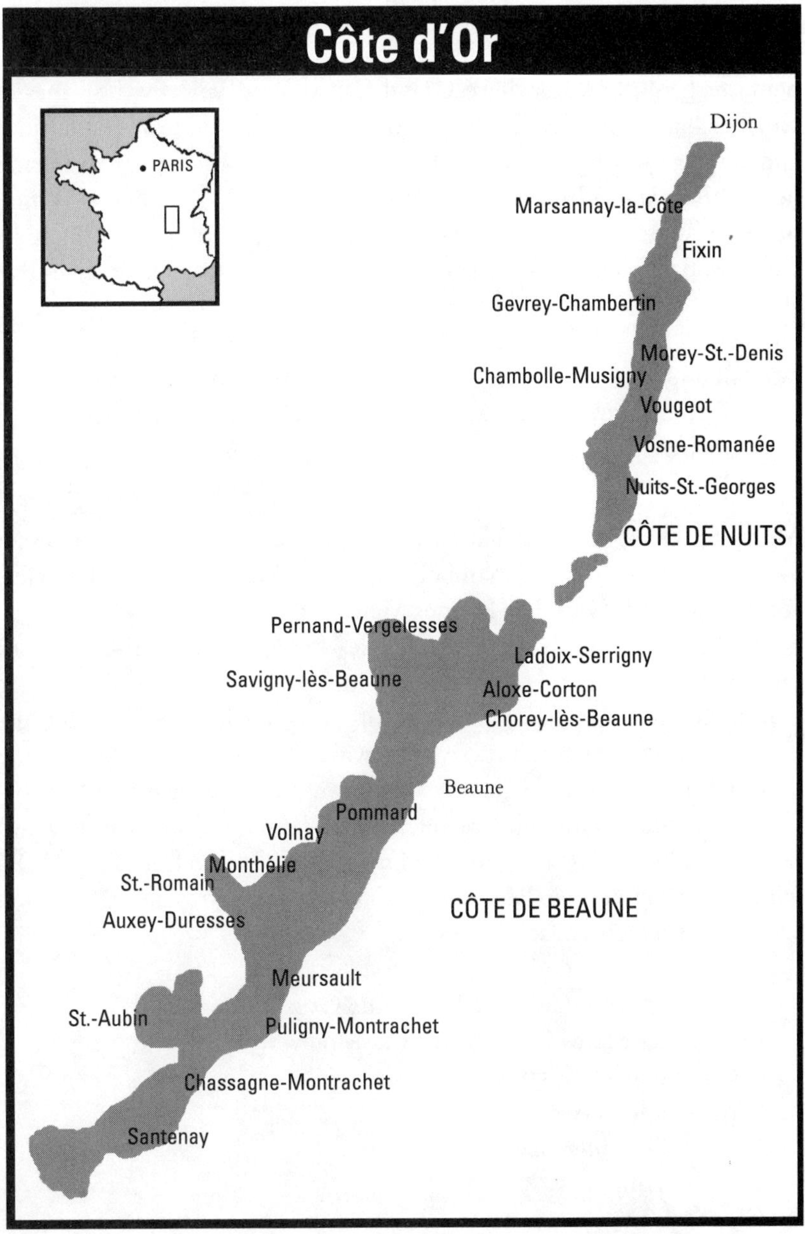

the largest communes of the Côte de Nuits, Gevrey-Chambertin is home to eight Grands Crus vineyards. That's more than a third of the twenty-three red Grands Crus vineyards located in the entire Côte de Nuits. Of the eight Grands Crus, the highest reputation belongs to Chambertin and

Chambertin Clos de Bèze, and as a result only these two are entitled to place the name Chambertin first. The remaining six must list the vineyard name first. All, however, have Grand Cru status. Typically the wines of Gevrey-Chambertin are big, well structured, highlighted with dark fruits, and very age-worthy. (Incidentally, Napoleon's favorite wine was Chambertin.) *Recommended producers:* Amiot, Domaine Dujac, Leroy, Ponsot, Serafin, Rousseau, Roumier, H. Lignier, R. Groffier, Le Clerc, Roty, Faiveley, Bachelet, Fourrier, Trapet.

Chambertin Grands Crus Vineyards

Chambertin	Griottes Chambertin
Chambertin Clos de Bèze	Latricières Chambertin
Chapelle Chambertin	Mazis Chambertin
Charmes Chambertin	Ruchottes Chambertin

Morey-St.-Denis Less well-known than its neighboring communes of Gevrey-Chambertin and Chambolle-Musigny, Morey-St.-Denis hosts five red wine Grands Crus. Les Bonnes Mares is the best known of the five; it is located partly in Chambolle. Clos des Lambrays represents the least known of all of Burgundy's red Grands Crus. At their best, the wines of this commune are highly aromatic, elegant, and well balanced. I often describe the nose as rich strawberry. The wines from vineyards closer to the Gevrey side can possess a good deal of power, while the wines from vineyards closer to Chambolle are often more refined. There are over two dozen Premiers Crus vineyards in Morey-St.-Denis, and the Village AOC wines can be quite fine. *Recommended producers:* Pierre Amiot, Drouhin, Dujac, H. Lignier, Ponsot, Groffier.

Morey-St.-Denis Grands Crus Vineyards

Les Bonnes Mares (located partly in Morey-St.-Denis and partly in Chambolle-Musigny)
Clos de la Roche
Clos de Tart (*monopole*)
Clos des Lambrays
Clos St.-Denis

Chambolle-Musigny There are two Grands Crus vineyards in Chambolle-Musigny, of which one, Bonnes Mares, is partially located in Morey-St.-Denis. Of the two, Bonnes Mares is often the bigger wine. At their best, the wines are elegant, fragrant, silky, and well textured. There are more than twenty Premiers Crus vineyards, of which Les Amoureuses and

Les Charmes are the best known. *Recommended producers:* Drouhin, G. Mugneret, Dujac, Faiveley, Groffier, Leroy, Comte de Vogue, Jadot, Hudelot-Noellat, Barthod.

Chambolle-Musigny Grands Crus Vineyards

Bonnes Mares (located partly in Morey-St.-Denis and partly in Chambolle-Musigny)
Les Musigny (red and white)

Vougeot The Grands Crus vineyards of Clos de Vougeot account for 80 percent of the total production of Vougeot wines. Unfortunately not all of it is worthy of the status. To put it simply, too much Clos de Vougeot is being produced in vineyards not suited to be called Grand Cru. To add to the confusion, far too many landowners are involved in wine making. This is unfortunate because these wines can be excellent when properly selected. Buy with caution and know the producer. *Recommended producers:* J. Gros, Leroy, Groffier, Mongeard-Mugneret, Drouhin, Arnoux, Jaffelin, Henri Clerc, Daniel Rion, Confuron, Grivot, Jadot, Meo-Camuzet, Roumier.

Vougeot Grands Crus Vineyards

Clos de Vougeot

Vosne-Romanée This is the big daddy of the Côte de Nuits, the home of the most sought-after and expensive Pinot Noirs in the world. They also represent, along with Gevrey-Chambertin, the biggest-style red wines of Burgundy. The most famous producer of Grand Cru red wine in Vosne-Romanée is the Domaine de la Romanée-Conti, which owns property in five of the six Grands Crus. The best expressions of the Grands Crus wines are complex, powerful, fleshy, concentrated, deeply colored, and often obscenely expensive. As with many things that are wildly expensive, these wines can also be disappointing and often not worth the cost. There are thirteen Premiers Crus vineyards in Vosne-Romanée that are capable of producing great wines at a fraction of the cost of the Grands Crus. The Village AOC wines are labeled Vosne-Romanée, and in the hands of a good wine maker, they can be very good. *Recommended producers:* Domaine de la Romanée-Conti, Leroy, Henri Jayer, Grivot, Bouchard Père et Fils, Drouhin, Dujac, Faiveley, Mongeard-Mugneret, Meo-Camuzet, Latour, Jean Gros, Daniel Rion, Arnoux, Hudelot-Noellat.

Vosne-Romanée Grands Crus Vineyards

La Romanée	Les Richebourgs
La Romanée-Conti	La Romanée-St.-Vivant
La Tâche	La Grande Rue

Flagey-Echézeaux Considered similar to Vosne-Romanée wines, the wines of Flagey-Echézeaux possess less finesse. They can be big, robust, well colored, and flavorful. Of the two Grands Crus, Les Grands Echézeaux is considered slightly finer and is usually more expensive. *Recommended producers:* Domaine de la Romanée-Conti, Mongeard-Mugneret, Drouhin, Dujac.

Flagey-Echézeaux Grands Crus Vineyards

Echézeaux
Les Grands Echézeaux

Nuits-St.-Georges It is the town of Nuits that gave its name to the Côte de Nuits. This large village is a major commercial center as well as a grape-growing region. The wines of Nuits-St.-Georges are predominantly red, although a tiny amount of a rare and often overpriced Nuits-St.-Georges Blanc is produced. There are no Grands Crus vineyards, but there are more than thirty-five Premiers Crus sites. The best of these are found near the neighboring commune of Vosne-Romanée to the north, just south of Nuits, and in the adjoining commune of Prémeaux. Les St.-Georges, Les Boudot, Les Poirets, and Clos de la Maréchale are some of the top Premiers Crus. At their best these wines are dark, fairly tannic, sturdy, rustic, and initially slow to open up. With time the wines soften and round out quite nicely. While prices for the top Premiers Crus have escalated recently, the Village appellation wines of Nuits-St.-Georges have become consistently good and fairly priced. *Recommended producers:* Chopin-Groffier, Grivot, Rion, R. Chevillon, Henri Jayer, Leroy, Faiveley, Chauvenet, Jadot, Domaine de l'Arlot, Mongeard-Mugneret.

2. CÔTE DE BEAUNE

Ladoix The northernmost wine commune of the Côte de Beaune, Ladoix is an appellation that has become more popular of late. It can be a confusing commune because nearly 50 percent of its best red wine vineyards are sold under the more prestigious appellations of Corton, Aloxe-Corton Premier Cru, or Aloxe-Corton, while the remaining wine is sold as either Ladoix, Côte de Beaune, or Côte de Beaune Village. Most of the wines produced are red; they are often light to medium colored and sometimes lean. *Recommended producers:* Cornu, Prince Merode, Chevalier Père et Fils.

Aloxe-Corton The commune of Aloxe-Corton is the only commune that produces both a red and a white Grand Cru. The red Grand Cru, called Corton, is also the only red Grand Cru in the Côte de Beaune. Red Corton is produced from the lower vineyards, while the white Grand Cru of Corton-Charlemagne is produced from the upper vineyards. Corton-Charlemagne is a big, powerful, deeply colored white wine that can be exquisite and quite full-bodied. It is a white wine that must be aged before its true glory is revealed. The red Grand Cru vineyard of Corton, also called Le Corton, is quite large, and its wines represent some of the best values of all the red Grands Crus. Red Corton is big, powerful, rich, and deeply colored; it shares some of the more masculine qualities of Côte de Nuits wines, while enjoying some of the elegance of the Côte de Beaune. Corton also requires some patience and time in the wine cellar for best drinking. Several Premiers Crus vineyards are labeled Aloxe-Corton Premier Cru. *Recommended producers:* Bonneau de Martray, Coche-Dury, Faiveley, Dubreuil Fontaine, Louis Latour, Roumier, Prince de Merode, Rapet, Cornu, Jadot, Tollot Beaut, André Nudant, Hospices de Beaune, Bouchard Père et Fils.

Aloxe-Corton Grands Crus Vineyards

Corton (red)
Corton-Charlemagne (white)

Pernand-Vergelesses When you think of the great Grand Cru white wine of Corton-Charlemagne, you think of Aloxe-Corton, but quite a large parcel of vineyards that are entitled to be called Corton-Charlemagne are actually located in the village of Pernand-Vergelesses. A good white Pernand-Vergelesses, like some of the Premiers Crus, offers a great value. It's a baby Corton-Charlemagne at a third of the price. As this piece of information becomes more public, I can assure you the price will rise. The good ones are yellow gold, stony, mineral, and full-bodied and do require some aging for best drinking. A lovely red Pernand-Vergelesses is also produced from the Pinot Noir grape and is earthy, aromatic, and often light in color. *Recommended producers:* Dubreuil Fontaine, Leroy, M. Rollin, Guyon, Louis Latour, Bonneau de Martray.

Chorey-lès-Beaune One of the less popular Villages of Burgundy, Chorey-lès-Beaune has become an affordable alternative to some of the better-known and more expensive Village wines. These wines are often sold as Côte de Beaune Village and are light in color and accessible, with little need of or benefit from aging. There are no Premiers Crus vineyards in Chorey-lès-Beaune. *Recommended producers:* Cornu, Arnoux, Drouhin, Germain, Tollot Beaut, Nudant.

Savigny-lès-Beaune This is a good-size wine commune that concentrates on red wine produced from the Pinot Noir. The wines produced are medium-bodied, aromatic, simple, and best consumed three to five years old. The Premiers Crus vineyards offer wines with more complexity that can be aged longer. The wines of this commune are often good values as well. *Recommended producers:* Simon Bize, Bruno Clair, Drouhin, Albert Morot, Mongeard-Mugneret, Chanson, Tollot Beaut.

Beaune Lending its name to the Côte de Beaune, the old walled town of Beaune is the wine capital of Burgundy. The famous Hospices de Beaune, which is now a museum, is where the Hospices de Beaune wine auction is held each year. The results of this auction help set the prices for upcoming Burgundy vintages. The predominantly red wine–producing commune of Beaune produces lovely, soft, fruity wines of light to medium color. While these wines are best enjoyed in their youth, they are capable of aging quite gracefully if stored well. There are no Grands Crus vineyards, yet there are many fine Premiers Crus sites, most notably Les Bressandes, Les Grèves, Les Boucherottes, and Le Clos des Mouches. Le Clos des Mouches also produces an excellent white wine by the Burgundian *négociant* Domaine Drouhin. *Recommended producers:* Drouhin, Faiveley, Robert Ampeau, Jaffelin, Lafarge, F. Gaunoux, Hospices de Beaune, Jacques Germain, Latour, Jadot, Tollot Beaut, Albert Morot, Leroy.

Pommard Pommard produces big, round, rustic, deeply colored, and fairly tannic wines that can be quite age-worthy. While some show great finesse and complexity, others can seem a bit alcoholic and hard. Although there are no Grands Crus vineyards, more than a third of the commune is rated Premier Cru. Of the many Premiers Crus holdings, the two best are Les Epenots and Les Rugiens. There are those who feel that these two vineyards deserve Grand Cru status. *Recommended producers:* Comte Armand, de Courcel, Gaunoux, Domaine Leroy, Hospices de Beaune, Jadot, Pousse d'Or, Château de Pommard, Drouhin.

Volnay If I were given only one vote on which commune's vineyards should be considered for red Grand Cru status, my vote would most certainly be for the vineyards of Volnay. Located between Pommard to the north and Monthélie and the Côte de Beaune's first major white wine commune of Meursault, Volnay often produces the most elegant, refined, and — if I may use the phrase — wonderfully feminine yet powerful red

Burgundy of the entire Côte de Beaune. There are twenty-six Premiers Crus vineyards in Volnay, with Clos des Chênes, Clos de Ducs, Caillerets, La Bousse d'Or, and Santenots rated among the best and most consistent. Incidentally, Santenots is actually located in Meursault, and its white wines may be called Meursault. *Recommended producers:* Marques d'Angerville, Faiveley, Bitouzet-Prieur, J. F. Coche-Dury, Drouhin, Leroy, Comte Lafon, Lafarge, Domaine de la Pousse d'Or, Ampeau.

Monthélie, Auxey-Duresses, St.-Romain Because of escalating wine prices of the established villages, these three rather unknown wine communes have begun to receive some attention and appreciation for their value. Located around and behind Meursault and Volnay, these communes rarely produce wines that challenge the complexity of a good Volnay, Meursault, or Puligny. They do, however, admirably fill a niche for those who want to drink Burgundy but cannot afford to. The red wines can be attractive and pretty, while the whites range from crisp to soft and nutty. In most cases these wines are best consumed within a few years of their release. There are no Grands Crus in these communes.

Meursault With Meursault begins the most highly regarded stretch of Chardonnay vines in the world. The three communes in the stretch are (north to south) Meursault, Puligny-Montrachet, and Chassagne-Montrachet. Of the three, Meursault is the largest village in size. There are no Grands Crus vineyards in Meursault — unlike in Puligny and Chassagne — but there are many excellent Premiers Crus. My favorites among them are Les Genevrières, Les Perrières, and Les Charmes. A small amount of red Meursault is made from Pinot Noir, but these wines seem something of a curiosity. The wines of Meursault are sturdy and often deeply colored. Terms like toasty, hazelnut, creamy, full, opulent, and chunky are often used to describe them. Good Premiers Crus are best when given four to six years to soften and round out (the trend in the United States has been to drink them much too young). *Recommended producers:* J. F. Coche-Dury, Jean-Michel Ganoux, Comte Lafon, Michelot-Buisson, Guy Roulet, Grivault, Hospices de Beaune, Leroy, Château de Meursault, Bitouzet-Prieur, Rougeot, Jobard, Germain, Ampeau.

Blagny Located between Meursault and Puligny-Montrachet, the hamlet of Blagny cultivates both Chardonnay and Pinot Noir. The Chardonnay is sold as Puligny-Montrachet, Meursault-Blagny, or Meursault Premier Cru. The appellation Blagny is exclusive to red wines. Best described as rustic style and less than refined, these wines are a good value. *Recommended producers:* Domaine Leflaive, Jobart.

Puligny-Montrachet Though smaller in size than Chassagne or Meursault, the commune of Puligny-Montrachet has earned the reputation of producing the greatest Chardonnays in the world. Of Burgundy's six white Grands Crus, four of them lie at least in part in Puligny. Le Montrachet, the greatest Chardonnay vineyard in the world, lends its name to the other Grands Crus vineyards of Puligny and Chassagne listed here. Le Montrachet and Bâtard Montrachet are located half in Puligny and half in Chassagne. The vineyards of Montrachet are so sacred and sought after that owning just a few rows of vines in one of them could easily set you back a million dollars.

Montrachet offers its taster the finest expressions of the Chardonnay grape. It is powerful yet refined and full flavored, often possessing a long, rich, creamy finish that can last for the better part of a minute. Drinking young Montrachet as well as some of the other Grands Crus of Puligny can be a disappointing experience, as these wines need years to develop and open up. Thus it is not surprising that Montrachet is also the world's most expensive dry white wine. It is not unusual to pay $400 or more for a single bottle.

Is it worth it? you may ask. The answer to that is, of course, personal, but judging from the fact that restaurants and retailers fight for their allocations of Montrachet each year, there is certainly a demand. The Grands Crus wines of Bâtard, Bienvenues Bâtard, and Chevalier, though less expensive, are still quite pricey. Keep in mind that while the greatest Chardonnays are produced from these vineyards, so too are some of the most overrated. Do some research and buy from a reliable producer and source. For the rest of us mere mortals there is some good news: Puligny-Montrachet also has eleven Premiers Crus vineyards that produce wine that can be excellent, though less concentrated. There is also a fair supply of Village AOC wine that is much easier to find than both Grand Cru and Premier Cru; however, the quality can often seem diluted and inconsistent. Again, be sure to buy from a reputable house. *Recommended producers:* Laguiche, Pernot, J. M. Boillot, Marc Colin, Domaine Leflaive, Sauzet, Roger Caillot, Louis Carillon, George Deleger, Robert Deleger, Drouhin, Amiot-Bonfils, Ampeau, Ramonet, Niellon, Domaine de la Romanée-Conti, Comte Lafon, Latour, Jadot, Morey.

Puligny-Montrachet Grands Crus Vineyards

Le Montrachet (in part)
Bâtard Montrachet (in part)
Bienvenues Bâtard Montrachet
Chevalier Montrachet

Chassagne-Montrachet Chassagne is the last and southernmost white Grand Cru–producing commune in Burgundy. Half the wine production in Chassagne is red wine, and many good, steady examples are produced. Stylistically the reds range from soft to rustic, medium-bodied, medium-colored wines with cherry fruits. I often describe red Chassagne as blue-collar Pinot Noir. There are no red Grands Crus vineyards in Chassagne; however, the Premiers Crus vineyards of Clos Saint-Jean, Les Chenevottes, and Les Vergers are consistently good producers.

There is no doubt that Chassagne's greatest wines are white. At the top of the scale are the Grands Crus vineyards of Montrachet and Bâtard, which are shared with Puligny, as well as the entire, less familiar, small Grand Cru vineyard of Les Criots Bâtard Montrachet. When bought untested and without guidance, the Village- and Premier Cru–level white wines of Chassagne often represent a much better value and a safer choice than the white wines of both Puligny and Meursault. Some of the top Premiers Crus vineyards are Les Ruchottes, Les Caillerets, and Les Embrazées. Depending on a vineyard's location, the flavor profile for white Chassagne ranges from full and firm, with good, even racy, acidity to a more elegant, refined, lighter, gentler version. Both styles are capable of aging well. Even the simpler Chassagne AOC wines can be high in quality at the hand of one of Chassagne's many top producers. *Recommended producers:* Neillon, Colin Deleger, Bachelet Ramonet, Marc Morey, Benard Morey, Albert Morey, Delagrange Bachelet, Jacques Delagrange, Marc Colin, Domaine Ramonet.

Chassagne-Montrachet Grands Crus Vineyards

Montrachet (in part)
Bâtard Montrachet (in part)
Les Criots Bâtard Montrachet

Santenay Santenay lies at the end of "the golden slope" as well as at the end of the Côte de Beaune. Both red and white wines are produced, with the reds showing more promise than the whites. There are no Grands Crus vineyards; however, there are eleven rated Premier Cru. Of the group, Les Gravières is the most respected. The styles of the red wines of Santenay run from soft, light, and stylish to firm, burly, and dense. While once a great value, the wines of Santenay — like those from everywhere else in Burgundy — have begun to escalate.

ENJOYING THE WINES OF BURGUNDY

There are many different applications for white Burgundy. For simple sipping as an aperitif, Bourgogne Blanc and Mâcon are light, refreshing wines that do the job well and inexpensively. Aligoté, the other permitted white grape type in Burgundy, also excels as a starting wine. If you prefer more flavor, add a touch of Cassis and serve an authentic Kir. A crisp Chablis is masterful when paired with shellfish like shrimp and oysters. The bigger, fuller white Côte de Beaune wines of Chassagne-Montrachet, Puligny-Montrachet, and Meursault are wonderful with most types of white fish, either baked or grilled. Lobster, as well as white meats such as chicken, turkey, pork — even veal — are all good partners for these wines. As far as Montrachet goes, whenever I get the rare opportunity to sample one, I tend to have it solo, although it can be sublime with foie gras.

How about red Burgundy? With the wide variety of wines, styles, and producers of Burgundy, there is just not enough time or space to answer such a question. I have to admit that for me red Burgundy is one of the most versatile and food-friendly red wines produced anywhere. Depending on your choice of commune, producer, and vintage — and it is now your job to sample these — there are simply no red meats (or white meats, for that matter) that red Burgundy cannot properly accommodate. The lighter-style red Burgundy is one of the few red wines that can even successfully cross the "red wine with fish" barrier that has been considered a dining faux pas for so many years. Try cheese and Chambertin, Beaune and turbot, Volnay and chicken, Nuits-St.-Georges and beef, or a fine, old Vosne-Romanée on its own.

The Côte Chalonnaise

Located south of the Côte de Beaune and just north of the Mâconnais is the Côte Chalonnaise. Of all the regions of Burgundy, the Côte Chalonnaise is the least well known. The soils of the Chalonnaise are similar to those of the Côte de Beaune, being a combination of limestone, gravel, and some clay. The vineyards are located at slightly higher altitudes than Beaune's and are more exposed to nature's elements, mostly wind.

Both red and white wines are produced in the Chalonnaise at a ratio of 75 percent red to 25 percent white. In order of importance: Chardonnay and Aligoté are planted for the whites, Pinot Noir and Gamay for the reds. There are four appellations of importance: Rully and Montagny, which are exclusively white wine regions, and Mercurey and Givry, which — with the exception of Mercurey Blanc — are red. Both Rully and Mercurey possess select vineyards rated Premier Cru, and their wines cost a bit more than the simpler Village wines. Because its famous neighbor (Côte de Beaune) gets most of the attention, Chalonnaise's less popular wines provide some of Burgundy's best values. Its wines often offer some of the same qualities of the Côte du Beaune's wines, although they are seldom capable of the same depth of complexity or ageability. *Recommended producers:* Domaine de la Folie, Michel Juillot, Domaine de la Renarde, Jaf-flin.

Mâconnais

South of the Chalonnaise region we come into the Mâconnais. This is a predominantly white wine–making region, with Chardonnay the grape of choice. Small amounts of rosé and red wines are also produced from the Gamay and the Pinot Noir. Pinot Noir produced in the Mâconnais is entitled to the Bourgogne appellation; when blended with Gamay, it is called Bourgogne Passe-Tout-Grains. The most famous and possibly the best white AOC of the Mâconnais is Pouilly-Fuissé. The other major AOCs are Mâcon, Mâcon Supérieur, Mâcon Village, Mâcon (followed by the name of the village), St.-Véran, Pouilly-Loché, and Pouilly-Vinzelles.

White wines are produced chiefly in the southern part of the Mâconnais, where the soil is a mixture of marl, clay, and chalk. Wines from this region can be quite a bargain, especially if you are looking for a consistent, everyday, drinking Chardonnay that is relatively easy to find. For the most part, wines from the Mâconnais are best consumed in their youth, when they showcase their fresh fruit and simple charms. On occasion, however, Pouilly-Fuissé and sometimes St.-Véran, if carefully harvested from old vines and low yields, are capable of producing stellar, age-worthy white wines that can develop and last five to ten years. The best example is Château Fuissé Vieilles Vignes from J. J. Vincent. *Recommended producers:* Louis Latour, J. J. Vincent, La Foret, Jean Bernard, Olivier Merlin, Auvigue, Jean Theveney, Noblet, Drouhin, Georges Duboeuf, Trenel.

Beaujolais

Ten miles south of Mâcon begins the hilly wine region known as Beaujolais, which is located in the department of the Rhône. Ninety-eight percent of all Beaujolais is red, produced from the Gamay grape, although a Beaujolais blanc is produced in small quantities. There are four AOCs: Beaujolais, Beaujolais Supérieur (slightly higher in alcohol), Beaujolais-Villages, and Cru Beaujolais. The vineyard area covers a span thirty-six miles long and just over six miles wide. This large area is divided into northern and southern sections.

Southern Beaujolais, or "Bas" Beaujolais, as it is called, has primarily clay and chalk soils. Most Beaujolais and Beaujolais Supérieur wines are produced here. These wines are light violet in color, soft, very fresh, fruity, and meant to be consumed upon release. To the north, Beaujolais wines of a higher distinction known as Beaujolais-Villages are produced in a granite-based soil. Beaujolais-Villages may be produced from any of thirty-nine approved villages.

Still in the north, the region of "Haut" Beaujolais, with a high soil concentration of granite and schist, produces the region's finest wines, called Cru Beaujolais. Crus Beaujolais are more deeply colored, fleshier, more complex, and more flavorful than the other Beaujolais wines and will benefit from short-term cellaring (two to four years, depending on which Cru). Ten Crus Beaujolais are produced: Brouilly, Moulin à Vent, Morgon, Côte de Brouilly, Fleurie, Chiroubles, Juliénas, Chénas, St.-Armour, and Régnié.

Every fall a wine called Beaujolais Nouveau, representing wine from the harvest just past, is produced. The release of this wine is a celebration of the harvest and has become quite an amusing marketing ploy as retailers and restaurants race to be the first to offer it. The wine is generally high in natural acidity, purple, quite fruity, low in alcohol, and very simple. It is best consumed chilled and rather quickly. *Recommended producers:* Georges Duboeuf, Sylvian Fessy, Jadot, Domaine Perrier, Descombes, Verger, Château de la Chaize, Trenel.

ENJOYING BEAUJOLAIS

Beaujolais is one of the few red wines that benefit by being chilled. Chilling keeps the wine's high acidity approachable and its fruit refreshing. A wine meant for fun and easy, uncomplicated consumption, Beaujolais is best enjoyed in simple, casual settings. Beaujolais-Villages and Cru Beaujolais are more complex and can accommodate different types of food. Simplicity, however, is still the key.

Côtes du Rhône

The Rhône Valley begins just south of Lyon and continues in a narrow strip that runs adjacent to the Rhône River for 125 miles south to Avignon. Unlike the cooler climates that accommodate many of France's other

RED BORDEAUX VERSUS RED BURGUNDY

I am often asked to describe the basic differences between red Bordeaux and red Burgundy wines. The differences are due, of course, to vineyard, location, climate, soil, and grape types used. But knowing these facts offers little immediate information for the novice or the just curious. I've listed some basics below to serve as a quick guide.

- Bordeaux is usually deeper in color than Burgundy.
- Bordeaux is generally more age-worthy than Burgundy.
- Bordeaux is generally bigger bodied and heavier than Burgundy.
- Bordeaux is not as versatile a food wine as Burgundy.
- Generally, young Burgundy is easier to consume than young Bordeaux.
- Burgundy is generally softer than Bordeaux.
- Bordeaux is most often a blend of several red grapes, while Burgundy — with the exception of Beaujolais — is always exclusively Pinot Noir.
- Bordeaux produces a more consistent wine year after year than Burgundy does (owing to the fickle nature of Burgundy's Pinot Noir grape).

great wine regions, the climate here is predictably warm, even hot. Because of this heat the wines of this region are bigger, more rustic, and more alcoholic (riper grapes produce more alcohol) than the wines of many other regions throughout France. The Côtes du Rhône appellation produces the majority of wines (both red and white) and offers the region's best wine values. Wine labeled Côtes du Rhône may come from anywhere within the Côtes du Rhône. Slightly better in quality is the AOC classification of Côtes du Rhône with the name of a specific village attached to it — Côtes du Rhône Gigondas, for example. The best appellations are the individual ones: Hermitage, Côte Rôtie, and Châteauneuf-du-Pape.

The Rhône Valley is divided into two distinct wine-making regions known as the northern and the southern Rhône. Red wine rules in the Côtes du Rhône, as more than 90 percent of production is red. The northern Rhône also contains the white wine appellations of Condrieu and Château Grillet (France's smallest AOC area), both exotic, rare, and expensive. Côte Rôtie, Hermitage, Crozes-Hermitage, St.-Joseph, Cornas, and St.-Péray represent the red wine appellations of the northern Rhône and are produced exclusively from the Syrah grape.

Côte Rôtie (roasted slopes) and Hermitage are clearly the northern Rhône's greatest wines. They are deeply colored, robust, and massive when young and require additional aging before consumption. Crozes-Hermitage, considered the baby brother of Hermitage, is produced from the lower vineyards surrounding Hermitage. Crozes-Hermitage matures earlier and is slightly less complex than Hermitage. When properly aged, these wines become softer and rounder; they remain full in style and often display wonderful roasted and spicy aromas. St.-Joseph wines are softer and much more approachable when young. While considerably less complex than Hermitage and Côte Rôtie, they are quite often a very good value. Another less well-known wine is Cornas, which is often tannic and coarse in its youth and soft and silky when aged. Like St.-Joseph, Cornas can represent a good value. White Hermitage, Crozes-Hermitage, and St.-Joseph wines are produced, but they are seldom seen. In my opinion they are overpriced and a bit of an acquired taste.

The southern Rhône produces almost 90 percent of all Côtes du Rhône wines and, like the northern Rhône, predominantly red wine. The region's most famous wine is Châteauneuf-du-Pape. It can be made from any combination of thirteen permitted grape types, although Syrah and Grenache usually dominate the blend. The soil, which in some areas is buried under several feet of fist-size stones, is chiefly rocky granite. The large stones absorb and retain the sun's heat during the day and then slowly release it long after the sun has gone down. As a result of this slow and prolonged heating, the grapes often pick up additional ripening. Châteauneuf's style can be robust and chunky or softer and more approachable, depending on its blend and the wine maker's direction. The bigger, more robust versions of this wine often require many years to soften. Patience is rewarded, as what develops in better vintages is a rich-textured, mouth-filling, full-bodied wine that can become quite refined. White Châteauneuf is produced in very small quantities and is a novelty. It is not the most food-friendly wine, however, as it is often ripe and high in alcohol.

Gigondas and Vacqueyras are the other red wine appellations of the southern Rhône, and while not as well known, they produce medium- to full-bodied reds at a very fair cost. Some of France's best rosé wines called Tavel and Lirac are also made in this region. Produced chiefly from Grenache, these orange- and pink-tinged wines are fun, refined, refreshing, and affordable. If you have a sweet tooth, the village of Rasteau produces a high-octane, yet floral and sweet, white dessert wine known as Muscat Beaumes-de-Venise from the Muscat grape.

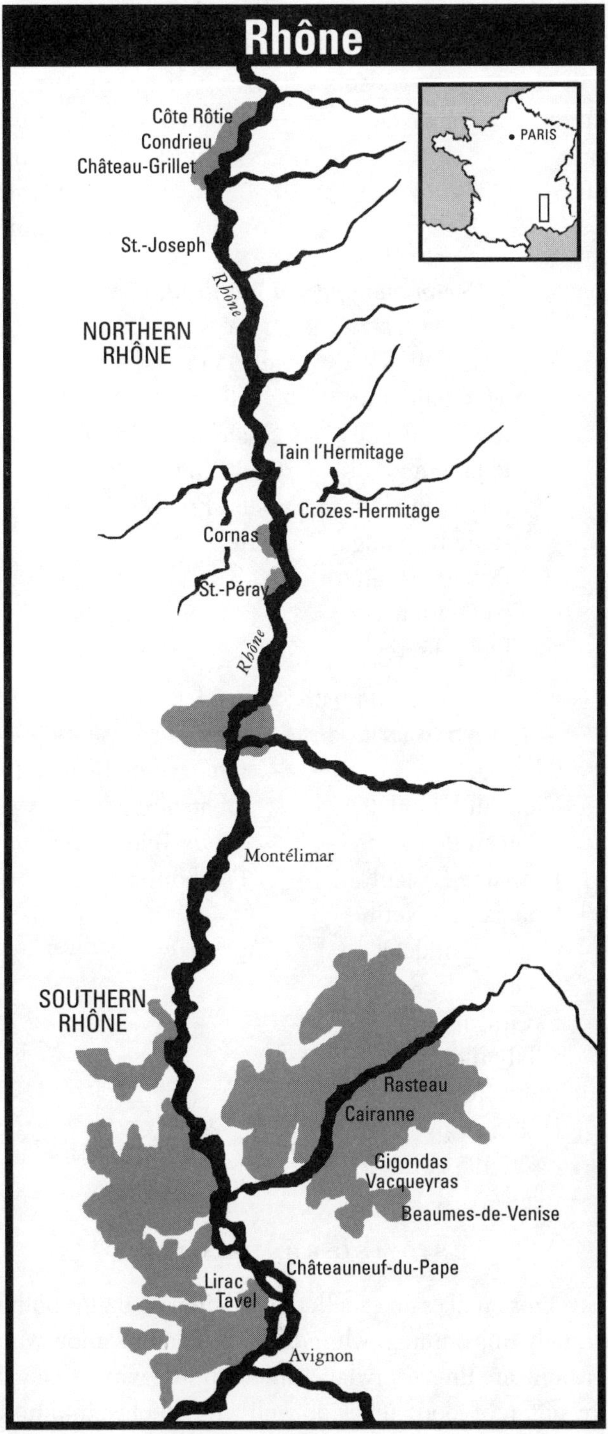
Rhône
PARIS
Côte Rôtie
Condrieu
Château-Grillet
St.-Joseph
Rhône
NORTHERN RHÔNE
Tain l'Hermitage
Crozes-Hermitage
Cornas
St.-Péray
Rhône
Montélimar
SOUTHERN RHÔNE
Rasteau
Cairanne
Gigondas
Vacqueyras
Beaumes-de-Venise
Châteauneuf-du-Pape
Lirac
Tavel
Avignon

Major Permitted Grape Varieties

NORTHERN RHÔNE		SOUTHERN RHÔNE	
WHITE GRAPES	RED GRAPES	WHITE GRAPES	RED GRAPES
Marsanne	Syrah	Clairette	Cinsaut
Roussanne		Ugni Blanc	Grenache Noir
Viognier			Carignan
			Syrah

Recommended Rhône Producers

NORTHERN RHÔNE

RED WINE	WHITE WINE
M. Chapoutier	E. Guigal
E. Guigal	Château du Rozay
P. Jaboulet	Château Grillet
J. L. Chave	Delas Frères
Rene Rostaing	Perret
Robert Jasmin	
Vidal Fleury	
Delas Frères	

SOUTHERN RHÔNE

RED WINE	WHITE WINE
Château de Beaucastel	Château de Beaucastel
Château Fonsalette	Château La Nerthe
Château Pignan	Vieux Telegraphe
Domaine Raspail	P. Jaboulet Aine
Château La Nerthe	
Cru de Coudelet	
Château du Rayas	
E. Guigal	
P. Jaboulet	
Vieux Telegraphe	
H. Bonneau	
La Vieille Ferme	

ENJOYING RHÔNE WINES

Chilled Tavel rosé makes an excellent aperitif wine that is both refreshing and charmingly unassuming, while the simple appellation wines labeled Côtes du Rhone are fine, everyday-drinking house wines that will complement many different foods. They do well with chicken and turkey, for example. They are reasonably priced, widely distributed, and, for the most part, ready to be consumed when purchased. Red Côte Rôtie, Hermitage, Crozes-Hermitage, and Châteauneuf-du-Pape are much more full flavored. They are good partners for heavier meat dishes such as lamb, stews, game, and full-flavored cheeses. I do recommend these wines be at least four to five years old before serving. If you cannot wait, however, I strongly recommend decanting them prior to the meal. This procedure will aid in softening the wine's firm tannins. After dinner Muscat Beaumes-de-Venise provides a tasty and refreshing finish.

Provence

Provence is the oldest wine-growing region of France, as well as one of the most beautiful. With wines classified as AOC, VDQS, Vins de Pays, and Vins de Table, Provence has a wine that will fit everyone's budget. Of the AOCs, Côtes de Provence is the largest and is best known for its delightful rosés. The four other major AOCs are Palette, producing fine red, white, and rosé wines; Cassis for bone-dry, high-acid whites; Bandol, with its full-bodied rosés; and Bellet for its refreshingly light red, white, and rosé wines. Château Simone of Palette is said to produce Provence's best wine.

Permitted Grape Varieties

WHITE GRAPES	RED GRAPES
Clairette	Carignan
Ugni Blanc	Cinsaut
Sémillon	Grenache Noir
	Mourvèdre
	Cabernet Sauvignon
	Syrah

ENJOYING PROVENCE WINES

The wines of Provence are best enjoyed when simply opened and consumed — no special fanfare or occasion is necessary. The rosés make perfect picnic wines and excel when you are swinging slowly in a hammock. The white wines are good aperitifs, and the reds are excellent for summer barbecues.

Languedoc Roussillon

Between the southern section of the Côtes du Rhône to the north and the Mediterranean Sea to the south lies the largest vineyard in all of France.

The vast Languedoc Roussillon represents nearly 40 percent of the total vineyard area of France. Chiefly Vins de Pays and Vins de Table wines are produced in this region, and thus it is less well-known and enjoys a lower status than other, major wine regions. However, it does represent a large percentage of all the French wines consumed worldwide, and the wineries of this region have made considerable strides in improving the quality and image of their wines. This hard work is beginning to pay off as the wines improve while remaining a good value. Some fine AOC wines are also produced — Côtes du Roussillon, Côte du Roussillon-Villages, Fitou, Corbières, and Coteaux du Languedoc, to name a few. Delicious Vins Doux Naturels, sweet dessert wines, are produced in good quantities from Grenache, Maccabeu, Muscat, and Malvoisie grapes.

The Loire Valley

The Loire Valley, one of the most beautiful regions of France, takes its name from the Loire, France's longest river. The valley begins at the Atlantic Ocean in the western central portion of the country and reaches past Touraine. Rich in history, the Loire Valley offers the tourist more than natural beauty. An assortment of medieval castles and fortresses built and occupied during the fifteenth and sixteenth centuries, as well as large, elegant châteaus erected during the seventeenth and eighteenth centuries, are still standing today.

Castles are not the only reminders of a time long past, as fine wines have been produced in the Loire Valley for centuries. A number of world-famous wines — Pouilly-Fumé, Muscadet, Sancerre, and Vouvray, for example — are from this region. Seventy-five percent of the wine produced in the Loire Valley is white, with the remaining 25 percent divided among rosé, sparkling, and red wines. The most important grape types of the region are Sauvignon Blanc, Muscadet (Melon de Bourgogne), and Chenin Blanc for white wines; and Cabernet Franc, Grolleau, and Gamay for its reds and rosés. While there are numerous wine-producing areas in the Loire, the most important are the Pays Nantais, Anjou, Touraine, Pouilly-sur-Loire, and Sancerre.

Pays Nantais The Pays Nantais is home to the world-famous Muscadet and is located in the western portion of the Loire Valley. Muscadet is produced from the Melon de Bourgogne grape, also known as the Muscadet grape. This unique grape was first introduced into the region at the end of the seventeenth century after a severe frost killed off most of the vineyards. The Muscadet grape is harvested early and produces a crisp, lemon-tart wine that is high in natural acidity, making it an ideal wine for shellfish. Meant to be consumed upon release, Muscadet is best purchased in the most current vintage and served well chilled. Muscadet is often bottled right off its natural sediments, also called *lees,* immediately after fermentation. When this is the case, the Muscadet is called *sur lie.*

There are four different Muscadet AOCs. The simplest and least restrictive is Muscadet AOC. The smallest AOC is Muscadet des Coteaux de la Loire, and the largest is Muscadet de Sèvre-et-Maine (which adds the names of the local Maine and Sèvre Rivers to the AOC name). It is in the Muscadet de Sèvre-et-Maine appellation that Muscadet *sur lie* is produced. Recently a fourth Muscadet AOC, Muscadet Côtes de Grand Lieu, has been added, and this appellation is reserved for the best Muscadet vineyards of a specific area. Some good VDQS wines such as Gros Plant du Pays Nantais are also produced in the region. *Recommended Muscadet producers:* Gadais, Marquis de Goulaine, Sauvion.

Sancerre and Pouilly-sur-Loire Located in the eastern section of the Loire Valley, Sancerre and Pouilly-sur-Loire produce the region's two best-known dry white wine AOCs of Sancerre and Pouilly-Fumé. Produced exclusively from the Sauvignon Blanc grape, these wines can be quite excellent and pair especially well with seafood. To my mind Pouilly-Fumé is capable of being a more complex wine than Sancerre, owing in part to the slaty silex soils found in the vineyards that produce it. When these soils are combined with a competent wine maker, a deliciously crisp, refreshing wine with smoky (hence the term *fumé*) and minerally aromas is produced, accentuated by its trademark tangy finish. Sancerre, located just across the river, produces less complex wines, yet they represent a better value for everyday drinking while sharing many characteristics with good Pouilly-Fumé. *Recommended Pouilly-Fumé producers:* Didier Dagueneau, Serge Dagueneau, Jean Pabiot, Marc Deschamps, Ladoucettes, Guyot. *Recommended Sancerre producers:* Crochet, Reverdy, Jolivet, Roger Neveu.

Touraine In the center of the Loire Valley lies the large wine district of Touraine. The best white wines are produced from the Chenin Blanc grape, with the best-known being Vouvray. Vouvray offers many different expressions of the Chenin Blanc grape — dry, semisweet, and occasionally very sweet. Most dry versions are consumed young, while well-made sweet versions can last for many years, even decades. Good-quality *méthode champenoise* sparkling wines are also made in Touraine.

Chinon and Bourgueil provide red wine lovers with the Loire's best red wines. Produced from the Cabernet Franc grape, Chinon is a flavorful wine highlighted by fresh raspberry fruit when young. When carefully selected, Chinon is quite capable of being aged. *Recommended Vouvray producers:* Huet, Foreau.

Anjou-Saumur The silica-schist and chalk soils of the Anjou region produce some fine wines. For red wine, Cabernet Sauvignon and Cabernet Franc grapes are best suited. When Cabernet Franc is used, the wines are known as Cabernet d'Anjou. Fine examples of dry rosé are also produced from the Cabernet Franc.

Excellent white wines are produced from the Chenin Blanc grape, the best of which are dry and produced in the district of Savennières. These wines can be teeth-rattlingly dry, minerally, and green tinged. When carefully selected, they can age for decades. If high natural acidity is not to your liking, you may wish to avoid this wine, especially when young. La Coulée de Serrant is the best and most expensive example of Savennières.

Deliciously sweet wines are produced in limited quantities in the districts of Coteaux du Layon, Bonnezeaux, and Quarts-de-Chaume from grapes affected by the botrytis mold. These wines are gold, often with green hues, and are capable of improving for many decades. Saumur produces both red and white wines; however, its predominantly chalky soils are ideal for producing the sparkling wine AOC of Saumur and Crémant de la Loire.

Bordeaux

If there is a hierarchy in wine, the undisputed king — at least for red wines — is Bordeaux. I am not saying that the best red wines produced are Bordeaux, although many professionals are inclined to that opinion. Bordeaux is, however, the wine with the highest reputation. It is the wine that most often fetches the highest prices on retail shelves and wine lists and at wine auctions. Ask a hundred wine collectors to bring out their most prized bottles of wine, and ninety will bring out a bottle of red Bordeaux. The world wine market is driven higher by the prices of red Bordeaux, and when the wine market takes a tumble, you can be sure that this event is somehow tied to the wines of Bordeaux.

How can one wine region be so famous? How can it have such an effect on so many others? Bordeaux has simply been doing it better than anyone else for the longest stretch of time. How long? Since long before the Romans showed up in 56 B.C. — for over two thousand years, in fact — Bordeaux has been cultivating vineyards and wine. History shows that at least some of the credit for the fame and worldwide recognition of Bordeaux must be given to the English. In 1152 a royal marriage put the region under English control, and Bordeaux soon became a bustling seaport, providing the perfect opportunity for its wines to be exported and accepted into the important and powerful English market. And accepted Bordeaux's wines were, as they quickly became England's wine of choice, a relationship that continues to this day. "Clairet" was the name the English gave these wines ("claret" today), which were made in a much lighter style at that time than they are today.

Bordeaux is located in southwestern France and situated on the Garonne River. To the north, the Garonne meets the Dordogne River to form the Gironde. The Gironde is a tidal estuary, as well as the name of the department where Bordeaux is located. The combined influence of the nearby Atlantic Ocean and that of the Garonne, the Dordogne, and the Gironde plays a key role in producing Bordeaux's most favorable soils, microclimates, and growing conditions. Along with its king-size reputation for quality, the vineyard appellation of Bordeaux is also one of the largest in France, with more than a quarter of a million acres of grapevines in the department. One of every 3½ cases of French wine imported into the United States is Bordeaux.

A wide variety of wines — both red and white — is produced in Bordeaux, but the region is best known for its reds. Unlike other major winemaking regions of France, where the wines are produced from a single grape type, the mastery and magic of Bordeaux wines are most often achieved by the blending of different grape types. For red Bordeaux, the permitted grape types are Cabernet Sauvignon, Merlot, Cabernet Franc, Malbec, and Petit Verdot. For white Bordeaux, Sauvignon Blanc, Sémillon, and Muscadelle are permitted. How much any one grape type dominates differs dramatically from region to region. Cabernet Sauvignon, for example, is much more influential in a finished wine from Pauillac; in Pomerol the Merlot grape is more dominant.

The individual vineyards and properties of Bordeaux are called *châteaus*, although a few properties — Domaine Chevalier of Graves, for example — prefer the use of the *domaine* prefix, which is actually much more common in Burgundy. When we hear the word *château* we may imagine an elaborate and grandiose mansion surrounded by acres of vineyards. While many châteaus do conform to this image — Château Margaux and Château Mouton-Rothschild are two good examples — others are much simpler. Unlike Burgundy, where the yield of one producer's wine for one vintage can be as little as a few cases, the châteaus of Bordeaux produce thousands of cases. There is also only one producer for each château or property in Bordeaux. This makes purchasing Bordeaux much simpler than purchasing Burgundy, since there can be any number of producers from the same vineyard in Burgundy each year. Burgundy's Clos de Vougeot, for example, can have as many as fifty or sixty different producers each year, while in Bordeaux there can be only one Château Latour.

THE CATEGORIES OF BORDEAUX WINES

Bordeaux wines are sold in five different categories. The highest category in terms of quality is a château-bottled wine. To be château bottled a wine must be made entirely from grapes grown on the named estate. The wine must also be produced, bottled, and aged on the premises of that estate. Examples of château wines are Château Lafite-Rothschild and Château Lynch-Bages.

In the next category are wines produced at one château or estate and sold in barrels to a shipper who, in turn, bottles the wine. This is a practice that is far less common today than it once was.

The largest category of Bordeaux carries a regional appellation. Wines from anywhere within the region — for example, Bordeaux, Pauillac, or Graves — are produced and labeled as being from that region.

The fourth category encompasses a Bordeaux wine sold under the name of the grape type used to produce it — Cabernet Sauvignon, for example. When wines are sold in this manner they must be produced entirely from the named grape.

Proprietary label is the last level and usually represents wine that has been bought and blended by a shipper or merchant and given a brand name, the rights to which belong to that shipper. Mouton-Cadet is a well-known example of a proprietary wine.

MAJOR RED WINE DISTRICTS OF BORDEAUX

Bordeaux is a region made up of many different wine-producing areas, each with its own soils, drainage, and climates. There are two major groupings that I will discuss. The first, located on the left bank of the Gironde estuary, is made up of Médoc and Graves. The wines from this region are thus often referred to as the "left bank wines." The second grouping produces the family of Libournais wines. These communes are located on the right bank of the Dordogne River, and their wines are often referred to as the "right bank wines."

MÉDOC

The Médoc produces red wines exclusively and is divided into two parts: Médoc to the north and the Haut-Médoc to the south. The Haut-Médoc

Bordeaux

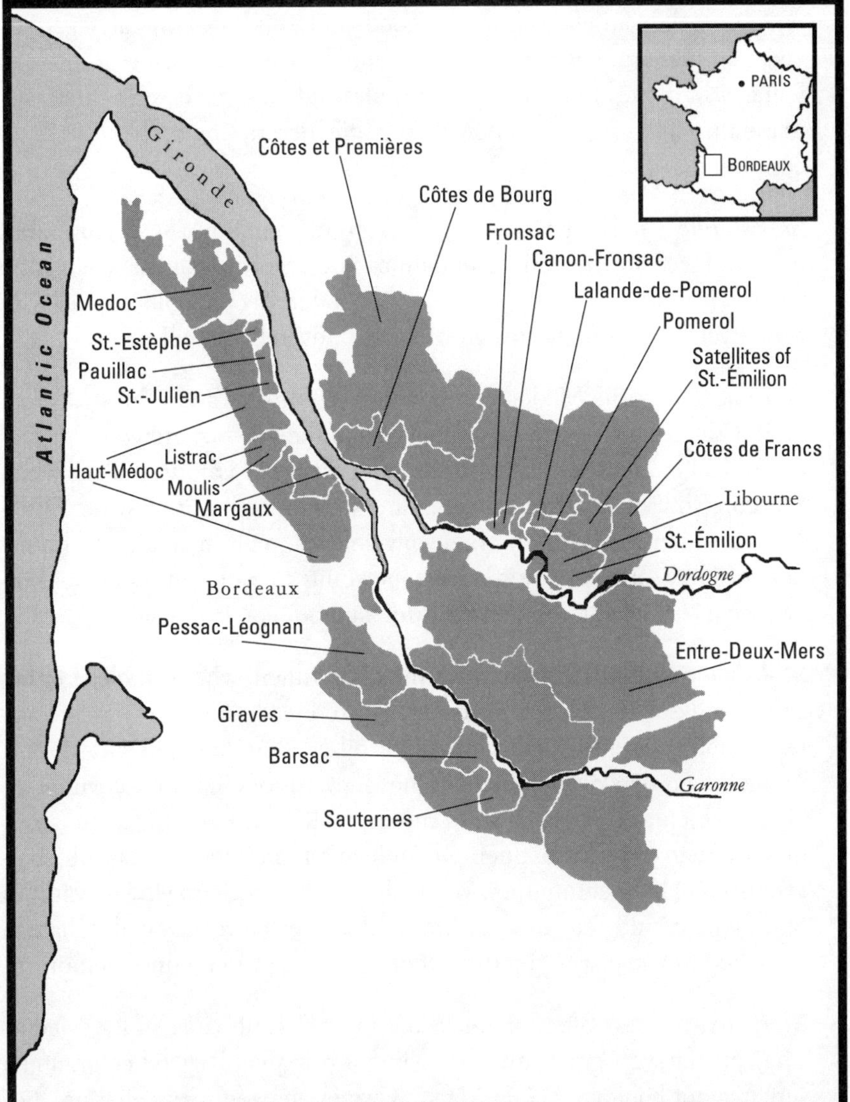

is further divided into separate communes, of which six are of special merit. Listed north to south, they are St.-Estèphe, Pauillac, St.-Julien, Listrac, Moulis, and Margaux.

Cabernet Sauvignon constitutes the majority of the blend for most left bank wines. In good and very good vintages the wines are deeply colored and austere, with hints of aromas like black currants, black cherry, truffles, Cassis, and even gravel. When aged in French oak casks, these wines take on more weight and body from the wood's tannin, while familiar, cigar-box cedar aromas are slowly incorporated into the wine. Top wines from good vintages have the ability to age for decades and, in some cases, actually demand this kind of aging. Following is a brief description of the four major communes.

St.-Estèphe The Haut-Médoc's northernmost commune, St.-Estèphe at its best produces big, full, and firm tannic wines. Slow to mature when compared with other Médoc wines, they are often deeply colored and with good fruit. There are no first-growth vineyards in St.-Estèphe.

Pauillac This is the Médoc's most famous commune and is located south of St.-Estèphe. Pauillac is home to three of the five first-growth vineyards of Bordeaux: Château Lafite-Rothschild, Château Latour, and Château Mouton-Rothschild. Pauillac wines are the most age-worthy wines of the Médoc. When young, they are deeply colored, high in acidity, and quite tannic. They soften slowly and have the ability to evolve into some of Bordeaux's most elegant, refined, flavorful, and opinionated wines.

St.-Julien South of Pauillac, we come to St.-Julien, where an elegant, fragrant, and softer style of Bordeaux is produced. These wines are approachable sooner than the wines of the other communes of Haut-Médoc. Along the borders of St.-Julien are the vineyards of Château Léoville-Las-Cases, which are separated from those of Château Latour of Pauillac by little more than a ravine. Such proximity often produces wines with characteristics of both communes. While there are no first-growth vineyards in St.-Julien, should the wines of the Médoc ever be reclassified, Château Léoville-Las-Cases would most certainly receive serious consideration.

Margaux Margaux often produces the most elegant wines of the Médoc. They provide very good structure (without being hard), good color, and a very fragrant bouquet. While Margaux wines are worthy of cellaring, they are approachable sooner than the sturdier wines of Pauillac or St.-Estèphe. Château Margaux is rated first growth and is the top status wine of Margaux.

THE 1855 CLASSIFICATION OF THE RED WINES OF BORDEAUX

In 1855 under the direction of Napoleon III, the vineyards of Bordeaux were classified for the Universal Exhibition of Paris. Only the red wines of

Bordeaux, along with the sweet wines of Sauternes and Barsac, were included. The classification was intended to be a reflection of each vineyard's reputation as well as its wine's market price. Of the red wines selected, all but one, Château Haut-Brion of Graves, were from the Médoc.

In the Classification of 1855 the highest-rated vineyards were classified as first growths, followed by second, third, fourth, and, finally, fifth growths. Amazingly enough, how a château was originally rated and where it was placed over a century ago is still reflected in the price and perception of that château's wines today. While there has been no major revision to the Classification of 1855 — except that Château Mouton-Rothschild was elevated from a second growth to a first in 1973 — there are many who feel that a major reappraisal is long overdue.

Premiers Crus (First Growths)	*Commune*
Lafite-Rothschild	Pauillac
Margaux	Margaux
Latour	Pauillac
Haut-Brion	Pessac (Graves)
Mouton-Rothschild (1973)	Pauillac
Deuxièmes Crus (Second Growths)	
Rausan-Ségla	Margaux
Rauzan-Gassies	Margaux
Léoville-Las-Cases	St.-Julien
Léoville-Poyferré	St.-Julien
Léoville-Barton	St.-Julien
Durfort-Vivens	Margaux
Gruaud-Larose	St.-Julien
Lascombes	Margaux
Brane-Cantenac	Cantenac
Pichon-Longueville-Baron	Pauillac
Pichon-Longueville, Comtesse de Lalande	Pauillac
Ducru-Beaucaillou	St.-Julien
Cos d'Estournel	St.-Estèphe
Montrose	St.-Estèphe
Troisièmes Crus (Third Growths)	
Kirwan	Cantenac
D'Issan	Cantenac
Lagrange	St.-Julien

Langoa-Barton	St.-Julien
Giscours	Labarde
Malescot-Saint-Exupéry	Margaux
Boyd-Cantenac	Cantenac
Cantenac-Brown	Cantenac
Palmer	Cantenac
La Lagune	Ludon
Desmirail	Margaux
Calon-Ségur	St.-Estèphe
Ferrière	Margaux
Marquis-D'Alesme-Becker	Margaux

Quatrièmes Crus (Fourth Growths)

Saint-Pierre	St.-Julien
Talbot	St.-Julien
Branaire-Ducru	St.-Julien
Duhart-Milon-Rothschild	Pauillac
Pouget	Cantenac
La Tour-Carnet	St.-Laurent
Lafon-Rochet	St.-Estèphe
Beychevelle	St.-Julien
Prieuré-Lichine	Cantenac
Marquis-de-Terme	Margaux

Cinquièmes Crus (Fifth Growths)

Pontet-Canet	Pauillac
Batailley	Pauillac
Haut-Batailley	Pauillac
Grand-Puy-Lacoste	Pauillac
Grand-Puy-Ducasse	Pauillac
Lynch-Bages	Pauillac
Lynch-Moussas	Pauillac
Dauzac	Labarde
Mouton-Baronne-Philippe	Pauillac
De Tertre	Arsac
Haut-Bages-Libéral	Pauillac
Pédesclaux	Pauillac
Belgrave	St.-Laurent
De Camensac	St.-Laurent
Cos-Labory	St.-Estèphe
Clerc-Milon	Pauillac

Croizet-Bages	Pauillac
Cantemerle	Macau

Cru Bourgeois The term *Cru Bourgeois* is used to describe the wines of the Médoc, Haut-Médoc, and Sauternes that are ranked just below the Crus Classés (first to fifth growths, as classified in 1855). Crus Bourgeois wines were first classified in 1932. The list was expanded in 1962, and in 1978 it was revised to its current form. There are three levels of quality in this classification. Crus Grands Bourgeois Exceptionnels is the highest level, followed by Crus Grands Bourgeois, and then Crus Bourgeois. Because these wines do not have the same status as Crus Classés wines, their prices are lower. Many châteaus listed in this classification — Margaux's Château d'Angludet, St.-Estèphe's Château Phélan-Ségur, and Moulis's Château Chasse-Spleen are good examples — provide excellent wines as well as value.

The 1978 Classification of Crus Bourgeois of the Médoc and Haut-Médoc

GRANDS BOURGEOIS EXCEPTIONNELS

Agassac	Dutruch-Grand-Poujeaux
Andron-Blanquet	Fourcas-Dupré
Beausite	Fourcas-Hosten
Capbern	Du Glana
Caronne-Sainte-Gemme	Haut-Marbuzet
Chasse-Spleen	Marbuzet
Cissac	Meyney
Citran	Phélan-Ségur
Le Crock	Poujeaux

GRANDS BOURGEOIS

Beaumont	Morin
Bel-Orme-Tronquoy-de-Lalande	Moulin-à-Vent
	Le Meynieu
Brillette	Les Ormes-de-Pez
La Cardonne	Les Ormes-Sorbet
Colombier-Monpelou	Patache d'Aux
Coufran	Paveil-de-Luze
Coutelin-Merville	Peyrabon
Duplessis (Hauchecorne)	Pontoise-Cabarrus
Fontesteau	Potensac
La-Fleur-Milon	Reysson
Greysac	La Rose-Trintaudon

Hanteillan
Lafon
De Lamarque
Lamothe
Laujac
Liversan
Loudenne
MacCarthy
De Malleret
Martinens
Ségur
Sigognac
Sociando-Mallet
Du Taillan
La Tour-de-By
La Tour-du-Haut-Moulin
Tronquoy-Lalande
Verdignan

BOURGEOIS

Aney
Balac
La Bécade
Bellerive
Bellerose
Bonneau-Livran
Le Boscq
Le Breuil
La Bridane
De By
Cap-Leon-Veyrin
Carcanieux
Castéra
Chambert-Marbuzet
La Clare
La Closerie
Duplessis-Fabre
Fonréaud
Fonpiqueyre
Fort Vauban
La France
Gallais Bellevue
Grand-Duroc-Milon
Grand-Moulin
Haut-Bages-Monpelou
Haut-Canteloup
Haut-Garin
Haut-Padarnac
Houbanon
Hourtin-Ducasse
De Labat
Lamothe-de-Bergeron
Le Landat
Landon
Lartigue-de-Brochon
Cru Lassalle
Lestage
MacCarthy-Moula
Monthil
Moulin Rouge
Panigon
Pibran
Plantey-de-la-Croix
Pontet
Ramage-la-Bâtisse
La Roque-de-By
De la Rose-Maréchale
Saint-Bonnet
Saransot
Soudars
Tayac
La Tour-Blanche
La Tour-du-Mirail
La Tour-Haut-Caussan
La Tour-Saint-Bonnet
La Tour-Saint-Joseph
Des Tourelles
Vieux Robin

GRAVES

South of the city of Bordeaux is Graves, a region whose very name evokes its gravelly soils. Here, as in other left bank vineyards, Cabernet Sauvignon is the most cultivated grape. Both red and white wines are produced (55 percent red to 45 percent white). In general the red wines are the more notable, but it must be acknowledged that the best-known, dry white wines of Bordeaux are from Graves.

The best red wine vineyards in Graves are located in the northern section within the Pessac-Léognan appellation. The vineyards of Graves were classified in 1959, and the top vineyards are rated as Crus Classés (classified growths), a term of prestige that is most often included on the label. The lone exception is Château Haut-Brion, which was rated as a first growth (the highest classification for a Bordeaux wine) along with the wines of the Médoc in the 1855 classification.

The 1959 Classification of the Graves

RED WINES	COMMUNE
Bouscaut	Cadaujac
Haut-Bailly	Léognan
Carbonnieux	Léognan
Domaine de Chevalier	Léognan
De Fieuzal	Léognan
Olivier	Léognan
Malartic-Lagravière	Léognan
La Tour-Martillac	Martillac
Smith-Haut-Lafitte	Martillac
Haut-Brion	Pessac
La Mission-Haut-Brion	Talence
Pape-Clément	Pessac
Latour-Haut-Brion	Talence

WHITE WINES	COMMUNE
Bouscaut	Cadaujac
Carbonnieux	Léognan
Domaine de Chevalier	Léognan
Olivier	Léognan
Malartic-Lagravière	Léognan
La Tour-Martillac	Martillac
Laville-Haut-Brion	Talence
Couhins-Lurton	Villenave d'Ornon
Couhins	Villenave d'Ornon

THE LIBOURNAIS

The second grouping of Bordeaux wines is called the Libournais. Included in this group are the communes of St.-Émilion, Montagne-St.-Émilion, Lussac-St.-Émilion, Puissequin-St.-Émilion, Pomerol, Lalande-de-Pomerol, Fronsac, and Canon-Fronsac. Of this grouping, the communes known for producing the best wines are St.-Émilion and Pomerol.

St.-Émilion Twenty miles northeast of the city of Bordeaux lies the medieval wine district of St.-Émilion. The right bank wines of St.-Émilion are exclusively red and contain a high proportion of the Merlot grape. Because of the higher concentration of Merlot, St.-Émilion wines are often approachable earlier than other Bordeaux wines. When selectively chosen, St.-Émilion wines are among the best of Bordeaux; they are deeply colored and medium- to full-bodied and can be quite fleshy.

There are three top-quality classifications for the wines of St.-Émilion. From the highest category of quality to the lowest, they are Premiers Grands Crus Classés, of which there are thirteen (headed by Château Ausone and Château Cheval Blanc in a separate category "A"), Grands Crus Classés (there are fifty-five), and Grands Crus (there are hundreds). The vineyards of St.-Émilion are classified every ten years and were last classified in 1996.

Premiers Grands Crus Classés

A: Château Ausone
Château Cheval Blanc

B: Château Angélus
Château Beau-Séjour-Bécot
Château Beauséjour
Château Belair
Château Canon
Château Figeac
Château La Gaffelière
Château Magdelaine
Château Pavie
Château Trottevieille
Clos Fourtet

Grands Crus Classés

Château Balestard la Tonnelle
Château Bellevue
Château Bergat
Château Berliquet
Château Cadet Bon
Château La Tour du Pin Figeac (J. M. Moueix)
Château La Tour Figeac
Chateau Lamarzelle
Château Laniote

Château Cadet-Piola
Château Canon la Gaffelière
Château Cap de Mourlin
Château Chavin
Château Clos des Jacobins
Château Corbin
Château Corbin-Michotte
Château Curé Bon
Château Dassault
Château Faurie de Souchard
Château Fonplégade
Château Fonroque
Château Franc Mayne
Château Grand Mayne
Château Grand Pontet
Château Guadet Saint-Julien
Château Haut Corbin
Château Haut Sarpe
Château L'Arrosée
Château La Clotte
Château La Clusière
Château La Couspaude
Château La Dominique
Château La Serre
Château La Tour du Pin Figeac (Giraud-Bélivier)
Château Larcis Ducasse
Château Larmande
Château Laroque
Château Laroze
Château Le Prieuré
Château Les Grandes Murailles
Château Matras
Château Moulin du Cadet
Château Pavie Decesse
Château Pavie Macquin
Château Petit Faurie de Soutard
Château Ripeau
Château Saint-Georges Côte Pavie
Château Soutard
Château Tertre Daugay
Château Troplong-Mondot
Château Villemaurine
Château Yon Figeac
Clos de l'Oratoire
Clos Saint-Martin
Couvent des Jacobins

Pomerol It is said that good things come in small packages, and in fact, in Pomerol, the smallest of the major wine districts of Bordeaux, great things are often found. Located northwest of St.-Émilion, the right bank wine district of Pomerol produces red wines made predominantly from Merlot. Château Pétrus, Pomerol's most famous wine as well as one of the world's most sought after, is made with upward of 90 to 95 percent Merlot. No white wine is produced in the district.

The soils of Pomerol are high in iron oxide, which many believe is one of the reasons the wines produced here are unique. The best Pomerol wines are some of Bordeaux's fullest and richest. They can age for decades, but they can be so flavorful and plummy, you may not want to wait. The vineyards of Pomerol have not yet been classified, although a pecking order has been established, with Château Pétrus as its greatest property. Recently the wines of Château Le Pin have also received considerable attention, and the gap between the two is said to have narrowed. Following is a list of the other châteaus of Pomerol.

Other Recommended Châteaus of Pomerol

Certan-de-May	Le Gay
Vieux-Château-Certan	L'Église-Clinet
Trotanoy	Beauregard
La Pointe	La Fleur-Pétrus
Lagrange	Latour à Pomerol
Lafleur	Petit-Village
La Conseillante	Gazin
L'Évangile	

OTHER WINE-PRODUCING REGIONS OF BORDEAUX

While the red wine districts I've just discussed are the most famous, half of all the red Bordeaux produced comes from the lesser-known districts of Blaye, Premières Côtes de Blaye, Côtes de Bourg, and the Premières Côtes de Bordeaux. These wines are most often sold under the regional appellation of Bordeaux or purchased and blended for some of the large *monopole* or proprietary wine labels. They have become more consistent of late and can be bought for a fraction of the price of the wines from the better-known red wine districts of Bordeaux.

BORDEAUX AND BORDEAUX SUPÉRIEURS

Wines labeled Bordeaux and Bordeaux Supérieurs represent the regional appellation for both red and white Bordeaux wines. The wines labeled Bordeaux Supérieurs have been selected as the best of the regional appellation wines. The grapes for these wines may come from anywhere within the Gironde district. Wines of these classifications represent a good value and are meant to be consumed upon, or soon after, their release.

WHITE WINE DISTRICTS OF BORDEAUX

With Bordeaux's red wines receiving the lion's share of the glory, it's easy to overlook the wonderful white wines of Bordeaux. White Bordeaux is made in a variety of different styles, from the bone-dry whites of Graves to the thick, luscious, sweet offerings of Sauternes and Barsac. The grapes used in producing white Bordeaux are Sauvignon Blanc, Sémillon, and Muscadel. As a general rule, the dry versions of white Bordeaux are bottled in green bottles, while the sweet Bordeaux are bottled in clear bottles.

Graves The white wines of Graves are produced in a number of different styles and are almost always produced dry. White Graves is at its best in its youth when it's refreshing and lively, although certain châteaus such as Laville Haut-Brion and Haut-Brion have been producing more age-worthy and oak-influenced versions. A Graves Supérieurs is also produced, usually as a semidry version with more body than Graves. The white wines of Graves were classified in 1959, with the best rated as Crus Classés (see Graves classification of 1959, page 213).

Entre-Deux-Mers Nestled between the Dordogne and Garonne Rivers lies the triangular-shaped Entre-Deux-Mers, which translates as "Between Two Rivers." This has become one of Bordeaux's most important producers for everyday-drinking white Bordeaux wines.

Sauternes and Barsac In the southernmost section of Bordeaux is the world-famous wine district and appellation of Sauternes. Five communes, including Sauternes, are permitted to use the Sauternes appellation. The commune of Barsac has its own appellation (Barsac AOC) and may use either.

A thick, honeyed, golden sweet wine, Sauternes is produced by leaving the grapes on the vine long after harvest has finished everywhere else in Bordeaux. When nature complies, a mold called *Botrytis cinerea* ("the noble rot") forms on the grapes, causing them to shrivel and dehydrate. This results in grapes with an extremely high concentration of sugar. The arrival of the botrytis mold is not guaranteed, as a proper balance of climatic conditions — fog, moisture, humidity, and sun — is needed for its growth. Because each grape cluster must be picked at the optimum stage of development, the pickers may have to make as many as five or six different passes through the vineyards over a period of several weeks. This labor-intensive practice ultimately translates into a higher cost for the consumer — Sauternes is fairly expensive.

Because Sauternes is such a heavy and bold wine, drinking an entire bottle can be difficult. Most producers offer half bottles as a solution. The château with the highest reputation in Sauternes is Château d'Yquem, which — by a large margin — produces France's most expensive and sought-after sweet wines. The 1855 classification of the vineyards of Sauternes and Barsac follows.

Grand Premier Cru	*Commune*
D'Yquem	Sauternes

Premiers Crus	
La Tour-Blanche	Bommes
Lafaurie-Peyraguey	Bommes
Clos Haut-Peyraguey	Bommes
De Rayne-Vigneau	Bommes
Suduiraut	Preignac
Coutet	Barsac
Climens	Barsac
Guiraud	Sauternes
Rieussec	Fargues
Rabaud-Promis	Bommes
Sigalas-Rabaud	Bommes

Deuxièmes Crus	
De Myrat	Barsac
Doisy-Daëne	Barsac
Doisy-Dubroca	Barsac
Doisy-Védrines	Barsac
D'Arche	Sauternes
Filhot	Sauternes
Broustet	Barsac
Nairac	Barsac
Caillou	Barsac
Suau	Barsac
De Malle	Preignac
Romer-du-Hayot	Fargues
Lamothe-Despujols	Sauternes
Lamothe-Guignard	Sauternes

ENJOYING BORDEAUX WINE

White Bordeaux (dry) Well-chilled, select white Bordeaux can be served as an aperitif. When I use the word *select,* I am referring to a white Bordeaux that has not had extended contact with new oak barrels. Heavily wooded wines, in my opinion, can be a bit too much as an opening act. Seafood and poultry are also recommended for these wines. White Bordeaux with more influence of oak works well with more flavorful grilled fish such as tuna or salmon.

White Bordeaux (sweet) While many enjoy a glass of sweet Sauternes or Barsac before a meal, these wines are most often served at the end of a meal with, or as, dessert. The classic match for sweet white Bordeaux, however, has always been a slice of foie gras.

Red Bordeaux Red Bordeaux has always been a wine best served with flavorful (not spicy) red meats such as beef, lamb, and game. White meats such as chicken, veal, and turkey can also provide good company for red Bordeaux wines. But when choosing a wine to serve, one must always take into account a wine's present stage of development. The tannins and astringency that accompany many young red Bordeaux can easily overpower many fine dishes.

As a general rule, I suggest drinking the simpler regional AOC Bordeaux wines, Crus Bourgeois, and Bordeaux Supérieurs at a younger age. Drink the classified growths a minimum of six years after the vintage date. Red Bordeaux can also pair well with certain cheeses such as Brie and Camembert. While the tannins of young Bordeaux can dominate too refined a dish, when served with cheese these tannins are actually softened and made more accessible.

9

GERMANY, ITALY, NEW ZEALAND, CHILE, SOUTH AFRICA, AUSTRALIA, AND SPAIN

Germany

Germany, one of the oldest wine-producing countries in the world, has a glorious wine tradition dating back to 100 B.C. With such a history, it is curious that the wines of Germany are among the most misunderstood in the world. The confusion surrounding German wines is widespread and does not discriminate. It is experienced by wine retailers, restaurateurs, sommeliers, and, of course, you, the consumer. Much of this misunderstanding stems from complicated wine laws, labeling practices, and pronunciations that have always confused the foreign consumer. While the government's good intention of providing a quality-controlled, definable, and traceable product is commendable, many feel that too much information is offered for the average wine drinker. The intense and successful marketing of inexpensive proprietary wines — Blue Nun and Black Tower are two examples — has compounded the confusion. These inexpensive sweet wines became so popular that they were soon perceived as models for all German wines. While wines of this sort can be well made, enjoyable, and affordable, they do not in any way represent the quality end of the German wine industry. It's a shame that so many wine drinkers miss the many pleasures and great values that high-quality German wines provide.

After much thought about how best to explain the intricacies of German wine while holding your interest, I've decided on the simple approach of providing only essential information. I know that wine purists and those knowledgeable about German wines will find fault with this. My goal, however, is to make the novice comfortable with wine. So here goes.

GERMAN GRAPE TYPES

There are good reasons why more than 80 percent of all the wine produced in Germany is white. The chief one is climate: Germany is the northernmost grape-growing region in Europe. Of the world's wine harvests, Germany's lasts the longest, often well into November. Matching this long, slow, cool growing season with the proper grape types is of the utmost importance. Most respected red grape types require a much warmer climate to achieve proper maturity. So while red wines are produced in Germany, for our purposes when you think German wine, think white wine.

Of the many different white grape types cultivated in Germany the three best known are the productive Müller-Thurgau, the full and flavorful Silvaner, and the noble and most widely planted Riesling. Of the three, it is the late-maturing Riesling grape, also known as the white Riesling and Johannisberg Riesling, that produces Germany's best wines. Most German wines are labeled after the grape type used to produce them, and the wine must contain a minimum of 85 percent of the labeled grape type.

The Riesling For some reason, be it marketing or a lack thereof, the Riesling grape often takes a backseat to more popular grapes like Chardonnay and Sauvignon Blanc. It wasn't always this way. At the turn of the century it was common for top German Rieslings to command twice the price of top French Bordeaux. In fact, the German Riesling is as noble as, and even more versatile than, any other white grape in the world — including the French Chardonnay. Selectively chosen, Riesling, unlike Chardonnay, has the potential to age gracefully for decades, even centuries.

Some major characteristics separate German Riesling from Riesling produced elsewhere. The first of these is alcohol content. German Ries-

---

German vineyard in Calmont

COURTESY OF GERMAN WINE INFORMATION BUREAU

lings are considerably lower in alcohol, ranging from 7 percent to 11 percent. A second characteristic is the Riesling grape's versatility. Nowhere in the world is this more evident than in the vineyards of Germany. Here Rieslings of great breed are produced dry, semidry, medium sweet, sweet, or extremely sweet. Possessing one of the most fragrant aroma profiles of any grape type, German Rieslings can display floral scents as well as those of apricot, peach, honey, apple, melon, and pear. Another trademark of German Rieslings is that they are wonderfully framed by a refreshing bounty of crisp acidity. It is this same acidity, a result of the long, cool growing season, that gives German Rieslings the ability to age so well.

GERMAN WINE CLASSIFICATIONS

In France wines are classified by the vineyard and district where the grapes are grown — for example, Chambertin in Burgundy or Pauillac in Bordeaux. In Spain Riojas are classified as reserva, or gran reserva, depending on the length of time the wine has been aged in oak barrels and in bottles. Many New World wine regions classify their wines according to the grape type used to produce them — for example, Chardonnay, Merlot, or Zinfandel. In Germany, however, wines are classified according to the grapes' natural sugar content at the time of harvest.

Because of Germany's cool northern climate, the proper ripening of grapes can be a struggle and is never guaranteed. This is one reason Riesling grapes are left on the vine to ripen longer than any other wine grape type. Such long harvests are not without risk, as any extended or sudden cold frosts can quickly destroy an entire crop. German grape growers do everything they can to extract the sun's warming rays. They plant their vineyards on the sunniest plots of land or close to rivers so that additional sunlight reflected off the water can be absorbed by the grapevines. While most wine regions make a single pass through the vineyards at harvest time, in Germany quality-minded estates pick each grape cluster individually as it ripens. This results in as many as four to six pickings during the harvest. Simply put, the riper the grapes, the higher they may be classified. Remember that higher sugar levels do not guarantee a finer wine, as the vineyard, soil, and producer are also important quality factors.

In Germany there are two quality wine categories, Tafelwein and Qualitätswein. These terms are important and are listed on the wine label. As with elsewhere in the world, sometimes nature does not comply and the grapes do not ripen enough to produce the desired level of alcohol. On these occasions the addition of sugar before fermentation is permitted in a practice called *chaptalization.* Chaptalization is permitted for Tafelwein and QbA (Qualitätswein bestimmter Anbaugebiete) wines, but it is not permitted for the QmP (Qualitätswein mit Prädikat) classification of wines, which must by law be produced using only the grapes' natural sugars.

Tafelwein Translated, Tafelwein means simply "Table Wine." There are two classifications of Tafelwein. Wines in the first category, Deutscher Tafelwein, come from one of the broad Tafelwein regions. These are enjoyable, simple wines meant to be consumed early. The second classification is Landwein, which means "Special Wine." These wines are more complex and must be produced from slightly riper grapes in a dry or semidry style. Wines labeled Tafelwein are seldom exported.

Qualitätswein These are quality wines made from ripe, very ripe, or overripe grapes. The two classifications of Qualitätswein wines are Qualitätswein bestimmter Anbaugebiete, or QbA, and Qualitätswein mit Prädikat, or QmP.

QbA. The majority of German wines are QbA wines and must be produced within one of the thirteen growing regions using only approved grape types that have been ripened sufficiently. These wines represent a higher level of quality and are more regulated than wines classified as Tafelwein.

QmP. Wines labeled QmP are subject to the same regulations as QbA wines, but they offer additional distinctions or merit. Germany's greatest wines are of this classification. Following, in order of grape ripeness, are the six different levels or distinctions of QmP wines. These terms are also found on the wine's label, and it should be noted that grape ripeness and the level of sweetness of a wine are not necessarily the same.

1. *Kabinett* (cab-in-net). The first level of ripeness. This, the lightest of QmP wines, is refreshing in style and produced dry, semidry, or semisweet.
2. *Spätlese* (shpayt-lace-ah). The grapes for this wine are picked at least one week past the normal harvest. Fuller in flavor and body, it is produced dry, semidry, or semisweet.
3. *Auslese* (owsh-lace-ah). This wine is produced from a late harvest of very ripe grapes. Intense, flavorful, and heavier in style, it is most often produced as a semisweet or sweet wine.
4. *Beerenauslese* (BA) (bear-en-owsh-lace-ah). Produced from overripe grapes that are selected individually, this is a dessert wine, heavy in weight, flavor, and sweetness.
5. *Eiswein* (ice-vine). A wine that is produced from grapes of the Beerenauslese distinction that have been harvested while naturally

frozen. To produce Eiswein, the grapes must be picked and pressed while still frozen. Very concentrated, sweet, high in acidity, and expensive.

6. *Trockenbeerenauslese* (TBA) (trocken-bear-en-owsh-lace-ah). This wine is produced from extremely overripe (raisinlike) grapes that are selected individually, grape by grape. These grapes are affected by *Botrytis cinerea,* the noble rot mold, which provides additional flavor and complexities. It takes twenty times more grapes to make a bottle of Trockenbeerenauslese than to produce a typical bottle of dry wine. Deeply colored, with honeylike sweetness and refreshingly high natural acidity, these wines are intense, complex, and among the world's fullest and most age-worthy. Rare, as they are not produced each year, these wines are quite expensive.

THE STYLES OF GERMAN RIESLINGS

Germany's wines enjoy a sweet reputation, yet many are made in drier styles. In the QmP category, what is basically the same wine can be produced in a dry, semidry, or sweet style. A Riesling, for example, could be Riesling Kabinett trocken (dry), Riesling Kabinett halbtrocken (half-dry), or Riesling Kabinett (usually sweeter than the first two). This formula remains basically the same for wines of the Spätlese and Auslese levels, while the remaining three levels — Beerenauslese, Eiswein, and Trockenbeerenauslese — are dessert-style wines and always sweet.

The logical question is, how do the wine makers produce the desired level of sweetness? There are two wine-making procedures that accomplish this feat. The first involves the addition of naturally sweet unfermented grape juice, called *sweet reserve,* to the finished wine. The wine maker controls the level of sweetness by adding more or less sweet reserve. The second method, also the one most often used in the production of higher-quality German wines, is to arrest fermentation. This is performed by lowering the temperature of the fermenting wine, thereby stopping the fermentation. Left in the wine is the sweet, unfermented sugar, which is called *residual sugar,* or R.S. The sooner the fermentation is halted, the sweeter the wine.

GERMAN WINE REGIONS

The major wine regions of Germany are concentrated in the southwestern section of the country, with the best lying in proximity to either the Rhine or the Mosel River or one of their tributaries. These bodies of water have a warming influence that helps temper Germany's cool climate. The vine-

VDP eagle quality seal
COURTESY OF GERMAN WINE INFORMATION BUREAU

yards are planted on extremely steep, south-facing slopes, and harvest is an extremely difficult task that must be accomplished by hand. There are thirteen wine areas in Germany, each with individual microclimates and soils. The wine areas best suited to Germany's noble Riesling grape are the Mosel-Saar-Ruwer, Rheingau, Rheinhessen, Pfalz, and Nahe.

RECOMMENDED GERMAN WINE PRODUCERS

The best guarantee when searching for a high-quality German wine is the name of a good producer. With over fifty thousand producers to choose from, however, finding the good ones can seem a daunting task. To ease your way, I have listed here several recommended producers from each of the five major wine regions. When in doubt, however, look for the VDP eagle logo on a bottle's label (see illustration). This symbol represents an elite group of fewer than two hundred of Germany's top producers. The term *Weingut* means "Estate" and often precedes the name of the producer.

Mosel-Saar-Ruwer

Joh. Jos. Prüm
Egon Müller
von Hövel
Gutsverwaltung von Schubert
Dr. F. Weins Prüm
Reichsgraf von Kesselstatt
Dr. Loosen
Fritz Haag
Karthauserhof

Schloss Lieser
Forstmeister Geltz Zilliken
Selbach-Oster
Joh. Jos. Christoffel
Reinhold Haart
Willi Schafer

Rheingau

Robert Weil
Georg Breuer
Gutsverwaltung Geheimrat
Josef Leitz
Johannishof
J. Wegeler Erben
Schloss Reinhartshausen
Freiherr zu Knyphausen
Franz Künstler

Rheinhessen

Gunderloch
Sankt Antony
Keller
Freiherr Heyl zu Herrnsheim
Schales

Pfalz

Dr. Bürklin-Wolf
Koehler Ruprecht
Georg Mosbacher
Reichsrat von Buhl
Dr. von Bassermann Jordan
Pfeffingen Fuhrmann Eymael
Müller-Catoir
Biffar

Nahe

Hermann Dönnhoff
Emrich Schönleber
Schlossgut Diel
Crusius

READING GERMAN WINE LABELS

In an attempt to simplify the often overwhelming and confusing information found on German wine labels, American wine importer Rudi Wiest promotes a new, introductory-level wine category called "Estate Riesling." Wines of this category are most often of the QbA level. Listed with the term *Estate Riesling* are the name of the producer, the grape type, the vintage, and a one-word description, such as trocken (dry) or halbtrocken (semidry), used to describe the wine's level of sweetness. When neither trocken nor halbtrocken appears on the wine's label, it is safe to assume that the wine will be slightly sweeter in style than halbtrocken. Estate Rieslings must come from vineyards owned exclusively by the estate and from 100 percent of the varietal listed. While the Estate Riesling category is meant to make buying German wines easy, wines labeled as such also represent fine values.

GERMAN WINE BOTTLES

As a general rule, the standard German wine bottle is tall and slender, with green glass used for the wines of the Mosel-Saar-Ruwer region and brown glass for wines from the Rhine. The Bocksbeutel, a low, flagon-shaped green bottle, is also used in the wine region of Franken.

ENJOYING GERMAN WINES

I've always believed that the best way to introduce beginners to wine is through the easy appeal of German wines. From the informal picnic to the savviest of restaurant tables, when it comes to white wines, Germany offers some of the world's most versatile. Germany's wines are extremely flexible because of the many different styles in which they can be produced. Dry, semidry, or extremely sweet, German wines are one of the few wine groupings that are just as great without food as with it. When you further consider the good value they represent (since most people haven't discovered them yet!), it makes great sense to add them to your entertaining repertoire.

Start any occasion with a glass of young Riesling Kabinett or Spätlese trocken or halbtrocken. If you prefer bubbles, have one of Germany's fine sparkling wines known as Sekt. QbA and QmP Rieslings Kabinett and Spätlese, offered in trocken, halbtrocken, or slightly sweeter style, are great as aperitif or introductory wines. QmP wines of this style are best at two to

READING GERMAN WINE LABELS

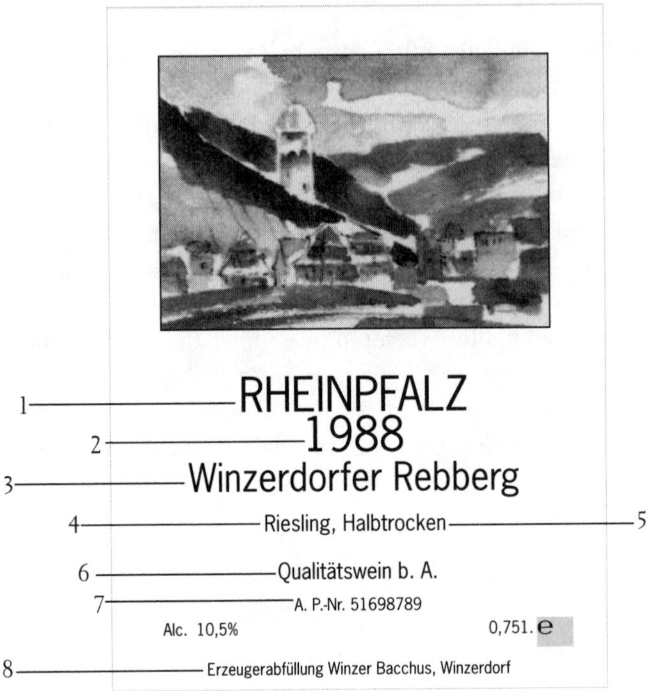

1 RHEINPFALZ
2 1988
3 Winzerdorfer Rebberg
4 Riesling, Halbtrocken 5
6 Qualitätswein b. A.
7 A. P.-Nr. 51698789
Alc. 10,5%
0,751. e
8 Erzeugerabfüllung Winzer Bacchus, Winzerdorf

1. The specific growing region: one of the eleven designated regions in Germany.

2. The year in which the grapes were harvested.

3. The town and the vineyard from which the grapes come. (In this case a hypothetical example.)

4. The grape variety.

5. The taste or style of the wine. In this case, semidry.

6. The quality level of the wine, indicating ripeness of the grapes at harvest.

7. The official testing number: proof that the wine has passed analytical and sensoric testing required for all German Quality Wines.

8. Wines bottled and produced by the grower or a cooperative of growers may be labeled "Erzeugerabfüllung" (estate-bottled). Other wineries and bottlers are identified as "Abfüller."

COURTESY OF GERMAN WINE INFORMATION BUREAU

four years of age. Some of the favorable food combinations for these wines are shellfish, crab, baked hams, fresh fruits, pizza, and mild cheeses — Monterey jack, for example. Slightly riper and sweeter Rieslings, like ripe Spätlese and Auslese, have more weight and possibly more residual sugar and are at their best at four to eight years of age. They pair well with fuller, more flavorful foods such as chowders, crab, oysters, sausage, liver, duck in sweet sauces, sweet-and-sour pork, fruits, turkey, and sesame chicken. Eiswein, Beerenauslese, and Trockenbeerenauslese, Germany's sweet to extremely sweet dessert wines, can also be quite excellent on their own after a meal. Goose liver, cheesecake, rich cheese, and fruit-style desserts are all quite comfortable with these styles of wines. These wines are best enjoyed when they are, at minimum, eight to ten years of age. Whatever the occasion, German Rieslings may be the only white wines in the world that can so well accommodate a meal from its beginning to its end.

Italy

More wine makers are found in Italy than in anywhere else in the world. Here the baker is a wine maker, as is the banker, the soccer player, the mechanic, the policeman — even the clergyman. If you're not a wine maker yourself, chances are very good that someone sitting around your dinner table is or has been. With grapevines found everywhere, from the simplest garden plot to the most breathtaking hillside, Italy has been called the world's largest vineyard. Hundreds of different grape types are grown, ranging from the traditional Sangiovese and Nebbiolo, to the more internationally popular Cabernet Sauvignon and Chardonnay, to the less well-known native Corvina and the Rondinella. Nowhere else in the world can such a diverse assortment of grape vines and vineyards be found, and nowhere else in the world are wines produced in such a wide range of different styles and flavors.

Such nationwide involvement with wine accomplishes two very important things. First it helps to demystify wine, and second, it incorporates wine into every aspect of the culture. In Italy a bottle of wine on the table is as commonplace as the bottle of Coke is on the American table. Additionally, many Italians also have their own wine cellars, humble though they may be. Simply enjoying wine seems to be an Italian pastime. Other cultures may treat wine as a symbol of status, power, and breeding, but in Italy wine is taken out of the trophy case, poured into a glass, and enjoyed. It is seen as something that will quench one's thirst while offering pleasure, two of Italy's favorite pastimes. This is not to say that the wines of Italy do not merit the same high praise and status that the best wines of France, Germany, Spain, and America enjoy, only that the Italian people haven't lost sight of how to enjoy them. In fact, in the arena of great wines, Italy enjoys its fair share of entries, especially the famous red wines of Tuscany and Piedmont.

The history of wine in Italy can be traced back over three thousand years to a time when the common people considered the natural transformation of grape juice into wine as magical, an act of the gods. It was the

Romans, of course, who completed the introduction and cultivation of wine throughout most regions of what we now know as Italy. Hundreds of years later, during the nineteenth century, wine making had become more of a craft, as improvements in all phases of it began to raise the overall quality of Italian wine. Unfortunately, Italy, like most of Europe, did not escape the devastation of phylloxera in the late 1800s, and many thousands of acres of vines sickened and died. It was also around this time that Italian influence began to be felt in the New World, as Italian immigrants introduced their wine-making skills into mainstream America. California wine history is paved with the achievements and successes of such wine makers. Simi, Foppiano, Pedroncelli, Sebastiani, Mondavi, and Gallo are but a few of the many Italian immigrants who helped improve both wine and wine making in America.

Back in Italy, grape growers dug out their phylloxera-infested vines and replanted their vineyards with the most suitable grape types. In the decades following World War II, the Italian wine industry grew, and Italy became the world's largest producer of wine. Overproduction and a lack of serious regulations, however, caused both the image of Italian wines and the wines themselves to become low cost and low quality. This must have been deeply frustrating to the handful of dedicated wine makers who were producing world-class wines at the time. It was their bad luck to be guilty by association.

The rebirth of the Italian wine industry began in the late sixties, as grape growers and wine makers began to rethink their priorities and to emphasize quality instead of quantity. This change in direction, which continues today, led to stricter wine-making and grape-growing practices and labeling regulations, which led to the creation of the DOC (see following) wine laws in 1963.

Although it was initially resistant to changes in its wine-making philosophy and traditions, Italy has begun to accept some modern wine-making technology and gently blend it together with age-old traditions. It will take a while before a unified direction for the Italian wine industry becomes clear. However, all the ingredients are in place for a very bright future.

ITALIAN WINE LAWS

Like most quality-minded wine-producing regions, Italy has adopted strict laws to protect the quality and authenticity of its wines. But unlike other European countries, which established these practices centuries ago, Italy's wine regulations have evolved a great deal during the past few decades. Following is a description of the four quality levels of Italian wines. Italian wines can be labeled by region (Chianti, Soave, Barolo), after the grape type (Dolcetto, Chardonnay), or under proprietary names (Solaia, Tignanello, Dreams).

Vino da Tavola The most basic classification of Italian table wine, Vino de Tavola is produced where no delimited zone exists or outside the guidelines of existing wine regulations. While most wines that fall into this category are simple and inexpensive, some of Italy's most exciting and expensive handcrafted wines, including the new Super Tuscans, are also included in this category. Hopefully, upcoming legislation will help define this category better.

IGT (Indicazione Geografica Tipica) This is the Italian equivalent of the French Vin de Pays classification, which represents select wine-growing areas or regions.

DOC (Denominazione di Origine Controllata) Modeled after the Appellation Contrôlée system of France, Italy's wine classification DOC was formulated in 1963. The DOC category guarantees the origin of a wine from a delimited zone and also regulates alcohol content, grape types, yields, and certain aging requirements. Today DOC wine laws continue to be refined and remodeled. As of this writing there are some 240 approved DOC zones located throughout Italy.

DOCG (Denominazione di Origine Controllata e Garantita) This is Italy's highest classification of wine. Considered the elite of the DOC classification, wines with DOCG status have an additional guarantee of authenticity and are produced under stricter regulations and guidelines than DOC wines. Currently there are thirteen approved DOCG wine zones. They are Barbaresco, Barolo, Brunello di Montalcino, Chianti, Vino Nobile di Montepulciano, Albana di Romagna, Gattinara, Carmignano (red wine only), Torgiano Rosso riserva, Taurasi, Montefalco Sagrantino, Vernaccia di San Gimignano, and Moscato d'Asti/Asti Spumante.

ITALIAN WINE REGIONS

Italy can be divided into four general areas: the south (including the islands), the center, the northern center and northwest, and the northeast. There are twenty different wine regions located throughout these areas, and each of these can be further subdivided into provinces. There are so many different regions and provinces, it would be impossible to explore them all in an introductory guide such as this. Instead my focus will be on

Italy's most important wine regions, Tuscany and Piedmont. Following is a list of the twenty regions broken down geographically.

Southern Italy and the Islands

Sardinia	Apulia
Sicily	Basilicata
Campania	Calabria

Central Italy

Latium	Marches
Tuscany	Molise
Umbria	Abruzzi

North Central and Northwest Italy

Piedmont	Lombardy
Valle D'Aosta	Liguria
Emilia-Romagna	

Northeast Italy

Trentino-Alto Adige
Veneto
Friuli-Venezia Giulia

THE WINES OF TUSCANY

The beautiful rolling hills of Tuscany produce five of Italy's thirteen top-ranked DOCG wines, including Chianti, Italy's most recognized red wine. Add the more than twenty DOC areas also located in Tuscany and you will begin to understand the importance of this region. Tuscany's most famous and greatest wines are red, produced primarily from one of Italy's two great red grapes, the Sangiovese. A fine white DOCG is Vernaccia di San Gimignano, produced from the native Vernaccia vine. Vin Santo, a sweet, exotic dessert wine that is produced from dried grapes and aged for many years in small oak barrels, is the crown jewel of Italy's sweet dessert wines. Chardonnay, Pinot Grigio, Pinot Bianco, and Sauvignon Blanc are a few of the other white varietals that have enjoyed success as Tuscan wine makers have tried their hands at different varietals.

Chianti The most famous red DOCG produced in Tuscany, Chianti is made almost exclusively from the Sangiovese grape. Chianti can be produced within one of seven subzones, with the highest reputation belonging to the area known as Chianti Classico, located in central Tuscany. Chianti Classico wines are often identified by the symbol of a black rooster found on the cap of the wine bottle. Wines labeled Chianti riserva have received additional barrel aging and are usually higher in quality and more expensive. While the name Chianti is well known, its reputation is divided between the inexpensive, easy-drinking jug wine so often seen in the straw flask to the rare, elegant, age-worthy version that has become one of Italy's most sought-after red wines. The gap between the two has narrowed of late as quality-minded producers have become inclined to produce better wines for higher prices. Chianti is very versatile in its uses and often of excellent value. *Recommended producers:* Antinori, Badia a Coltibuono, Castellare, Castello di Ama, Fontodi, Il Palazzino, Ruffino, Terrabianca Felsina, Frescobaldi.

The Super Tuscans There has been a growing trend to produce wines with more of an international appeal (some call them "Bordeaux style" wines), using untraditional Italian grape types, production methods, and blends. Super Tuscans are often classified as Vini da Tavola because they disregard the strict rules that govern DOC and DOCG classifications. However, they do represent some of Italy's most exciting and delicious red wines. Leading the charge since the 1970s has been the wine estate of Antinori, whose Tignanello and Solaia are two well-known examples of Super Tuscan wines. Other recommended Super Tuscans are Carmartina, Le Pergole Torte, Castello di Ama, Terrabianca Campaccio, and Sassicaia.

Brunello di Montalcino This is considered by many to be Tuscany's greatest red wine, and it is classified as DOCG. Brunello, the grape used, is a clone of the Sangiovese grape, and here, in Montalcino, it is capable of producing wines of great weight and flavor that require many years to soften. Biondi-Santi is the estate most famous for this wine; however, its prices are often out of orbit. Rosso di Montalcino is a more affordable alternative. Classified as DOC and also produced from Brunello, it is aged considerably less in oak, thereby producing a softer, more approachable version of Brunello di Montalcino. *Recommended producers:* Barbi, Poggio Antico, Il Poggiolo, Frescobaldi, Costanti, Banfi, Biondi-Santi.

Carmignano Produced in small quantities, Carmignano is a fine red Tuscan wine classified as DOCG. Produced from a blend of Sangiovese (85 percent) and Cabernet Sauvignon (15 percent), Carmignano can be elegant and long-lived. *Recommended producers:* Il Poggio, Ambra, Capezzana.

Vino Nobile di Montepulciano This Tuscan red DOCG is produced from vineyards located just east of Montalcino in Montepulciano. Until recently, Vino Nobile, a onetime favorite with the nobility, has not lived up to its reputation. Perhaps achieving DOCG status has given producers something to strive for, because quality is now on the rise. Produced mostly from the Prugnolo grape (the local name for the Sangiovese), Vino Nobile at its best blends Brunello's strength with Chianti's elegance. Rosso di Montepulciano is a softer, more approachable DOC wine produced with less oak. *Recommended producers:* Polizano, Dei, Boscarelli, Avignonesi, Gattavecchi.

THE WINES OF PIEDMONT

The other major red wine–producing region of Italy is Piedmont, located in north central Italy. Piedmont, long esteemed for its culinary delights as well as its wines, is also home to the highly prized wild white truffles found in certain soils in and around the town of Alba. Unlike Tuscany, where almost all wines are red, Piedmont is home to many fine white wines such as Moscato d'Asti (DOCG), Arneis, and Gavi, as well as the world's most popular white sparkling wine, Asti, also known as Asti Spumante (also DOCG). However, as good as these whites can be, Piedmont's great reds, produced from Italy's other great red grape, the Nebbiolo, are accorded a higher distinction. Here the sturdy, thick-skinned Nebbiolo produces Italy's most powerful, flavorful, and greatest red wines, the Barolo and Barbaresco. Two other red grape types cultivated with great success in Piedmont are Barbera and Dolcetto. In all, there are four DOCG wine areas, complemented by more than thirty DOCs, in Piedmont, which ties Tuscany as Italy's second largest producer of highly classified wines.

Barolo This prestigious DOCG red wine was named after a small town near Alba in Piedmont. Barolo has been called the "king of wine" and the "wine of kings." Once you experience some good examples of this Nebbiolo-based wine, you will begin to understand its nobility. Often described as chewy, tannic, austere, thick with scents of warm tar, Barolo — especially when produced in the traditional rustic style — can be quite hard and unapproachable in its youth. When it is aged properly and given time to mellow, however, these harsh elements begin to soften and reveal many layers of complexity bound by thick, sturdy fruit and firm acidity.

Lately there has been an obvious attempt by many top producers to produce Barolo in a more approachable style by highlighting the wine's fruit and color while softening harsh tannins. Several different villages or zones, such as La Morra or Serralunga, produce Barolo in their own style, and the name of the village is usually listed on the label. A Barolo riserva that has been aged in barrels for an extended period of time is also produced, though it is not necessarily to everyone's taste. It is important to buy Barolo from a good and consistent producer; good Barolos are seldom inexpensive. *Recommended producers:* Pio Cesare, Manzoni, Marcarini, Ceretto, Conterno, Chiarlo, Giacomo, Gaja, Prunotto, Conterno Fantino, Colla.

Barbaresco This DOCG red wine is produced from Nebbiolo vines planted in the Langhe Hills near Alba. Barbaresco, along with its famous neighbor Barolo, produces the world's best, most powerful, and most ageworthy Nebbiolo-based wines. In general, Barbaresco is more approachable and somewhat softer than Barolo, but the hand and inclination of the wine maker play a key role in the wine's final outcome. Barbaresco is also often aged in oak for a shorter period of time than Barolo, which in turn aids in making it more accessible. A number of different styles of Barbaresco are produced, from the friendly, up-front fruit version to the more rustic traditional. One major determining factor remains the particular vineyard where the grapes are grown, of which there are many. Sori Tildin, San Lorenz, and Costa Russi are three good examples. The other important factor is, of course, the producer. *Recommended producers:* Ceretto, Marchesi di Gressy, Gaja, Pio Cesare, Bruno Rocca Rabaja, Bruno Giacossa, Colla.

Dolcetto This DOC wine is soft, charming, and flavorful. Well colored and perfumy, Dolcetto is a friendly, approachable wine best consumed when young. Dolcetto d'Asti and Dolcetto d'Alba are two of the top Dolcetto DOCs available. *Recommended producers:* Altare, Vietti, Marcarini, Conterno Fantino, Colla.

Barbera Along with Nebbiolo, Barbera is the most widely planted grape in Piedmont. It was once considered capable of producing only second-rate wines, but wine makers have recently begun to reduce yields and reassess this grape's capabilities. Their dedication and efforts have been rewarded as these new and improved Barberas have begun to receive high praise from critics and consumers alike. Barbera is classified as DOC and is now being produced in a wide range of styles from the lovely, flavorful, fresh, and fruity to the more complex, oak-influenced style. Barbera d'Alba,

Barbera d'Asti, and Barbera del Monferrato offer the best examples. *Recommended producers:* Aldo Conterno, Prunotto, Chiarlo, Gaja, Martilde, Frescobaldi, Bricco Mondalino.

Gattinara A DOCG, Nebbiolo-based red wine from northern Piedmont, Gattinara is a softer and lighter expression of the Nebbiolo grape than the powerful Barolo. It can be excellent, but there is much variation among producers. *Recommended producers:* Rainoldi, Vallana, Le Colline.

Ghemme A DOC, Nebbiolo-based red wine, whose vineyards lie across those of Gattinara, Ghemme can be a good value.

Carema Another Nebbiolo-based DOC, Carema is produced in small amounts from steep vineyards that are difficult to harvest. It is light, perfumed, and elegant in style.

OTHER POPULAR ITALIAN WINES

Amarone A DOC wine from Veneto, Amarone is a unique version of Valpolicella (see following). It is produced from a blend of grapes that have been placed on mats for months until they have shriveled sufficiently before being fermented. Typically high in alcohol and fermented dry, this wine has a bittersweet flavor that some consider an acquired taste. The best Amarones are of the Classico distinction and require some cellaring. Good ones can age for decades. *Recommended producers:* Bertani, Speri, Quintarelli, Bolla, Tommasi, Dal Forno.

Bardolino This popular DOC from Veneto produces light, fresh, simple, easy-drinking red and rosé wines that are fairly consistent and inexpensive.

Grignolino Produces simple and pleasant light red and rosé wines, which are best consumed young and slightly chilled.

Spanna A red wine from Piedmont, Spanna is the local name of the great Nebbiolo grape. While not the most concentrated Nebbiolo-based wine, Spanna can be a great value for the type. Best when produced in a full, traditional, and rustic style. *Recommended producer:* Vallana.

Valpolicella A DOC wine from Veneto, Valpolicella is produced in a wide range of styles from blends of several grapes. The best is called Valpolicella Classico. For the most part, these wines are light and meant for easy drinking, although some are produced in a much heavier style. *Recommended producers:* Dal Forno, Bolla, Bertani, Speri, Allegrini, Zenato.

Cabernet Sauvignon, Merlot, Cabernet Franc, Pinot Noir These transplanted classic French Bordeaux varietals, which have been grown in Italy over recent decades, have garnered much attention and some great success. Of the four, Cabernet Sauvignon has clearly been the best.

WHITE WINES OF ITALY

The best wines of Italy are, without question, red, but to overlook its fine, user-friendly whites would be a sad faux pas. Italy produces huge amounts of white wine, placing it at the top of the list as the world's largest exporter. With a few exceptions, most of Italy's white wines are much less complex and less expensive than Italy's best reds. I realize that terms like "less complex" and "less expensive" can produce an unfavorable impression, but that is not my intention. Italian white wines are among the world's most consistent, food-friendly, and easiest-to-drink white wines, and they can be had at affordable prices. Soave, Frascati, Pinot Grigio, Trebbiano, and Orvieto are some examples of excellent, versatile Italian white wines that because of this consistency and value make wonderful house wines for either the restaurant or the home.

Italy's current wine renaissance has influenced the quality of white wines as well as reds. Serious and talented producers like Lageder, Puiatti, Jermann, and Schiopetto have made substantial contributions, upgrading the quality, the image, and the prices of Italian white wines. White wines are produced in almost every region of Italy; however, the best vineyards seem to be concentrated in the northeast regions of Veneto, Friuli-Venezia Giulia, and Trentino-Alto Adige.

ENJOYING ITALIAN WINES

Start off any occasion, or create one, with a cold bottle of a semisweet Asti Spumanti sparkling wine as an inviting and refreshing aperitif, but keep in mind that you may want to save a glass or two for dessert, especially if that final course involves fresh fruit. If you prefer a still white wine to begin, there are many possibilities: Pinot Grigio, Frascati, and Soave are all excellent and very affordable choices. These wines can easily continue on as first-course wines, especially if simple, freshly steamed seafood or shellfish is in your plans. If you desire a bit more weight in your white, try a vintage Tunina or one of the fine Chardonnays or Sauvignon Blancs that are available. These wines work well with grilled chicken, lobster, shellfish, tuna, light pasta, and stuffed ravioli dishes.

When you're in an easy red wine mood, try a simple Chianti with chicken pâté on toast or vegetable soup, or a Barbera with breaded veal cutlets — even a young Dolcetto or Rosso di Montalcino with pizza and pasta with red sauce. For heartier dishes, such as beef stews and steak, go with a full-bodied Barolo or Barbaresco. Chianti riserva, Super Tuscans, and other Sangiovese-based wines will match up very well with lamb and risottos, while the bittersweet Amarone works well with most game and stews.

For ripe and aged cheese, like Parmesan and Gorgonzola, select robust Nebbiolo-based reds like Barolo, Barbaresco, or Spanna, while the softer, milder cheeses such as Ricotta and Mozzarella call for medium-bodied whites. Moscato d'Asti, Vin Santo, Malvasia, and Asti Spumante are all sweet-style wines that can comfortably accommodate many different styles of desserts and act as the finishing touch to any meal.

New Zealand

This small nation is a very welcome newcomer to the international wine scene. Located roughly 1,000 miles southeast of Australia, New Zealand is approximately 1,100 miles long and 160 miles wide. Its vineyards are quite favorably influenced by its cool maritime climate. Its two main islands, North Island and South Island, are home to nine major wine-producing areas, five located on North Island and four on South Island. On both islands the drier, more hospitable climate found on the east coasts is most favorable for grape growing.

South Island's Marlborough region, with its stony river flats, well-drained soils, sunshine, and long growing season, has become New Zealand's most famous and most respected wine region. It was from plantings in Marlborough that the successful marriage of Sauvignon Blanc and New Zealand was first realized. It is interesting to note that grapevines have been planted in Marlborough only since 1973. At that time an acre of land could be had for the cost of a cab ride from Manhattan to Kennedy Airport, about thirty dollars. Hawke's Bay and Gisborne are two other grape-growing regions that show excellent promise.

What is most exciting about New Zealand is the fact that it has produced world-class wines from the Sauvignon Blanc grape in little more than two decades. The unoaked versions of New Zealand's Sauvignon Blancs are flavorful, herbaceous, crisp, lively, racy, grassy, tropical, and trademarked by a clean lime-flavored tang on their finish. They have caused more than one Frenchman to sigh and lift his beret. When you consider the high cost of the better French Pouilly-Fumés and Sancerres, there is little reason for anyone not to consider New Zealand's more affordable efforts. The oaked version (often overoaked) of Sauvignon Blanc has become more fashionable of late, and while oak does add to the wine's complexity, it can sometimes mask some of the wine's fresh and invigorating fruit flavors.

The winery that first thrust New Zealand into the spotlight for Sauvignon Blanc was the Cloudy Bay Winery. With the help of some brilliant marketing and some timely press, New Zealand Sauvignon Blanc, it seemed, had found both its market and its niche. Why, then, with all this momentum in place, have New Zealand producers become so tempted to look for other wines to produce? Does New Zealand make some good Chardonnay? Yes. Does New Zealand produce some decent Riesling? Yes, again. How about Pinot Noir and Cabernet Sauvignon? Once again, the answer is yes. But why bother producing a good wine when you can produce a great one? That great wine is Sauvignon Blanc, and New Zealanders should revel in it. You don't see Burgundy's wine makers trying to cultivate anything other than Chardonnay and Pinot Noir, nor do you see German grape growers planting Chardonnay because it's the flavor of the month. Time will tell (it always does). One can only hope that nature, not marketing, will dictate which grapes New Zealand decides to concentrate on in the future.

For the most part, New Zealand's wines are labeled by the grape type used, as long as they contain a minimum of 85 percent of the stated grape type. To be vintage dated, 85 percent of the grapes used must be of the listed vintage. While there are almost three hundred wineries in New Zealand, Corbans and Montana Winery (known as Brancott Vineyards in the United States) are the best known and together are responsible for 70 percent of New Zealand's total wine production. *Recommended producers:* Cloudy Bay, Corbans, Montana/Brancott Vineyards, Villa Maria, Selaks, Te Mata, Martinborough, Matua Valley.

ENJOYING NEW ZEALAND SAUVIGNON BLANC

New Zealand Sauvignon Blancs, especially those without oak, are wonderfully refreshing when served as an aperitif wine, during an afternoon barbecue, or simply while lounging in a hammock. They are excellent as palate-cleansing first-course wines, especially when paired with fresh seafood and shellfish. The sturdier oaked versions carry more weight and are less flexible in their applications, but they tend to accommodate heavier styles of fish as well as most light meats.

Chile

South America's finest red wines, as well as its best values, are produced in Chile. Blessed with a warm and consistent climate, here the ripening of grapes is seldom a problem. Rain is scarce, however, and many vineyards must be irrigated. The best vineyards are located in central Chile near the capital of Santiago, where they are protected by the Andes mountains.

The unique and isolated location of these vineyards protected them against phylloxera during the nineteenth century. While wine had been made in Chile for centuries, it wasn't until phylloxera's destruction of French vineyards led out-of-work French wine makers into Chile that its wines took on any distinction. Along with their wine-making knowledge, these wine makers also brought cuttings of such noble grape types as Cabernet Sauvignon, Merlot, Malbec, Pinot Noir, Chardonnay, Sauvignon Blanc, and Riesling. Chile does have its share of native grape types, the most notable being the País; however, it is with the above-mentioned grape types, transplanted from France, that Chile has had its greatest success. The fact that the vineyards of Chile remain phylloxera-free to this day explains why many vineyards contain a large proportion of cherished old vines. While most of the world's grapevines have been grafted onto phylloxera-resistant rootstock, the vines of Chile have not, saving both time and money.

White wines of average quality are produced from Chardonnay, Sauvignon Blanc, and Riesling, but the best wines produced are red, most notably Cabernet Sauvignon and Merlot. Quality has increased dramatically over the last two decades as modern technology, coupled with a more wine-friendly government, has permitted this old yet ignored industry to grow. Chile, recognized worldwide as producing great value for its red wine, has drawn considerable outside interest and investment, most notably from Bordeaux's famous Château Lafite-Rothschild, California's Robert Mondavi Winery, and the Torres winery of Spain. *Recommended producers:* Los Vascos, Santa Rita, Concha y Toro, Caliterra, Almaviva, Miguel Torres.

South Africa

It's a singularly gratifying moment when an author can finally sit back and say, "This book is finished!" My moment came early in 1999, after a humbling 2½-year process of tasting, typing, and research. Sadly, my sense of accomplishment did not last long. While this book was in production, I was invited to lunch at the restaurant Daniel in New York City to taste several wines of South Africa, a wine region about which I knew very little. The quality and value of those wines so impressed me that later that evening I found myself calling suppliers and exporters for more samples of these relatively unknown wines. Two days later I pleaded with my editor for a chance to include at least a short entry on the wonderful wines of South Africa. She kindly agreed, for which I am quite grateful.

South Africa is no newcomer to viticulture. In fact, the first vineyards were planted at the Cape in 1655 by the region's first governor, Jan van Riebeeck. These vineyards produced the Cape's first wine in 1659. South Africa's early wines were relatively unexciting, no doubt because the wine makers lacked grape-growing and wine-making experience.

Quality remained inconsistent throughout the seventeenth and much of the eighteenth century, but British occupation during the early to mid–nineteenth century gave a boost to South Africa's sagging wine industry and greatly increased both the demand for and the production of its wines. This success was short-lived, however, for as soon as Britain resolved its problems with France in 1861, the need for South Africa's wines lessened dramatically. War, infestation by phylloxera, and other events slowed the wine industry even further. A unified commitment to quality was also needed, and an organized wine growers' association, known as the KWV, was formed in 1918. Order was slowly restored to the troubled wine industry. With the freeing of Nelson Mandela in 1990, the end of apartheid, and President Bush's lifting of the boycott on South African products, South Africa began to redefine its wine-producing capabilities with an emphasis on quality. Today South Africa has quietly become the world's eighth largest producer of wine.

The southwestern Cape area of South Africa produces the best wines, with the most notable traditional regions being Constantia, Paarl, Stellenbosch, and Franschhoek. Today newer regions like Walker Bay and Elgin and rediscovered regions like Swartland have begun to challenge traditional perceptions. With a Mediterranean climate and a variety of soil compositions, South Africa produces excellent wines. Most popular of the white grape types are Chardonnay, Chenin Blanc, Riesling, Muscat, and Sauvignon Blanc. Cabernet Sauvignon, Merlot, Cinsaut, Pinot Noir, and a local grape called Pinotage (a cross between Pinot Noir and Cinsaut) produce the most successful red wines. Most of South Africa's wines are labeled by the grape varietal (Pinotage, Sauvignon Blanc, and so on) used in their production. To be labeled in this fashion, exported wines must be produced from a minimum of 85 percent of the named grape type. Excellent quality and high value are your reward for seeking out these relatively unknown wines. *Recommended wineries:* Brampton, Rustenberg, Meerlust,

Swartland, Thelema, Mulderbosch, Indaba, Kanonkop, Grangehurst, Buitenverwachting, Cabriere.

Australia

When Australia's first settlers landed, looked around, and took stock of their new home's natural inventory, they undoubtedly witnessed many unusual sights — kangaroos, koala bears, the Great Barrier Reef seething with marine life, and the expansive and desolate outback. What they did not find anywhere, however, were grapevines. Seems a shame, all that beauty and natural wonder with no wine-producing vines to help one enjoy it.

This sad scenario did not last long. During the late eighteenth century cuttings of vines were imported from Europe and were soon transplanted successfully. (Many of the early settlers were, incidentally, not of the most noble variety themselves, as Australia was actually founded as a British penal colony comprising lawbreakers, social outcasts, and their keepers.) While the transplanted vines did quite well for nearly two centuries, acknowledgment from the international wine-producing and wine-drinking communities has been forthcoming only in the last two decades.

It is really astonishing to see how far the Australian wine industry has come. Today nearly twenty million cases of Australian wine are exported around the world each year. There are many reasons for Australia's newfound acceptance in the world market, but the main ones are timing, technology, quality, and pricing. First of all, Australia was on the scene at just the right time. An international demand for good wines, especially Chardonnay, grew rapidly during the eighties and early nineties. The demand was particularly strong for French and Californian Chardonnay, and as the prices for these wines increased, the door opened wide for Australian wine makers to work their magic. Magic often goes by another name when discussing wine — technology. And while countries with traditional wine-making histories were slow to accept it, the liberal and experimental Australian wine industry welcomed technology, absorbing and refining it in the process. In a relatively short time, Australia found itself winning international medals, awards, and competitions with the best of them. While I am not a big believer in medals and awards, they do draw attention. Once given the opportunity, the down under wine makers capitalized on it by accurately reproducing the styles of the wines that were in demand, but at considerably lower costs. For a while many wineries went a bit overboard in incorporating too much new oak in their wines, but that trend, happily, has diminished of late.

The lion's share of attention was initially given to wines produced from the white Chardonnay grape, but the sleeping giant of Australia has always been the red Shiraz grape. Known as Syrah in other wine regions of the world, most notably the Côte du Rhône, the Shiraz is Australia's most widely planted grape, capable of producing world-class wines. Perfectly suited to selected regions and soils of Australia, the Shiraz can be produced in a range of different styles. Its best characteristic is its full, expansive, developed expression of fruit. This expression comes in many forms, including cassis, pepper, spice, and chocolate, but it is usually well developed. And unlike other great red wines that require years of cellaring before becoming approachable, most Australian Shiraz seems to be born pretty and approachable any time. In other words, it's too hard not to drink these wines young. Additional aging will help smooth out any rough edges while adding complexities and nuances. Price is another virtue of Australian Shiraz — dollar for dollar it is one of the best red wine values of the world.

Other successful red grapes, in order of importance, are Cabernet Sauvignon, Merlot, and Pinot Noir. Chardonnay, Sémillon, Sauvignon Blanc, and Riesling produce Australia's best whites. Being fairly isolated and uninvolved with other wine-producing regions during the nineteenth century had its advantages, as exposure to the vine-destroying phylloxera pest that devastated European vineyards was limited. As a result, some of the world's oldest Shiraz grapevines (on original rootstock) are growing in Australia, producing wines of extremely low yields and high quality.

AUSTRALIAN WINE REGIONS

Australia is divided into six separate states — Queensland, Western Australia, South Australia, New South Wales, Victoria, and Tasmania — plus the Northern Territory. The Northern Territory, Queensland, and the northern part of Western Australia are considered too warm, dry, and tropical to produce top *vinifera* wine grapes, and very little wine is produced on the island of Tasmania. The cooler southern states of Victoria, New South Wales, South Australia, and parts of the southern section of Western Australia are home to Australia's finest vineyards. Within each of these states exist many smaller wine areas, such as the German-influenced Barossa Valley located in South Australia, Western Australia's Margaret River, or Victoria's Yarra Valley, each with its own wine-producing inclinations. Wide variations in microclimates, drainage, and soils are also found throughout Australia. The most unique soil is a famous stretch of red loam-covered limestone called terra rossa, soil found only in South

Australia's Coonawarra area. This terra rossa soil has produced some of the country's most stunning red wines. It is a common practice, by the way, for wine makers to blend the wines of several of Australia's different states. This results in the production of wine from a rather large wine appellation, but it is a practice that offers the wine maker a much desired range of flexibility and consistency.

AUSTRALIAN WINE LAWS

Australia, unlike other wine-producing countries, welcomes and invites experimentation and change. Not being bound by centuries of tradition does have its advantages, and Australian wine makers seem to enjoy their freedom. Where else in the world can you find a sparkling Shiraz, and who do you think invented the wine-in-a-box concept? Though more liberal than most wine-producing countries, Australia does have some basic labeling regulations:

- If a wine is labeled by grape type, a minimum of 80 percent of that listed grape must be used.
- If two different grape types are used, with neither contributing 80 percent of the blend, then both grape types must be listed in order of importance or dominance. Example: A red wine produced from 55 percent Shiraz and 45 percent Cabernet Sauvignon must be listed as Shiraz/Cabernet Sauvignon.
- If a region or state is listed, a minimum of 80 percent of the grapes must come from the listed area, or the wine must have been made or blended in that region. Obviously the second part of this regulation makes it more than a little ambiguous.
- If a vintage date is stated, 100 percent of the grapes used must be of that vintage.

Following are some terms that are often found on wine labels:

Show Reserve This term brings attention to the fact that the wine has won an award.

Wood Matured This indicates that the wine has spent some time in contact with fairly new oak casks.

Reserve Bin or Bin # This indicates that the producer feels this wine is a higher-quality wine than his standard wine.

RECOMMENDED AUSTRALIAN WINE PRODUCERS

Finding a good Australian producer is rather easy, as many are fairly well distributed. You will discover that some wineries make different wines from different blends. Talk to your retailer for additional input and information.

While there are many top-rated producers in Australia, the crown jewel is Penfolds. Wine makers for over a century, Penfolds specializes in red wines produced mainly from Shiraz, Cabernet Sauvignon, or different combinations of the two. Penfolds is a name to seek out when buying Australian wines; even those not in the know can buy with confidence. The Grange Hermitage bottling, made primarily from the Shiraz grape, is Penfolds's and Australia's best and most sought-after red wine, capable of aging and improving for many decades. Following is a list of other recommended wine producers:

Peter Lehmann
Seppelts Great Western
Mount Langi Ghiran
Cape Mentelle
Rosemount Estate
Tim Adams
Richard Hamilton
Moss Wood
Leeuwin Estate
Lindemans
Orlando Jacob Creek
Howard Park
Deakin Estate
Petaluma
Mount Adam
Taltarni
Tyrrells
Wynns Coonawarra Estate
Wolf Blass
Katnook Estate

ENJOYING AUSTRALIAN WINES

When you think of Australian wine, you will never be too far off the mark if you think in terms of generous, full-flavored wine with a ripe and rich display of fruit. White Riesling is a simple, safe choice for an aperitif or lounging wine, while dry Sauvignon Blancs offer better acidity and pair well with most fresh seafoods, including, of course, Australia's famous shrimp on the barbe. I personally gravitate toward one of the less popular yet fine Sémillons or Sémillon blends, which are produced in a wide range of styles from dry or off-dry to luscious and sweet — all offering good viscosity and mouth feel. Chardonnays are often of the full-throttle variety, and although they can be a little hard on their own, they can shine with grilled fish and lightly smoked meats. Australian Chardonnays are best described as ripe, exotic, tropical, and best consumed two to five years after the vintage.

Shiraz, produced in so many different styles, can accommodate many different types of cuisine and may require some experimentation on your part. While the less complex Shiraz and Shiraz blends are wonderful for barbecues and pizza, the more complex versions work quite well with most red meats, especially beef, game, lamb, and flavorful game birds such as pheasant and squab. Stews, casseroles, and certain cheeses can also be enjoyed with Shiraz-based wines. At the moment Australian wines are quite a good value and worth seeking out, as prices for comparable wines — California Cabernet Sauvignon or Merlot, for example — can be quite a bit higher.

Spain

When the World's Fair is held in a major city in the United States, every store owner, street vendor, and retail outlet manager does anything and everything he can to maximize sales and profits from the influx of customers and tourists. With such economic opportunity at hand, stores open as early as possible and close late. And who would fault them? After all, money is money, and you must make it when you can — right?

Imagine my surprise and disbelief, then, as I walked the streets of Seville during the 1992 World's Fair in Spain. Without warning — and with the precision of a predawn military strike — all the shop owners simultaneously and with great courtesy directed their customers to the door and enveloped themselves in their much cherished custom of afternoon siesta. Why this disinterest in money? What kind of businessperson ushers his customers out of his store? Why not make money instead of lunch? The answer, of course, is that this is Seville, and Seville is Spain, and siesta is *tradition*.

From siesta to flamenco, running with the bulls, and dinner at ten P.M., Spain — right or wrong — has always been very serious about its traditions. Coming from a city (New York) in a country (the United States) that was founded on the principle of independence and various attitudes of nonconformity, I found tradition at such a level quite an experience. Wine is also a tradition in Spain. Here the history of wine making spans more than 2,500 years. Archaeological digs have revealed evidence that the Greeks in the Catalonia region near Tarragona and the Phoenicians in Andalucía near Málaga and Cádiz were involved in the cultivation of grapes and wine making. For many centuries the quality of Spain's wines was considered good. In the eighteenth century wine makers in the Rioja region looked to France for the technical advice that would help increase the aging and traveling capabilities of their wines. Combining Spanish wine-making traditions with French techniques created what many of us know as the classic "Rioja style" unique to this part of the world. Then, when phylloxera ravaged and destroyed French vineyards during the mid–nineteenth century, many talented French wine makers crossed the Spanish border, looking to make wine. Spain soon became the beneficiary of all the knowledge and tools the French wine makers brought with them. Later, phylloxera also descended on and destroyed some of Spain's vineyards, but by then the knowledge and skills required to graft rootstock had been developed.

In Spain wine has always been produced for pleasurable consumption, part of the daily routine. Go into a tapas bar in Logroño, Rioja, at lunchtime and you'll find people enjoying many small samplings of local food and wines, while they indulge in comfortable conversation among friends. Ten minutes after they've finished, ask them what they just drank. Odds are the answer will be, "I'm not sure, but it was good." Compare this with one of the new wave wine bars found in many major American cities today, where self-proclaimed wine aficionados (wine geeks with good jobs) compare wines and vintages in a language they seem to have created for the sole purpose of diluting everyone else's drinking pleasure.

Today Spain, like Italy, is experiencing a wine renaissance. New ideas, as well as updated wine-making equipment, are augmenting the great Spanish wine traditions already in place. Although there is a movement afoot to preserve and actually improve the quality of Spain's native grape varietals, an increasing amount of attention and vineyard acreage is being given to the more internationally recognized varietals such as Cabernet Sauvignon, Chardonnay, and Merlot. Although Spain produced some exceptional though rather idiosyncratic white wines, including the unique fortified Sherry wines, the majority of its whites were simple, pleasant, and easy to drink, but up until recently uninspiring. Sparkling wines known as Cava are produced in a wide range of styles and have become some of the most consistent, well-priced sparkling wine values in the world. There is little debate that Spain's greatest table wines are red, and they are capable of being truly great, possessing the individual characteristics that are unique to the native soils, grape varietals, and wine-making traditions of Spain. Of all the red native grape varietals planted (there are many) throughout Spain, the Tempranillo stands alone as the greatest. Although some bodegas in Rioja have pulled up Tempranillo and replanted with

Cabernet Sauvignon and Merlot in an attempt to cash in on the prestige these varietals are currently enjoying, these wines will never replace the great Tempranillo.

Extended barrel aging is another Spanish wine tradition, and no other wine-producing country ages its wines so long before releasing them for sale. It is also interesting to note that while many types of oak barrels are used in Spanish wine making, the oak of choice is the American oak. While the quality of Spanish wines has long been recognized by other European countries, the American wine-buying public has not known much about these wines and has even shied away from them. This is starting to change, however, and the wines of Spain are beginning to receive the warm reception they deserve. After all, wines of such value and quality cannot be ignored forever.

SPANISH WINE LAWS

Spain, like most other major wine-producing countries, takes protecting the authenticity and reputation of its wines quite seriously. Strict regulations on important matters such as grape type, planting of vines, yields, pruning, oak aging, and wine-making practices are carefully monitored and safeguarded. At the national level, the branch of government responsible for these regulations is called the Instituto Nacional de Denominaciónes de Origen (INDO). It works in concert with the individual regional governments that guarantee a wine's origin and quality. These individual regions, or DOs, are the equivalent of French AOCs or American AVAs; wines from these regions are considered quality wines by Europe's EEC. There are currently fifty-two individual DOs located in Spain. Each DO is governed by its own regulatory council, known as the Consejo Regulador, and is listed on the wine's label. There is also a superior classification within the DO called Qualified Denomination of Origin (QDO or DOC). Currently only Rioja falls into this category.

SPANISH WINE CLASSIFICATIONS

Wines are classified regionally (Rioja, Navarra, Penedès), but they are further classified by the amount of time they have been aged in both oak casks and bottles. Following is an explanation of the different classifications and their requirements. Keep in mind that the aging requirements given are minimum requirements only; many bodegas exceed them, often by great amounts. A wine's region and aging classification is found on the label with a smaller, additional label also located on the back of the bottle.

Regional name A wine named after the region it is from with no specific aging classification, Spain's simplest classification of wine. Wines in this category are immediately available for sale.

Vino de Crianza This term is applied to both red and white quality wines. Before release a red wine must age a minimum of two years, of which at least six months must be in oak casks. Although select Crianza wines can age after release, most are meant to be consumed upon release.

Vino de Reserva This term is applied to quality red wines that have undergone a minimum aging period of three years. At least one of those years the wine must be in oak casks, followed by a minimum of two years in the bottle. Wines of this classification often possess more complexity and oak influence than Crianza wines.

Vino de Gran Reserva This term is applied to quality red wines from excellent vintages that have been aged at least two years in oak casks and three years in the bottle. Gran Reserva wines have traditionally been considered Spain's finest wines.

THE DEBATE ON EXTENDED AGING

There has been a lot of debate about the importance placed on the amount of time Spanish wines are aged, especially in oak barrels. At the center of this debate is Spain's classification system, which seems to reward extended aging by giving a higher classification to wines that have been aged for extended periods of time. A higher classification implies better quality and yields higher prices. Many producers feel that with some vintages and in certain circumstances, a wine's quality can actually be diminished by such extended aging. Unfortunately, because they do not want what is perceived to be a lower classification, they choose to age the wine regardless of the consequences. This has resulted in many overoaked wines that often lack fruit and freshness. While traditional producers have held fast to the government's guidelines, there are new producers on the scene who choose to disregard these requirements in hopes of producing the best possible wine. This is not dissimilar to the concept that created the Super Tuscan phenomenon in Italy.

SPAIN'S MOST IMPORTANT NATIVE GRAPE VARIETALS

Red Varietals

Tempranillo
Graciano
Manzuelo
Cariñena
Garnacha
Monastrell

White Varietals

Viura/Macabeo
Albariño
Palomino
Garnacha Blanca
Moscatel
Pedro Ximénez
Godello
Airen

THE MAJOR WINE REGIONS OF SPAIN

Spain is the third largest producer of wine in the world, and quality DO regions are located throughout the country. In the north is Spain's most celebrated DO area of Rioja, with the neighboring region Navarra. To the south is Jerez, home of Spain's famous fortified Sherry wines. On the northeast coast is Penedès, located near Barcelona, while in the southeast is Alicante, Jumilla, and Valencia. Central Spain is where Europe's largest contiguous vineyard, La Mancha, is located, while Galicia lies along Spain's northwest coast. The wine regions and DOs that we shall cover here are Spain's most important.

Rioja The only Spanish wines that qualify as QDO are the wines of Rioja. Located in the central northern section of the country, the vineyards of Rioja follow the River Ebro. For centuries Rioja has been considered Spain's most famous and best wine region. It is divided into three individual subregions or subzones: Rioja Alta (the northernmost), Rioja Alavesa (on the Ebro's north bank), and Rioja Baja in the eastern and most southern section of Rioja. Each region has its own distinct climate and soil composition, and each produces wines with individual characteristics. There is an ongoing debate among Rioja producers about which of the three regions produces the best grapes. The consensus seems to indicate a split decision between the cooler regions of Rioja Alta and Rioja Alavesa, both of which are considered superior to the hot and dry region of Rioja Baja. Traditionally the wines of Rioja have been a blend of grapes produced in all three regions, as such a practice gave wine makers needed versatility as well as protection from a poor harvest occurring in any one region. Today a number of small producers are forgoing this practice to concentrate on estate-bottled wines, with some interesting results.

The soils of Rioja are a mixture of chalky calcareous clays, iron-rich ferruginous clays, and alluvial and sandy soils. Both red and white wines are produced, and although red Riojas receive most of the accolades, some excellent white Riojas are also produced. There are two styles of white Rioja. The first concentrates on fresh fruit and crisp acidity and is meant to be consumed when young. The second, more traditional style is quite heavily wooded, with additional aromas of nuts and oxidation that are quite age-worthy, though a bit of an acquired taste. White Rioja is most often produced from the Viura grape. For red Rioja, Tempranillo is the most celebrated red grape and constitutes the majority of most blends. It is complemented with Rioja's other main red grapes: Graciano, Garnacha, and Manzuelo. There has also been some experimentation — with limited success — with Cabernet Sauvignon and Merlot.

At the most basic level, Rioja wines are lightly colored, light-bodied, fresh, and simple. The Reserva and Gran Reserva bottlings in good vintages are much fuller, complex, and refined, with aromas of vanilla, crème brûlée, chocolate, and dark fruits. They are often highlighted by a silky smooth, soft, yet long finish. In the past there was a tendency for certain bodegas to overoak Reservas and Gran Reservas, but that tendency seems to be subsiding. It is not unusual for one bodega to offer different classifications of Rioja from the same vintage. One such example is the fine house of Cune, which often produces Rioja Crianza and different Rioja Reservas and Rioja Gran Reservas in any given year. Rioja wines can be classified (beginning with the most basic) Rioja, Rioja Crianza, Rioja Reserva, or Rioja Gran Reserva. *Recommended producers (bodegas):* Marques de Caceres, Muga, Cune, Valdemar, Marques de Murrieta, Tondonia, Martinez Bujanda, Rioja Alta, Remelluri, Sans Vicente, Roda, Fernando Remirez de Ganuza.

Navarra Remains of early wine making, traced back as early as the second century, have been found in the region of Navarra, which is located just above Rioja and bordering France. There are five subzones in the Navarra with varying climates and soil structures. They are Valdizarre, Baja de

Montana, Tierras Estrellas, Ribera Alta, and Ribera Baja. The most widely planted white varietals are Viura and Chardonnay. For red grapes there are Grenache, with many old vines still in existence, Tempranillo, Graciano, Merlot, and Cabernet Sauvignon. This region has traditionally been known for its rosés, but recently there has been a revival of estate-bottled wines, especially in the north, which will change the image of Navarra in the coming years. Two wineries to look for are Vega Sindoa and Guelbenzu.

Ribera del Duero Located 150 miles southwest of Rioja and following the course of the Duero River, the DO Ribera del Duero is quickly and not so quietly becoming recognized as one of Spain's greatest and most exciting red wine regions. With its continental climate, high altitude (2,500–3,000 feet), and short, hot summers, Ribera del Duero is an ideal location for growing Tinto Fino/Tinto del País grapes (local versions of Tempranillo), Garnacha, and Cabernet Sauvignon. Its soils are rich in chalk, with some alluvial influences. Here the emphasis is almost exclusively on red wine, and flavors range from soft and elegant to thick, chewy, and silky. The region's most famous bodega is Vega Sicilia, thought by many (myself included) to produce Spain's greatest red wine, called Unico. Red wines can be produced as regional, Crianza, Reserva, and Gran Reserva. This region's most sought-after wines can be expensive, but there are many excellent values to be found. Some fine rosés are also produced in Ribera del Duero. *Recommended producers:* Pesquera, Vega Sicilia, Teofilo Reyes, Vina Mayor, Emilio Moro, Arzuaga, Abadia Retuerta, Valsotillo.

Rías Baixas/Galicia Galicia is a predominantly white wine–producing region situated on the northwest coast of Spain and bordering the Atlantic Ocean. Located in the southern section of Galicia is the Rías Baixas, where the region's, as well as one of Spain's, best white wines, called Albariño, is produced. This is one of the few wines in Spain that are labeled after the grapes used to produce them. The Albariño varietal is believed by some to be related to the German Riesling. Albariño is a lovely, aromatically fragrant, unoaked wine with refreshing acidity. It is best when served young and well chilled. *Recommended producers:* Martin Codax, Fillaboa, Burgans, Lagar de Cevera.

Valdeorras is a steep mountainous region located approximately two hundred kilometers inland from the coast of Galicia. The soil is pure slate; the climate is continental, with Atlantic influences. The best-known grape is Godello, which produces a clean, crisp white wine. Bodegas Godeval has recently resurrected this varietal from obscurity and is the trendsetter for the DO.

Penedès Spain's best sparkling wine, Cava, was produced in the province of Barcelona as early as 1872. It is also produced in other regions of Spain, but more than 90 percent is produced in the Catalan region of Penedès. Cava is made according to *metodo tradicional (méthode champenoise)* guidelines and is produced in many styles, ranging from very dry to very sweet. They are extra brut, brut, extra seco, seco, semiseco, and, Cava's sweetest offering, dulce. The principal white grapes used for Cava are Viura (also called Macabeo), Xarel-lo, and Parellada, with Chardonnay beginning to become popular. Rosé Cavas are produced from Garnacha and Monastrell grapes. Spanish Cava, though quite different from French Champagne, offers excellent value and consistency for those who wish to drink sparkling wine on a regular basis. *Recommended Cava producers:* Juve & Camps, Codorniu, Gramona, Parxet, Leopardi, Marquès de Gelida.

Although most of the grapes in Penedès are used for the production of Cava, one bodega deserves special mention for its dedication and success with still wines. Torres produces quality wines at every price level from native varietals such as Tempranillo as well as through successful experimentation with Cabernet Sauvignon, Merlot, Pinot Noir, Sauvignon Blanc, and Chardonnay. Torres produces some of the world's best and most consistent wine values.

Priorat A small, rejuvenated red wine–producing DO, Priorat is located in the mountains above Tarragona, which is southwest of Barcelona. In steep hillside vineyards with little soil, vines are grown in beds of slate. Viticulture in this area dates to the twelfth century under the auspices of the local monasteries. The Garnacha and Cariñena varietals are the most widely planted and produce very low-yielding, concentrated, and intense red wines. *Recommended producers:* Costers del Siurana, Alvaro Palacios, Clos Mogador, Mas Igneus, Onix.

Up-and-coming regions Toro lies to the west of Ribera del Duero along the Duero River. Recently rediscovered, the region achieved great fame during the fifteenth and seventeenth centuries. Look for intense, full-bodied reds from this DO in the near future.

Jumilla is located in the provinces of Murcia and Albacete in southeast Spain. The vineyards vary in altitude from 1,200 to 2,400 feet. The climate is dry and continental. This DO is the birthplace of the varietal Monastrell, known as Mouvèdre in France and Mataro in the United States. The wines coming from this region exhibit great concentration, ripe fruit, and deep color.

Lanzarote, in the Canary Islands, produces delicious, exotic Malvasias, ranging from dry to sweet in a *terroir* of volcanic ash and desert climate.

Bodegas El Grifo is the first winery to be exported to the United States from this DO.

ENJOYING SPANISH WINES

The wines of Spain are among the most affordable, versatile, food-friendly wines found anywhere in the world. Although I haven't discussed Spanish Sherries, they add greatly to Spain's arsenal of wines. Fino and Manzanilla Sherries, served chilled and fresh, are aperitifs of choice in many parts of Spain. Although they have a higher alcohol content than most table wines, these fortified wines work very well with many types of foods, especially seafood and salty foods like ham and olives.

The aromatic Albariño is another fine choice for a refreshing start to a meal, as is the unoaked version of white Rioja. Both are wonderful with Spain's traditional seafood dish, paella, as well as with simple chicken dishes. Cava produced in a variety of styles has many applications. Try the extra dry or brut as an aperitif or the sweet dulce with fresh fruit, dessert, and cheese. From Friday night's pizza to Sunday's barbecue, basic Spanish reds like Rioja or Ribera del Duero Crianza can perform inexpensively and wonderfully. On those occasions when you want to get a bit more serious, try a fine, aged Rioja Reserva or Gran Reserva with lamb (a classic match) or a topflight Ribera del Duero with sturdier beef and game dishes. For dessert I recommend cream Sherry or a sweet Olorosa Sherry. And as a digestive, few things can match the intensity of a small glass of sweet, raisined Pedro Ximénez (P.X.). Sherry is a perfect way to conclude any meal or occasion.

AFTERWORD

Congratulations, you've made it to the finish line! You now have at your fingertips all the knowledge and expertise you need to understand and enjoy wine in any situation or environment. Best of all, you can enjoy wine undeterred by the pretensions that too often surround it.

We've covered a lot of ground — from wine evaluation and tasting to the wine cellar and the wine list, from wine making to the wine auction, from California to New Zealand. In closing, I should like to express my sincere hope that you have learned to trust your own judgment. Have confidence in your own palate — it is, after all, the only one you will ever need to impress. Good tasting and good health!

INDEX